MW00399671

Crack
and
Back

A Story of Gods'
Redemptive Powers

To Pastor Tom
Love Yoo !

Mark Barnes

[signature]

ISBN 978-1-63961-335-9 (paperback)
ISBN 978-1-63961-336-6 (digital)

Copyright © 2022 by Mark Barnes

All rights reserved. No part of this publication may be reproduced, distributed, or transmitted in any form or by any means, including photocopying, recording, or other electronic or mechanical methods without the prior written permission of the publisher. For permission requests, solicit the publisher via the address below.

Christian Faith Publishing
832 Park Avenue
Meadville, PA 16335
www.christianfaithpublishing.com

Printed in the United States of America

Contents

Acknowledgement

In his book, 'Crack & Back', Mark Barnes gives us a very candid View of his life. It is raw, honest and interesting. From his days as a crack addict until he found new life in Christ, he doesn't pull any punches in telling his story. I believe that as you read 'Crack & Back', you will be swept up in Mark's story and be greatly encouraged by the time the journey is done.

–Bayless Conley
Senior Pastor, Cottonwood Church

1

In the Beginning

Too many times I've heard that I have to write this book. From the beginning, when my buddy Bird would say it after I would tell him one of my crazy experiences that I had in Baltimore City while stuck on a crack binge for three days or sometimes even longer, he would say, "You have to write a book." Or when the first lady would walk down the aisle of the church under the power of the Holy Spirit and say, "Somebody in here is supposed to write a book." Or when T. D. Jakes said, "I normally don't preach for two days as a guest speaker at a church I'm visiting. But God has made me stay over an extra day because he wanted me to tell somebody that they have a book to write. Look at your neighbor and say, 'Get started, get started.'"

I can't tell you how many times God, through someone, has dropped a subtle reminder to me about writing this book. It was so easy to put it on the back burner. God has blessed me with new jobs and different opportunities, let alone the fact that I now live in Southern California, the place where it never rains. I must admit that I've been having a ball. But now that we have a pandemic shutting down everything, God reminded me that I now have the time.

At first, I struggled with how I would start this process. Then I heard a sermon at my church from Pastor Joel that we need to have mustard seed faith to move that mountain. To me, writing a whole book was definitely a mountain. He passed out mustard seeds to the entire congregation and said, "Just start." That was a word for me. I still didn't begin, but when the pandemic hit months later, that word popped back into my spirit: "Faith; the size of a mustard seed. Just start. Take down the mountain one piece at a time. Eat the elephant one bite at a time, even if the piece or the bite is the size of a mustard seed." It's funny what God uses to get our attention, but he made us, so he knows us.

So I began writing my story. God gave me the title in 2004, and I'm beginning in 2020. Talk about procrastination. One of my many character defects, but God can still use me. My prayer is that it helps someone. If he delivered me from the grips of crack cocaine addiction, he'll do it for you. He's no respecter of persons. Born in Baltimore City in 1960 to Homer and Earline Barnes. I don't remember much about my childhood, but I have one memory of my father. I was three to five years old, and he was carrying me down some steps in a row house in Baltimore City. That's it! That's the only memory I have of my father. I saw him thirty-six years later at my grandmother's funeral. My mother had to point him out because none of his three sons knew what he looked like.

My younger brother wanted to know if there was a way we could sue him for back child support. We all convinced him to let it go. Our mom did okay by herself. She let us know that he struggled with alcoholism, which was mainly why she divorced him. He looked okay, but you could tell that he had a tough life as he stood with his new wife. He gave us a halfhearted apology for his absence, and we got his number. He told us to call anytime so we could get together, which none of us did. That ship had sailed. We weren't mad at him; he was just a stranger to us and none of us were really too concerned about getting to know him. We were all grown men living our lives. I guess we kind of thought that may have been his job, to reach out to his sons. Never heard from him again. That's my father story—none, raised by a single-parent mom.

She graduated from Morgan State University with a degree in math. My mother was very intelligent. We started in the city, but after graduating with top honors, she started a job with the Federal Government in Aberdeen on the military base. Then, we were moving out of the city. We moved thirty miles north of Baltimore City to Aberdeen, Maryland. This was a slower country sort of town. We moved into our own house with a yard. I guess I was about six or seven years old when we hit Aberdeen. For a kid my age, that was like dying and going to heaven. We were still poor, but we didn't know it. Mom worked every day and came home and made dinner every night. This part of life was good. For a child my age, all I wanted was friends, and after school started that was no problem for me because, in Aberdeen, folks were a little more friendly.

Mom got her first car, an old white Buick. I guess it wasn't too old when Mom bought it, but it wasn't new. I remember on weekends, we all piled into it to go back to Baltimore because that's where all our relatives still lived. The car had an AM radio, and we could tell when we were getting close to Baltimore because the soul radio stations would start to come in tune as we got closer to the city. Aberdeen only had one radio station that played soul music, and it went off the air every day by 6:00 p.m. We looked forward to weekends in Baltimore. My aunt who lived in Cherry Hill had eleven kids, so that was always a good time. My grandmother lived in East Baltimore. All my uncles and aunts were much older than me, but it was always a treat to go visit them.

My grandmother was the spiritual leader of our family. We always knew if we went to see grandmother, we were going to church. You could always count on that one bologna sandwich at her house for lunch after church. We were lucky if it had cheese on it. I'll never forget looking forward to those sandwiches. Sometimes all my cousins would visit, and after church, Grandmother might make fifteen bologna-and-cheese sandwiches for all the grandchildren. We all sat together and ate, and after that, all the kids would go out and play while the adults would chitchat. My grandmother used to ride around on Sundays, and if she saw you and you were a kid, she would stop and ask you what you were doing. If you didn't have an answer, she would make you go to church with her. After the church service, she would take you home to your parents, and the parents didn't have a problem with it in those days. That's when it was okay for the village to raise the children. Try that nowadays!

That was when your neighbor could smack you upside the head if they caught you doing wrong in the streets. When they took you home and told your parents, you really got in trouble! I think that's part of what's wrong today. No more villages helping with the raising of the neighborhood children. Those were different times. After we got settled in Aberdeen, that became our Sunday routine, church in Baltimore, which was okay because we got to see our relatives every Sunday. So as years went by, I was meeting more and more friends and was well known in the neighborhood. It was a friendly neighborhood, and there wasn't a lot of crime. The worst thing we had to deal with was the neighborhood winos, and they were never a problem.

As kids, we used to taunt them and try to make them chase us. Overall, even they were friendly. Mom must have been doing better on her job because she decided to move. I was a kid, so I didn't ask why. So we moved to the other side of the tracks. The house was a little larger, not much, but the backyard was huge. This was Ohio Court. The only problem was the B&O railroad went right through our backyard. It was separated by an old, run-down fence. I remember as a kid jumping the fence and watching the trains go by and counting the cars. This neighborhood was a little nicer than the first, and it was easier to make friends. This is where I met my lifelong best friend Paul. I was now eight to nine years old, and I was playing sports.

My backyard was the baseball field, and if you hit the ball onto the railroad tracks, it was an automatic home run. My mother was quick with making me stay in the house if I did something wrong. I eventually got the nickname "Punishment" because my mother was quick to put me on punishment if I got in trouble.

Once, we were having a big baseball game in my backyard. Remember, my backyard was large so it could accommodate a whole baseball game. I still don't remember to this day why, but I got put on punishment in the middle of the game. Do you think the game stopped because it was in my backyard, and I was no longer able to play? Absolutely not! I had to watch all my friends play in my backyard through my bedroom window. That was a rough day. My childhood, I must say, was pretty average for a single-parent home because my mom was a good mother. We were the first in our court to get cable TV. That meant we could now watch channels 2 through 13 clearly. Being the first family to have cable TV in our court made me pretty popular with all my buddies, especially Paul who now wanted to come to my house to watch TV. And the TV show we never missed was the *Ultraman* superhero show.

During those days, I didn't own a bicycle but that was okay because we walked everywhere we wanted to go. Walking five miles was nothing. Since our community was safe, we did that all the time. By then, I was nine to ten years old, and I was starting to get around more and meeting a lot more friends. It was now time for the family to move again. Mom has found a larger house. She found a house in a community known as the Chesapeake Acres. This neighborhood was less than a mile from our first neighborhood (Ohio Court), so my buddy Paul was still able to come visit me. And this was also a Black community with lower- to middle-income Black families. We now had a house with a basement and a big yard. I failed to mention while living in Ohio Court my mother purchased my first drum set. My brother played the trumpet, so music was popular in our family. I got a three-piece Ludwig drum set. The only rule was, I couldn't play it when my mother came home from work. But all day long, especially during summer break, I would constantly play my drums. So when we moved to the new neighborhood in the house with the basement, it was much easier for me to practice. And I practiced all the time. The whole neighborhood knew about the kid with the drum set at the bottom of the block.

It's important that I go back to Ohio Court because when I got my drum set, I had another friend whose name was Eddie. Eddie was a White guy who lived in a neighborhood just across a big field from my neighborhood. His neighborhood was all White people while mine was majority Black with a few White people. Eddie also played the drums, but he didn't have a drum set to play. So when I got my set, Eddie would sneak over to my house to play my drum set. The reason Eddie had to sneak was because his parents were prejudiced against Black people. And Eddie told me about how his parents felt about Black people. To me and Eddie, this didn't matter because we were buddies. And he knew he was more than welcome to come to my house to play my drums because my mother was very nice to Eddie. As Eddie and I got to be close friends, his parents had to come to the realization that we were going to be friends no matter how they felt about me or Black people in general. So Eddie would invite me over to his house, but we had to stay outside. I wasn't allowed in Eddie's house. His parents must have felt pretty guilty of how they treated me because our friendship continued regardless of how his parents were.

So one day, Eddie said, "Hey, Mark, my parents would like you to come to dinner." I was shocked, but I was a kid, so it didn't really matter that much to me. I was looking forward to having dinner with my first White family. To them, it was a milestone because I was the first Black person to ever dine in their house. Actually, I was the first Black person to ever step foot in their house. Eddie used to always tell me how it was nothing for them to use the N-word on a regular basis during dinnertime. When the day came for me to join Eddie and his family for dinner, it was like any other day. The dinner table was set very nicely, and Eddie's mother brought the food out and served all of our plates. I don't remember us saying grace before dinner because that was mandatory in my house. But I actually enjoyed the dinner. No, she didn't serve fried chicken. We made small talk, his mother asked a few questions about my family, and we pretty much had a nice time together.

After dinner, his mother served dessert. We didn't always have dessert at my house, but my mother always served a well-balanced meal. To take it one step further, after we ate, Eddie and I were allowed to actually play inside the house. This was a historic day for me and Eddie's friendship. Eddie and I stayed friends all through high school. For a while, we played the drums in the marching band side by side. We would always joke about me being the first Black person to come to his house. To this day, Eddie is one of my best friends.

Now back to the Chesapeake Acres, my first lower to upper middle-class Black neighborhood. We were moving on up! Most of the parents in this neighborhood were college-educated, and there was a father and mother still in the home, just not mine. Some of the Black parents in this neighborhood had the nerve to be a little uppity. But it was a neighborhood where everyone knew each other, and there were plenty of kids in the Acres. Our community was one big block with a few cul-de-sacs around it. This was where I landed my first job; I was the neighborhood paperboy. I used to throw papers and tried my best to land them on your porch. I was even chased by a few dogs. That was how we did it in those days. Nowadays, papers are delivered from a car, if they're even delivered at all. The good thing about being the neighborhood paperboy was that you get to meet all your neighbors. And for the most part, most of the people in the neighborhood were nice to me. When we first arrived in this neighborhood, we were renting our house. Eventually, one of the houses in the same neighborhood came up for sale, so my mother purchased it. We finally owned our first home. This particular house was located right down the street from the first house we were renting. So we still lived in Chesapeake Acres.

When I was about eleven or twelve years old, I was starting to get pretty good on the drums because I used to practice during the summer months all day long. I got my first brand-new bicycle, and I was now playing baseball in the Little Leagues. In my youth, I was considered one of the better athletes in the neighborhood. One thing about living in the Acres was we loved playing sports. Whatever sport was in season, we played it. And that was back when you stayed outside until the streetlights came on, and you knew to get back home before the lights came on. They eventually installed a basketball court in my neighborhood. And as kids, we practically live there. It got to a point where our basketball court was packed with people playing all day long every day. And kids came from miles around to play at our basketball court. As it got more popular, it started to attract some undesirable kids. So what started out as a nice basketball court to play on, it started to become a hang out. You heard cussing, people were drinking beer, smoking weed, and every once in a while, a fight would break out. The families in the Acres were not having that kind of activity in their neighborhood. So the neighborhood parents got together, went to the county, and had them lower the basketball nets from ten feet high to five feet high. This ended all the basketball games at our basketball court.

There were many other courts in our town the kids could go to and play on, but that ended basketball in the Chesapeake Acres. As I started to grow into a handsome athlete, I started to get the attention of females. I always prided myself as a nice guy. I didn't cuss or do drugs at this time in my life. By now, I was about to go into the sixth grade, which is middle school. By eighth grade, I lost my virginity. Of course, I will never forget that day my girlfriend and I had sex in the woods. It was on the Aberdeen proving ground, the military base in our town. When my girlfriend and I finally got up from our first session, I noticed I had mosquito bites on my legs and arms that had to be six inches in diameter. It was like the mosquitoes just sat there and sucked my blood, and since I was so deeply engaged in what I was doing, I couldn't even feel them. She and I just laughed about it because for both of us, it was magical. And when I had my first ejaculation, I knew to pull out. So I have now discovered sex.

Sex was just like drugs because once you start, you can't stop. I'm not proud of the fact that I discovered having sex at such an early age but that's my story, and I'm sticking to it. My first girlfriend and I continued to have sex, but it was always protected. Thank God I never got her pregnant. We got through the summer as a couple, and now it was time to get to high school. My first two years of high school, even though I was a good athlete, were spent in the marching band because I loved to play the drums. Playing in the high school marching band was fun. We had away trips where we would visit different schools or play concerts at different venues. The most fun was on the bus ride home. It was usually dark because we traveled at night after the venue. That gave a young guy like me an opportunity to mess with the girls in the band.

Me and my buddy Dr. B, that was what we used to call him, (His name was actually Mark Benton) had quite the escapades on the bus rides. All I'll say about that is we were young and full of testosterone. But while it lasted, being in the band was a lot of fun. We would all brag about what we were able to pull off on the bus trip. But when you're young and dumb and full of cum, you'll try anything. During my high school years, I was in great shape; I was a jock. I stayed in the gym, and I had great stamina. I loved to jog, and the ladies loved us young jocks. With all the high school sex that was going on, also came some pregnancies. At that age, I didn't think I had any other choice but to have abortions. I'm not proud to say it, but I have had a few. Thank God for His grace and mercy and His forgiveness of my sins. I will see all of my babies in heaven.

My first two years of high school were a lot of fun; even though I was an athlete, I didn't play any sports until my junior year in high school. That was when I decided to start playing sports. So naturally I went out for the baseball team, and I made it. We had a very good team, and we went all the way to the playoffs and almost won it all. We lost the final game in the playoffs. Even though I was one of the better players on the team, I didn't get a starting spot. In the last two games of the regular season, they put me in to pinch-hit, and I hit two back-to-back home runs. My coach asked, "Where have you been all seasons?"

I answered him, "Right here on the bench, Coach."

After the coach saw that I could hit the ball, for the following playoff games, I was in the lineup as a pinch hitter. I also played on the football team in my junior year of high school, but I didn't get a lot of playing time there either. I didn't have a lot of experience playing football, but I could run fast. So that was how I made the team. Plus, I had very strong thighs, and I could squat more weight than anyone on the entire team. Since I didn't have great numbers in my junior year, I just looked forward to my senior year. I would be prepared, and things would be better. So the summer came and went, and now it was time for my senior year. Football was first. Of course I made the team, and the local papers had me rated as one of the top running backs in the county. I was the fastest sprinter on the team, I had strong legs, and it looked like I was going to have a very promising senior year.

We got through the summer practices, and now it was time for our first scrimmage game with me at the starting running back position. My first time carrying the ball, I gained a few yards. It felt good running the ball. The second time carrying the ball, I broke through the line and a couple of guys jumped on my back. Since my legs were so strong, I was able to carry them for two to three yards. Then all of a sudden, a defender came and hit me at my ankles because I wouldn't go down. I heard a slight crack, and I went down. When I got up from the pile, I noticed pain in my left ankle. I limped over to the sideline, and they started to administer ice to my ankle. I thought I would return to the game in a little bit, but the pain never subsided. I wasn't able to return to the game that day. I continued to come to practice, and the coach would always wrap and ice my ankle. He did this for a week. I refused to think anything was wrong with my ankle other than a bad sprain. But after a week of ice and wrapping, the coach suggested that I go get my ankle x-rayed. I did, and the doctor said I had a slight hairline fracture, and my football season was over. I actually shed some tears that day.

My football career ended during the first scrimmage, not even a real game. At this point, all I could do was get ready for baseball season. And that's what I did. I actually healed fast enough to return and play in the final game of the season. They let me carry the ball a couple of times, but I really didn't want to reinjure my ankle, so I took it really easy. Baseball season was just around the corner. We were picked to win it all this year since we almost won it all last year. And we had our ace, Cal Ripken Jr. who was already being scouted by the major leagues. Moving ahead, we had a great season, and we won the class A state championship. They haven't won it since. At the end of the season, I led the team in home runs, and RBIs in a single game. So I left my mark at Aberdeen Senior High School class of '78.

I must admit, my high school years were very memorable. From athletics to high school proms, it was a lot of fun. I didn't have the best grades in high school. I guess I was a C+ student. I didn't have the grades to get me into a university, so I had to go the community college route. I started out going to an interview at my mother's alma mater, Morgan State. But when I found out they didn't have a base-ball team, I knew that wouldn't be the school for me. So I decided to go to Essex Community College, and my major was going to be music. My first year, my grades were poor. I made the baseball team, and I had a mediocre season at best. At the end of the season, I hurt my shoulder. The one thing I got out of my first year at Essex Community College was some good friends and lessons on how to party. All my college buddies drank beer, but now I was starting to smoke marijuana. I barely squeaked through my first year of community college. And it was time to return for my second year.

The only reason I returned was because I wanted another chance at playing baseball. So when I didn't make the team, I was devastated. There really was no other reason for me to stay. Deep inside, I knew I didn't have what it took to make the team. Even though I questioned the coach about why he cut me, I knew he was fair in his decision. I continued partying with my college buddies, and my grades suffered. I dropped out and returned home. My mother was a little upset, but she was okay, as long as I got a job and went to work. And that was what I did.

I had been working in the dining facilities on the military base since high school, so it was easy for me to get my job back because I left in good standings with the boss. When I returned, I found out my buddy Paul was now the manager in charge. So it was easy for me to get a job, not only a job, but he shortly hired me as his assistant manager. This turned out to be a dream come true. Two young Black men managing a $1 million government contract. We were the bosses. We actually did a great job, and all of our employees loved us, most of which were Korean women. We were good to our employees, and they appreciated us tremendously. Sometimes too much. We made sure we never took advantage of the situation, but we did have fun, and that's all I'm going to say about that. My responsibilities were taking care of the payrolls, making sure everybody's check was right. I was good at it. Just overall managing the employees, making sure the mess sergeant had adequate kitchen workers in his dining facility at all times. It was a great job! This was a memorable time in my life. I lived at home with Mom. I didn't have any children. All I did was work and party.

2

Time to Get a Real Job

For me, this type of life was okay, but I knew since I had failed at college, I had to get some type of training if I wanted to get ahead in a career. The job I had had no sense of security. It was a government contract job that could end at any time. I always knew I wanted to be part of corporate America. There was a commercial I used to always see on television, and it advertised computer electronics training. The name of the school was RETS, which stood for "Radio Electronic and Television Schools." So I gave them a call and set up an interview with them.

After the interview, I took an entrance exam, passed, and I enrolled in the school. The only requirement to get into the school was a high school diploma and I had one of those. My classes were held on the weekends, so that worked perfectly with my work schedule. Even though I was still smoking and drinking, I was still able to pass the classes. Since I hadn't done well with college, I knew I had to do better with this technical training. So I took this training a little more serious than I did when I was in college. Out of two hundred people in my graduating class, I graduated in the top 5 percent. I was sure to find a good job. So I thought.

The school had placement assistance, and they did all they could to help us find work upon graduation. A year went by and I still hadn't found a new job in that industry. I didn't worry too much because I still enjoyed my present job working for my buddy Paul. My brother Kevin was working for the Xerox Corporation and I felt since I had electronics training, this would be a great opportunity for me. So I asked my brother to put in a good word for me and he did. I got my résumé together, I gave it to my brother, he gave it to the right person, and I received a call for an interview with Xerox. I was super excited to finally have a chance to work for a major corporation. I prepared myself with the help of my big brother, and I went into my interview.

I had always been good when it came to interviews. The interview went well, and as always, I played my "I played baseball with Cal Ripken Jr." card. During this time, Mr. Ripken was doing great with the Baltimore Orioles. I can't say it was the reason, but I did get hired with the Xerox Corporation. It always helped in the interview process to share a few stories of my times playing baseball with Mr. Ripken. So I got the job with Xerox; it finally happened: I landed a job with a major corporation. I had benefits, I got to travel, and everything that came with working for a big company. The starting pay wasn't the greatest, but at least I had health coverage. These were the days before urine analysis because I was smoking a lot of weed by this time.

Once I got hired, I had to go to the training facility to be trained on the products I would be working on. The training center was located in Leesburg, Virginia, and it lasted for three weeks. The facility was located deep in the woods, and it was the size of a small college campus. It had everything from all-you-could-eat dining facilities to gymnasiums, swimming pools, and bikes you could sign out. I had my own room, so I smoked weed when I got out of class. The facility was so deep in the woods, the deer would walk right up to you. You could actually feed them from your hands.

This training was more like being on vacation. The training wasn't difficult, so the time there was stress-free. The facility was international, so people were there from all over the world. I had a guy in my class I befriended; his name was Ahmad. He was from the Middle East and he spoke with a heavy accent. Ahmad was also a new hire. We became pretty cool, so I asked him if he smoked weed. At first, he didn't understand my question, and then I gave him the universal sign of two fingers to the lips, and he said, "Oh yeah, I do, sure!"

So I invited him to come to my room after we got out of class. It was always more fun to smoke with someone then to smoke alone. And the school location was the perfect place to smoke some weed because it was deep in the woods of West Virginia. We met in the cafeteria, we had dinner, and then we went back to my room. When Ahmad answered yes to my question about him smoking weed, it wasn't very convincing, but he said he did, and I believed him. I was actually used to hearing, "Yeah, man, you got some?"

That was how a seasoned smoker would answer. But what the heck, let's give this thing a try because I must admit, this was the first time I had ever smoked with someone from the Middle East. So we ate dinner and went back to my room. I already had a joint rolled up and ready to go. I lit it and took a big toke and passed it to Ahmad. He struggled a bit with the pass, but he got it. Then he took a toke on the joint and immediately started to cough. All I thought was that he was enjoying the weed because it was pretty good weed. I knew he would have a great buzz when it was all said and done. So we continued to smoke. Each time he took a hit, he would cough. This let me know I was definitely dealing with an amateur. We finished smoking the joint and I offered him a cold beer to which he refused. No problem, I'd drink alone.

After a few minutes, I noticed Ahmad was breathing heavy, like he was having a hard time catching his breath. So I asked him, "Are you okay?"

To which he answered, "No!"

I told him, "Hey, man, just calm down, and you'll be fine." He got up and started to pace back and forth, still trying to catch his breath. Now I was starting to get worried. Then he told me to call an ambulance! Now I was freaking out! I tried to convince him that he would be okay. We could go outside and get some fresh air. "You'll be just fine."

Again he said "Please call an ambulance!"

I explained to him, "If we have to call for an ambulance, we'll both lose our jobs!"

He said, "Don't worry. I won't say anything about us smoking weed."

In actuality, I knew that if this got out, I would definitely lose my job for getting an immigrant high during a training session. It would be all my fault! Somehow, we had to get passed this. All I could think was that I just got this job, and now I was about to lose it. I convinced Ahmad to go outside and get some air. We got on the elevator, and I was praying that there's no one else on it when we got on. Thank God there was no one on the elevator. We finally got outside and we walked.

After an hour of walking, he finally started to calm down. So before I walked him back to his room, I made absolutely sure that he was okay. In that moment, I saw my whole career with Xerox flash before my eyes. It was almost a fast end to what should have been a long career. Needless to say, I didn't smoke any more with Ahmad. I kept as low a profile as I could until the training was complete. Once the training was over, I returned to my job as a technician. I settled into this job very comfortably. I was an exceptional employee, and I got along with everyone. The company had an open-door policy, which allowed me to meet with my upper management staff. So being young and ambitious, I figured, Why not? I arranged a meeting with the regional manager in our office. That's right, brand-new in the company and I wanted to talk with my boss's boss.

It was a very exciting opportunity for me. I couldn't wait to sit down and have a face-to-face with the regional manager. I wasn't intimidated at all because I thought to myself, *What have I got to lose? This is my time to shine.* I could also share my aspirations with my growth in the company. When the day came, I went in to have my meeting with the regional manager whose name was Dave. Of course I shared my Cal Ripken Jr. story, but overall, we had a very good conversation. I left the meeting feeling very satisfied with our talk.

When the meeting was over, I immediately went to sit and talk with my boss to share with him how the meeting went. I told him it was a good meeting. I also let him know that David just told me about the company and the opportunities I could have as I continued to grow with the company. My boss shared with me that it was a good idea for me to sit down and have a conversation with Dave. That was that, and that was the end of the day. A day or two passed and I got a call from my boss to come to his office. There was something he had to discuss with me. Of course I was a little nervous about this since I just recently had my open-door meeting with Dave. So now, I was wondering if there had been a possibility that I had said something wrong in my meeting with Dave. I didn't have a clue.

I got to my boss's office and he said, "Come in and have seat, and could you close the door behind you?"

All I could think was, *What in the heck did I do?* So I sat down, and my boss said, "I don't know what you said to Dave, but he wants you to start immediately in management training."

My boss pulled out six manuals that stacked at least two feet high and said I was to begin reading the training manuals for a manager position. Dave thought after our conversation that I would be a prime candidate for management training. I didn't know what to say. He told me to begin reading the manuals and studying; he also said I was to start hosting the team meetings. The big boss apparently saw something in me; the question was, was I ready to take on such a large task? It was a lot of material to read and to pull this off, it would take total dedication. And I already had my doubts. I can't party and do this; it would be like working a full-time job and taking a full-time college semester.

I gathered all the manuals up and put them in my car and took them home. Now since getting the job with Xerox, I moved into my own place with my brother. So now I had a lot of responsibilities to go with my management training. A week went by and I had not cracked one of the manuals open. A couple more weeks went by and I hadn't hosted one meeting. It was getting really evident that this management training thing wasn't going to work out. The sad part was that even though Dave considered me for this opportunity, I couldn't take advantage of it. It didn't look good to my manager or to Dave, but eventually, it was business as usual, and I just carried on as a technician. Later on, I turned in all the manuals and I gave my boss some lame excuse because I wasn't able to complete the training.

Soon, things settled down and I went back to just being a tech. Then I got my company car. This was the first time in my whole life that I actually had a brand-new car with ten original miles on the speedometer. Finally, I was starting to experience some of the perks that came with working for a large corporation. I must admit, things were looking up. Having my own place, a good job, plenty of friends, my own car, or at least a company car. I was on my way to a happy destiny. Now living with my brother wasn't always an easy thing to do. My brother has always had a short fuse. I can't remember why, but for some reason, my brother decided to move out. We got along, but we didn't get along. So now I had to find another roommate, which really wasn't very hard to do because I had a lot of friends. And at that point in our lives, everybody wanted their own place.

It just so happened that one of my friends, Chris, had just gotten out of the military and he was looking for a place to live. The good thing about Chris was that we were childhood friends, and we loved to listen to jazz on his big tower speakers. Chris was very neat, and since he had just come back from Germany, he brought back a banging stereo system. Once Chris moved in, we put the apartment together like a true bachelor pad and the ladies loved it.

Being two young bachelors, we entertained a lot of ladies. Chris got a dog and named him; "Remy Martin". Yes, our dog was named after Cognac. Remy was a good dog; he just had a bad habit of sticking his nose into girls' crotches. Whenever we had female company, he would always stick his nose right in their private areas. He wasn't violent or mean, he was just playful. Chris and I got a kick out of it because we told the girls Remy was our coochie checker. If Remy didn't like it, we didn't like it—haha! We were a great host when it came to entertaining female company. And they always loved to come back and visit.

Once, some ladies came over and put on a lingerie party for Chris and me. That was a first for me. Of course, the evening ended in sex; we had some wild times. We partied, but not in excess. We drank beer, cocktails, smoked weed, and every once in a while, we snorted a little cocaine. In those days, cocaine was a rich man's high, so we didn't always partake, only when it would come through and that was rare. There was one experience I had smoking PCP. Chris had relatives in DC and at that time, that's where PCP came from.

One evening, when Chris came home, he brought some with him. We had some friends over, so he invited us all to smoke the PCP joint with him. I think it was a Friday night, we weren't doing anything special, so we all said, "Why not, let's do it."

We were passing this joint around the table. We got halfway through and put it out. Or maybe it just went out, and nobody had the guts to light it back up. While I was sitting in the chair, I was feeling a little weird, but nothing out of the ordinary. Then there came a knock at the door. So I got up to answer the door. When I stood to my feet, it felt like the hallway was leaning on a forty-five-degree angle, and the only way I could stand up straight was to lean against the wall as I walked down the hallway. I somehow was able to answer the door, get rid of whoever was at the door, and commence to walk back to my seat. Again, the floor was leaning on a forty-five-degree angle in my mind. So I had to hold onto the wall and walk all the way back to my chair, and literally fall into the chair. Of course, all the guys at the table busted out into laughter at me high as a kite on PCP.

For me, that was my last experience smoking that stuff. I swore then that I would never smoke PCP again. It wasn't an experience that I can say I enjoyed. All the guys at the table were high, and they seem to enjoy it, but for me, it was just too much. I didn't have any control. I guess after that experience I had, Chris never brought any more to the apartment. But once in a while, we would get some cocaine to snort. That usually was a special occasion because we really couldn't afford it. My neighborhood was majority White folks, and we got along with everybody, and everybody liked Chris and me; they even liked Remy. A couple of my neighborhood friends and I partied together. So when weed came through, everyone shared, just like when cocaine came through everybody shared.'

I had one friend; his name is Frank. Frank usually brought the cocaine. And he would sell it to us for reasonable prices. But he would also party with us. One particular day, Frank asked me if I'd like to sell some cocaine. I was already selling a little bit of weed, so I thought why not, this way we could party for free. I could sell some, and we could snort some. And I could make some extra money. So a couple of days later, Frank visited with his cocaine supplier. We hit it off right away, and when he asked me if I'd like to sell some, I said, "Sure, why not?"

So he said, "In a week, I'll bring some by, and I'll give you a week or two to get rid of it." So a week later on a Saturday morning, there was a knock at my door. When I went to answer the door, there was a car pulling off from in front of my apartment. It was the guy; I looked in my mailbox, and there was an eight ball of cocaine in my mailbox. I thought this was great door delivery service—no fuss no muss. So Chris and I snorted a little bit, then I bagged up some packages to sell, and the business had begun. It didn't take any time at all to sell enough to get my suppliers money back to him.

When I called him and told him that I was through and for him to come get his money, he was truly impressed. So he brought me another eight ball of cocaine to sell. And again, I turned it around quickly and had his money ready for him in just a couple of days this time. So when he visited again to get his money, he gave me a quarter of an ounce to sell. Now I was starting to make a lot of money, and I had plenty of cocaine to party with. The one thing about my supplier was he had the best coke around. He had the actual Peruvian flakes. And it was no question that it was excellent quality. The people I sold to loved it. That's why it was so easy to get rid of. Now being that the product was so good, I started to get a little more traffic at my front door then I would like. Since my neighborhood was a mixture of White and Black, I really didn't know who was cool, and who wasn't. So I had to tone it down a little bit.

And I started to do more delivering, and not allow people to come to my front door. While selling cocaine, I came across all types of users. This one particular gentleman who was a regular in the beginning asked me the question, if my coke was good. Of course, I said yes, but the way he would find out was brand-new to me. So he took a little bit and put it in the corner of his eye. I had never seen anyone do it this way. But apparently, it's pretty common.

Well, after he put it in his eye, he immediately said you have definitely got some good cocaine as his eyes began to tear up, which I already knew. Now the business is starting to pick up. I'm making a whole lotta money, and I've got plenty of cocaine to party with. Problem was I was still working a full-time job at Xerox. Some of my coworkers were my customers. This was always tricky because you didn't ever want a coworker to turn on you. I always kept them happy. At this point things were pretty good. My roommate and I were loving life. We both had good jobs and I was running my cocaine empire. We pretty much had a laid-back party house, plenty of weed to smoke, and plenty of cocaine to snort.

At that time, we didn't smoke too much weed or snort too much cocaine. We were just having a good time, entertaining the ladies and friends. Everybody loved to visit Chris and Mark's place. These were the times when using cocaine was fun. We enjoyed cocaine and smoking weed. We had plenty of money and very few problems. Cocaine was the perfect aphrodisiac when making love to the women that we would deal with. Then I met Sylvia and decided to settle down with one woman. I was getting older and the fast life with all the women was just too overwhelming. I was getting tired of living the fast life. It was time to settle down. Chris also had a steady girlfriend that he was committed to, so things were slowing down for the both of us. Not that we weren't still having a ball, but we weren't kids anymore, and it was time to make some changes.

3

Here Comes Shelby

The unexpected happened; I got my girlfriend pregnant. The one thing I wanted to do was to be a good father. I've never had a father growing up, so I was going to make sure I was present in my child's life. Even though I continued to sell drugs and party, and my clientele started to grow. I now had people who I supplied cocaine for and they were a part of my small empire. So in this crazy scene, I decided to move my girlfriend in with me. My roommate was really cool and was okay with moving out so my baby mama could move in. My plan was to raise my child with two parents in the household.

At first, things were good. My daughter Shelby was born and we were a happy family. My other neighbors that we were friends with, also were having children around the same time. As the children grew, they all played together. There were about five kids in the neighborhood that were around the same age; they were all my daughter's friends. When they were around two years old, all the kids had electric cars and when they drove in the cul-de-sac, it was like their own little speedway. It was so cute to see all the kids driving together in their electric cars. My daughter had everything; we spoiled her rotten. These were good times. We had barbecues together, birthday parties together, and went to amusement parks together. It was fun. All the dads would sit together and have beers, the wives or girlfriends would talk and have their good times. And later on, us men would snort a little bit of coke when the sun went down. It was all good. This went on for about four years with no major issues.

I toned down my cocaine selling for the sake of my child. But I did continue to sell; I had to always supply my people who sold for me. One day, one of the people I supplied stopped by like always to pick up his package; his name was Henry. Henry was a lifelong friend; we played baseball together as kids. I met him when I was ten years old, so we went way back. And now I was his cocaine supplier. I must admit the business was doing good. I was making some money—not a lot, just enough. Because my main concern was to have enough to party with, not necessarily to make a lot of money, but the money wasn't bad. Now Henry was a good salesman for me. He moved a quarter of an ounce every two weeks, which wasn't a lot, but for our needs, it was plenty. Combining his sales with mine, I was able to move an ounce every two weeks.

One Saturday, Henry came over to get his package. He always came early Saturday morning because my dealer always dropped my package off early on Saturday mornings. This particular Saturday, my girlfriend and daughter weren't home. So Henry came in and said, "Hey, Mark, you got to try this."

I say, "Try what?"

He went out to his car and brought back a shoebox. Now I was thinking, why in the world was he carrying a shoebox around in his car? He opened it and took out a large propane torch, a test tube, a box of baking soda, and a large glass bowl, similar to a water bong. Now I was curious to see what he was going to do with all of this stuff he removed from the box. By now, I had already given him his cocaine, so he cut out a small amount and put it on the glass. When you deal with cocaine, you always have to have a large glass, solely used for chopping it up and snorting lines. He added to the cocaine a small amount of baking soda. Mixed it up and put it in the test tube. Then he added some water to this concoction, mixed it around and began to heat it with the propane torch. I was watching his every move like a hawk because it was very intriguing. It was like he was a chemist. I was now watching it come to a boil.

Then he removed the heat, then continued the heat. Now the cocaine was starting to gather inside of the test tube. This was crazy; I had never seen anything like this done with cocaine before. Now the whole time he was doing this, he was swirling the test tube around. Before my very eyes, the cocaine in the test tube formed into a round pebble, about the size of a small marble. I couldn't believe it. Then he poured it all out onto a napkin and the pebble almost rolled onto the floor. It was a perfect little ball of hard cocaine. I couldn't wait to see what was next after witnessing this procedure. He took a razor blade and shaved some of it off. Then he took that and put it into the glass bowl.

Now remember, he was showing me something new, so you would think after all that, he was going to allow me to try it first. Not happening! The glass bowl he just filled with the cooked cocaine he lighted for himself. He took the same propane torch and slowly lit the glass bowl. He applied the heat and slowly pulled on the bowl with his lips, then he took away the heat and didn't pull anymore, then he again applied the heat and started to pull on the bowl again.

At this time, the bowl started to fill with white smoke but he didn't empty the bowl of smoke into his lungs just yet. He continued to apply the heat and slowly pulled on the bowl. What I could see was he was trying to get the bowl to fill completely up with smoke before he sucked it into lungs. And then it did. He started to pull and the bowl continuously stayed full of smoke as he slowly pulled the smoke into his lungs. It was like an artform; he had done this before and knew exactly what he was doing. When he continued to pull the smoke into his lungs until the bowl was completely empty, he held it, held it, and then blew out this big cloud of smoke and immediately put his head down.

After he had blown out the smoke from his lungs he put his head down, thirty seconds later, when he picked his head up, he had beads of sweat that had formed all over his entire face. I couldn't believe what just happened after he took a hit off the glass bowl. He's sweating like a pig and breathing heavy like he had just run a race. So naturally I asked him, "Are you okay?"

What came out of his mouth, no one could understand. He couldn't even talk; his mouth couldn't form the words to reply to my question. He just spoke some sort of gibberish. It took another minute before he could even speak again. I was looking at him like, what just happened? When he could finally talk again, I asked him, "Is it good?"

And he replied, "It is very good. Do you want to try?"

Being the trooper that I was, I said, "Sure why not? Hook me up!"

After seeing that, I was kind of glad that he did go first. My mind was thinking, *What kind of drug temporary hinders your ability to talk?* After seeing that, I was willing to try. You would think, after seeing that, why would I want to take the same trip? He still wasn't totally together. I had to give him another minute or two to gather his thoughts, so he could coach me through my turn. He cut a little piece off, put it on the pipe, and told me to bring it to my lips, but pull on it ever so gently. I did exactly what I was told. Then Henry applied the heat ever so gently and told me to pull ever so gently, and that was what I did. And just like with him, the white cloud started to fill the bowl. He would coach me on how to pull gently, gently, and how to start pulling more as he applied the heat.

When the white cloud reached its capacity, He told me to, "Pull, pull, pull!" I emptied out the bowl into my lungs. "Now hold it, hold it, hold it! Now blow it out!" And I did. Then I waited, and waited, and waited. And I said, "Ah, that was okay, but I prefer snorting." I did not get the same effect that Henry got. I did not go to the moon. It was just okay to me. No sweat formed on my forehead, my breathing didn't get heavy, it was just okay. Maybe I did something wrong; maybe I didn't pull correctly. I didn't know. All I knew was I did not get an affect nowhere near what my buddy got. And don't get me wrong; I definitely wanted the same effect that he got, it just didn't happen. So I told Henry to just take the rest of the rock he created with him. I was sure he was glad of that. But I didn't have all the tools required to take a hit. That was my first experience with hitting crack cocaine, and to me, it wasn't all that it was cracked up to be. I guess I'll remain a snorter.

Henry took a few more hits off of his rock before he left, each time getting the same effect, but not as good as the previous. To me, it just seemed like a whole lot of work to go through just to get high. I wasn't particularly attracted to that. I'd rather just cut up a few lines and take some snorts and call it a day. Plus, I couldn't get that high while raising my daughter in the same household anyway. You couldn't hide being that high, but you could always hide doing a few lines. I was really enjoying being a dad and raising my daughter. I loved playing with all the kids and they all loved Shelby's dad.

Now she was about five years old, and her friends actually came knocking at the door for her to come out and play. She was a good girl, and the neighborhood was safe, so it was always nice to have her go out and play with her friends. A month goes by, and my friend Henry stopped by to pick up his usual package and again this particular Saturday morning, my girlfriend and my daughter were not home. Henry came in and said, "Hey, Mark, do you want to try that again?"

Because Henry knew there was no way he could pull out his crack kit in the shoebox while my family was at home, so when he saw I was home alone, he asked the question if I'd like to try it again. I said why not; let's try again. Of course, he ran to his car and grabbed his shoebox with all of his paraphernalia in it. We again gathered around the kitchen table just like the last time. I took out my glass so he could put the cocaine on it for preparation. I gave him his package, and he immediately started to break out the crack kit props. This time, he seemed to be a little more rushed than before. There was more haste in his preparation for us to attempt to hit the pipe again.

Since I noticed him a little more eager than before, I commented, "Hey, dude, slow down. It's not going anywhere!" To which he just laughed and continued with the process. He did all the same steps as before, just a little faster with a little more precision. You could tell he had gotten better at it, and it was apparent he had been practicing. Once he finished cooking the rock, it came out a little bigger than before. This only told me that he had added a little more coke to the recipe than before. It was noticable that Henry wanted to smoke a little more than usual. All of these signs I noticed started to worry me. But I didn't make any mention of it, just duly noted what I saw. My main concern was that he always had the full amount of money when he returned to get his next package of cocaine. I also noticed that he wasn't talking as much, his prime objective was to finish cooking that rock up.

One thing was common: when he was done, he never offered to let me go first. It was obvious at this point that when he was done with the cooking part, he was ready for the smoking part. He was focused on getting his hit. So the minute the rock was done, he dumped it out, dried it off, shaved a little piece of it off (a little more than previously), and immediately started to put the fire on the pipe, and started the pulling process. This time, everything about what he did was a little bit more hurried and a little bit more anxious. When he finished pulling his hit and blew out the smoke, his eyes got big, his breathing got heavy, and the sweat started to bead up on his forehead. I remembered the last time he had a hard time speaking after his hit, and again, this time, he wasn't saying anything, just sitting there, looking spaced out. This time I asked a question just to see if he could answer.

So I asked him, "How was it?"

Then he put up one finger as if to say, "Hold on a minute." This let me know that again he couldn't talk; the crack once again had his tongue. A couple of minutes went by and he finally mustered up the ability to speak a few words. Barely understandable, he said, "It's good, man!" Once again, my friend had left the planet.

4

My First Real Hit

Just like the last time, he tried to introduce me to this new way to ingest cocaine; It was now my turn. I didn't make a big deal about it because I remembered the last time when I tried it, I wasn't too impressed because it didn't have the same effect on me that it had on Henry. He cut me off a piece, put it on the pipe, and started the heating process. A little heat, a small pull, a little more heat, a little more pull. Again, the combination of heat versus pull and the bowl started to fill with white smoke just like before. Then I was told to pull hard and I did. I took a full pull and all the smoke that filled the bowl shot into my lungs. And I was told to hold it, hold it, hold it, now blow it out.

When I blew out the smoke and the last bit of smoke left my lungs, I immediately heard bells ringing in my ears! I felt a high more intense than anything I've ever felt in my life! My eyes got big, my heart was racing, I was breathing heavy, and in a few short seconds, beads of sweat started to form on my forehead and across my face. I looked up at Henry's face and I knew he could tell; I had finally achieved that feeling that he got every time he hit the pipe. So now it was his turn to ask me: "How was it?"

Everything in me wanted to answer, and I tried to muster the words to reply, but all that came out of my mouth was gibberish. I couldn't speak intelligible words. When I realized that I couldn't talk, I stopped trying. I just relished in the new feeling I was experiencing. I couldn't control my mouth. Not only did I lose all control to speak, but I was actually drooling real spit, that I tried to wipe away before anyone could see it. A few minutes passed and I was able to finally say a few words, and all I could say was "That was unbelievable!"

When I finally regained control of all my faculties, I looked at Henry and said, "I'll never snort again." This was the only way to do cocaine, any other way was a waste. I did not realize what I had unleashed, but I was now a bona fide smoker of crack cocaine. Why I didn't get it the first time was beyond me, but I got it this time! So we cooked up some more and smoked for at least three more hours. And when we were done, we just packed up; Henry went home, and I went about my normal day. There was no phenomena of crave that we couldn't control. We were just done for the day with smoking.

So now, when Henry came to get his supplies on Saturday mornings, he brought his tools in, and we smoked for a while. I used to make sure Sylvia wasn't at home when Henry came to get his cocaine because we would probably indulge, but as time went on, we indulged even if she was there with my child or not. I just made sure they are both preoccupied; Shelby was outside playing with her friend and Sylvia was never interested in what we were doing; she knew I was taking care of business, and she left me alone to do that. When Henry fixed me up a hit and lit the pipe for me, I achieved that high every time. The only problem was he had all the instruments necessary to smoke. So I couldn't smoke unless he was there. The more we did it, the more I wanted to do it, whether he's there or not. I needed to learn how to do it on my own. I needed my own set of tools to pull it off. I needed to be trained and what better teacher to have then Henry.

I got my own test tube, propane torch, a box of baking soda, and my own bowl (crack pipe). So Henry showed me the ropes, and of course, I was a good student. I learned fast. Then I was bringing back nice little round pebbles of crack cocaine to smoke. I didn't realize it then, but that was probably the worst thing that could have ever happened to me in my life; to learn how to cook and smoke crack cocaine myself. But I did and I got me a shoebox to put all my stuff in. This way, I could take my show on the road, and I did just that. Now when I dropped off a package to one of my customers, I was able to ask the question, "Do you guys want to try something different, something new?" Nine times out of ten, they did.

I couldn't even recall how many of my loyal cocaine snorters I turned into crack smokers, but it was a lot. Some of them loved it; others were terrified because after a hit, it felt like their hearts were going to beat through their chests. Many thought they were on the verge of a cardiac arrest, so they would stray away from the smoking method. The only problem was the ones that did like it always needed me to cook it up for them and that took a lot of time, time I didn't have while I was making my rounds delivering my packages. Sometimes after a hit, my customer would just say go ahead and cook it all up for him or her. That was a sign that I just created a bona fide crack smoker. Which also meant that they needed their own bowls to smoke out of and that many people needed bowls, so I kept a few extras I could drop off with a few of my customers. This was before you could buy cocaine already rocked up. This was when it was called freebasing. It didn't take long before dealers were selling ready rock. That was what it was called then. I didn't do that to my cocaine because I still had customers that snorted.

Now that I had discovered my new love, I found myself running out faster, and I was doing more of my own supply, and I was not making the same amount of money that I used to make. My problem was I was a kind dealer, if you bought some from me, I would smoke some of my own with you. This also hurt my sales because I was spending more time with the people I sold cocaine to because I would sit there and smoke with them after selling it to them. Of course, I was also the cook, so I had to do all the cooking. I did teach a few people the procedure, and it was starting to spread, and people started having their own tools for cooking up their product.

During these times, I was still able to spend some time with my customers getting high and then continue with my business of dropping off packages. It took a lot of time to complete my day, but during those times, it just seemed like I was having fun. I was still enjoying smoking cocaine with my friends.

One story I will never forget was when I dropped off a package to my buddy Aaron. Aaron had a good job, he made good money, and he always got a hefty package from me. This was the day Aaron was to try his first hit off of the crack pipe. Aaron was always a good customer, and he was very cool about sharing his cocaine with me, or who was ever around. He was a good guy. He had bought from me before, but I had never showed him how to smoke it. I don't know why this particular day I did, but I guess it was his turn. I told him about it but never demonstrated it to him. He would ask, but I just left it alone.

Thinking back, I think he asked to try this particular day, so I said okay. Plus, I was starting to enjoy smoking more and more, so it was nothing for me to sit down and cook your cocaine up for you if you wanted me to. Because that way, I knew I was going to get to smoke it with you. So this day, Aaron put some out for me to cook up, and I added some to it and I cooked it up. Once I cooked up a nice little round pebble, And by this time, I was good at it, I could cook it up in no time. I took it out of the test tube, dried it off in a napkin, and shaved some off to put in the pipe. The difference between Henry and I was that I always let my customers go first. And by then, I was an excellent coach. I knew how to tell them to pull slowly, slow down, pull a little more, I applied a little more heat, and then I told him to pull until the bowl was completely empty, and he did. Then I said, "Hold it, hold it, hold it. Now, blow it out!"

Usually, I had people do this procedure while sitting down, Aaron happened to be standing during his first time. So the minute he finished pulling and all the smoke was out of the bowl and into his lungs, he turned around and grabbed his knees with his back facing me. He stayed in this position for approximately sixty seconds. When he turned around and faced me, he pointed to his face and his face was pouring with sweat. I mean sweat like I had never seen on someone before. And he, too, couldn't say one word; his mouth was temporarily out of order. In those days, we didn't compare that type of immediate sweating with the fact that your heart was pumping one hundred miles a minute. All we saw was, you must have gotten a great hit, and boy, this was some bomb cocaine. We were younger during these times, so our bodies probably were more apt to be able to handle it. Little did we realize how dangerous it actually was. That a hit of cocaine could take your body through so many changes in a small amount of time. But the euphoria you would realize from one hit was just amazing. Why we heard the bells ringing is still a mystery to me, but Aaron also said he heard bells ringing in his head after his hit.

After Aaron calmed down, we sat around and did a little more, then time was getting away, so I had to leave. I had more cocaine to drop off and the day was getting away from me. I had a few more customers that I introduced this new way of doing coke to, but I had to stop spending time at my customers' houses, smoking cocaine with them and try to concentrate on selling. As time went on, I was smoking more and more and selling less and less. When my dealer would show up on Saturday mornings to drop off my package, I didn't always have all of his money like I used to. I would have to quickly make it up out of my own paycheck. This should've been a red flag for me to notice, but I was so involved in smoking, my priorities started to get mixed up. It started to not be about the money and started to be more about the smoking and partying.

When my money was short, I would just tell him that some of my people that I supplied were a little short and I was waiting for them to pay me. This would work for a while because since I had a job, I was always able to make up the money. But I knew this wouldn't last forever, he had to realize things were changing with me. I could tell he was beginning to get concerned with my payment issues, and he would just make the comment, "Come on, man, get it together. I need my money."

I wasn't really concerned with him being a tough guy because he was a little scrawny White dude, and so what, I was a little short with his money; I would get it to him and he would be okay. One day, I was watching a Mike Tyson fight on television with a bunch of my friends. In the beginning of the fight, the camera would always span around to see what celebrities were sitting in the front rows. And there were celebrities all in the front row seats. As the camera continued to span, there was my dealer sitting in the front row of a Mike Tyson fight. I could not believe what I was seeing. That was when I realized I wasn't dealing with just an average guy; this dude was connected with the big boys. So that told me I had better get it together because apparently, this guy was connected with some pretty high-level folks. At least now, I knew why my coke was so good, this guy might be connected with the mafia, who knows?

Now I realized why he always told me if I wanted it, he could fill my whole washing machine up with cocaine. It just depended on how much I could handle. I knew now that I had better be careful, I didn't realize who I was dealing with, and I didn't want to piss him off because overall, he was a real nice guy. He never showed any type of anger or meanness whenever we would talk and for the most part, we got along pretty good. My usage continued and when he would show up for his money, I was continually short. Now he was starting to get upset and what he would do was give me less and less in my package size. So my packages went down from two ounces to one ounce, to a half an ounce, to a quarter of an ounce. This trickled down to my clientele; I had to give them less as well. Things were starting to unravel. He knew I was starting to mess things up. Even the people that I would supply would come to me with short money, which would really mess things up. It was getting more difficult to make up the money that I owed him, which also made it harder for me to pay my bills. My finances were in a mess. I couldn't really tell you where it happened, but somewhere along the line, I became addicted to my own product. For too long, I was getting high on my own supply, and now my supply was starting to run out. My drug problem was starting to weigh heavy on my relationship with my baby's mother.

As my drug-dealing career was slowly falling apart, something strange happened, which probably was the best thing that could've happened to me. I was pretty much at the end of selling cocaine, I really didn't have a lot. My dealer had pretty much cut me off, so I started finding others to supply me with some cocaine to sell because I still wanted to smoke, so in order to smoke, I had to sell. I would sell just enough to allow me to smoke for free. One day, some friends and I were sitting around my kitchen table just talking. Didn't have any drugs, wasn't smoking any weed, not even drinking any beer, just talking.

I heard a knock at my front door, so I went to answer it. When I opened the door there are two, White gentlemen in trench coats standing at my door. I asked, "Can I help you?"

One of the gentlemen answered and said, "Hi, we're selling magazines and we'd like to come in and show them to you. Do you mind if we come in and show you our magazines?"

I looked very puzzled, and I said, "No, not now. I have company. Now is not a good time."

So they said, "Do you mind if we have a drink of water?"

Now I was starting to get worried; this just didn't seem right. They actually asked me if they could come in and have a drink of water? I already knew what's going on; remember I'd been selling cocaine for quite some time now. These two gentlemen were undercover cops. So I finally got rid of them and I returned to my company. And the first thing I said was, "Hey, guys, 5–0 just came to my front door." I knew without a shadow of a doubt, I had just been visited by the police. I also knew that my dealing days were now over. Needless to say, I shut it down. I never sold another drug again. And the police never returned to my door again. I wish I could say I stopped using, but that wouldn't be true. With these recent events, my relationship was pretty much over with my child's mother, so I moved out and went to live with my uncle. He had a nice townhouse, and he needed a roommate to help share with the bills. I thought this would also give me a chance to get away from my madness and get a fresh start living with my uncle. I still paid all the bills at my child's mother's house because I couldn't stand to see them having to move out.

As long as I stayed off of the pipe, I could afford to do this. This lasted for a short time, because even though I slowed down my cocaine usage, I didn't stop. Because wherever I went, I always brought that crack pipe with me. Yes, I even turned my uncle on to a hit from the crack pipe. He wasn't too crazy about smoking cocaine, so I never offered it to him again. But just like a crackhead, I had to try. It did make his heart race and it did make him sweat, and that was enough for him to realize that he should not even think about trying to be a coke smoker.

5

Back Home with Mom

This relationship lasted just a short while before my uncle realized he had to get away from me and I realized there was no way I could afford to live there and pay the bills for my baby's mother's house. So I had to do what I didn't want to do, but I had to move back home with Mom. This way, I could save some money and get back on my feet. I just had to leave that cocaine alone. That was the toughest part, just stopping. Soon as I would save up some money, I would buy me a little bit of cocaine. I would package some to sell and the rest I had for myself to party with. It never failed, soon as I would start partying with my portion, when it was all gone, I would start unpackaging what I had to sell and start smoking it. This was a vicious cycle for me. I had to come to the realization that I just couldn't sell it; I had to stay away from it. It would just make me think back to the days when I was a great salesman when it came to selling coke. Until the day Henry showed up with the crack pipe. That was the beginning of the end.

As I realized I was fighting a losing battle, I managed to put together some sober days where weeks may go by and I wouldn't take a single hit of cocaine. During these times, things started to look up. I started playing basketball again. I started to jog again. I even got a gym membership, so I actually started to get back in shape. I jumped back into the dating scene since I was not with my baby's mother anymore. But it seemed the girls I come across also smoked coke, so again, this presented a problem.

If you were fighting a cocaine addiction, the worst thing you could do was to date someone who casually uses cocaine. Even if they just used it recreationally, you would go off the deep end because you would want to hit the pipe again, and you would. It would be very soon before once again, your finances would be all messed up. And no relationship could stand through that much turmoil. So I took a break from being in a steady relationship with anyone because I was a mess and I couldn't do anyone any good until I got myself together. Once again, I would put together some clean time, I would leave that pipe alone. I still drank, and I still smoked weed, but I hadn't touched the pipe in over a month.

So again, I was feeling pretty good about myself. Some friends and I put together a group. We called the group Zoom Productions. The purpose of the group was to throw parties. What we did was rent a facility, hire a DJ, and since I worked at Xerox, I was able to make these awesome flyers, and I was able to make thousands of copies to disperse among our friends. We posted the neighborhood on trees, telephone poles, on the sides of buildings, and barbershops. We painted the town with my flyers. And thanks to my friend Diane, who was brilliant at desktop publishing, she was able to put color pictures on these flyers, which made them very appealing. So the flyers would have all the information about our upcoming events, plus color pictures of all the guys in our group, and people loved them! When we had a party, the whole town showed up. We began to become very popular and our parties would draw huge crowds. It was established that if Zoom Productions was having a party, no one else would even dare try to have an event on the same evening.

Things were looking up, I was to save money again, and it had been a couple of months since I've had any crack. Zoom Productions was doing just fine. I struck up a conversation with a young lady who normally frequented our parties. So from there, we began to date. Her name was Terry. At this one particular party we threw, since we were now a couple, she was always there with me. She had some experience with crack cocaine, but we kind of didn't talk about it too much. We probably didn't because we both realized that it was a relationship killer, so we left it alone and enjoyed each other's company.

Even though I no longer sold cocaine, a couple of the guys in Zoom Productions did. I had purchased from them in the past, but I tried not to mix business with my issues. I wouldn't want it to be known that I had a crack problem. Since Terry had her own place and I was still living home with my mother, I decided to move in with her. I had some clean time, so I thought I was ready to move out of my mother's house.

Terry and I started out doing pretty good. One thing about Terry was she loved to drink, not a heavy drinker but loved to drink, nonetheless. At one of the Zoom parties, Terry and I were having a great time. The reason this night stuck out more than others was because we were drinking a little more than usual, and it was amazing how your defenses go down when you were drunk. Terry also knew the guys in the group that sold cocaine.

This particular night, she decided, unbeknownst to me, to purchase some. After the party, we got home, and she pulled out some rocks that she bought. I immediately got truly depressed because I knew I was powerless and I would not be able to say no. Terry had no knowledge of my history with cocaine; to her, we were just extending the party a little bit longer—no harm, no foul. But I knew this could set off another long binge of cocaine use, which was followed by spending all my money, and possibly ending another relationship. So we smoked. And we smoked until what she had purchased was all gone. Of course, since I hadn't smoked in a while, I had some money in the bank, so I came up with the bright idea of going to the bank and making some calls and getting some more. We had set off the crave, and we had to answer the call.

We continued to smoke, go to the bank, and get more money out until all the money was gone. Now all we were left with was no money or cocaine. One thing about Terry was she could always fall asleep immediately after smoking, but I couldn't. I had to stare at the ceiling until I eventually fell asleep. This sometimes would take hours. Finally, I fell asleep only to wake up the next day to the depressing thought of what I had done the night before on into the morning hours. And like I thought, this was only the beginning. Because now we would spend more money on the weekends at first smoking cocaine together. Which soon spilled over into the week-days. And it was never a good thing when you and your partner both used, because eventually we both continued to smoke.

Bills got behind, arguments started, and we just couldn't get along anymore. We actually had a good relationship, had it not been for us picking up that pipe yet one more time. I eventually moved back home with Mom, and another relationship was over. I don't think we lasted a year before our relationship bit the dust. It was nice while it lasted. Whenever problems would arise, I would always be able to fall back on my mother who was always there for me. Whether it be financial or the need to come back home for a place to stay, she was always there. My brothers were getting tired of me not being responsible and having to come back home to live with Mom. I was becoming a burden. Even though my mother's business did well and she was okay financially, my brothers still thought that I needed to be more of an adult. The only good thing about it was Mom lived alone, and it was good to have someone in her house with her.

Another thing I wasn't proud of was while living in my mother's house, I would still smoke crack in my bedroom while she was just in the next room, adjacent to me. This really wasn't cool, but I did it anyway. This wasn't cool because after I would take a hit, I would get super paranoid, and think at any moment my mother was going to come into my room. I was truly tweaking. This was one of the reasons why I didn't smoke in my mother's house. I would actually drive around in my car and smoke. Being back home in my mother's house was a deterrent to me smoking. This allowed me to also gain some sober time because smoking there wasn't fun. I just knew I had to stop smoking this stuff. And knowing this I would stop for a while, then out of the blue I would come up with a reason to go and get some rocks. It was like my mind would convince myself that today is a good day to take a hit.

Then I didn't realize that was the enemy talking to me, and I was taking the bait. I also had a few friends that every once in a while, we would get together and smoke. I had been away from my last girlfriend for a couple of weeks, and I felt like I was doing pretty good. And my group Zoom Productions was having a party. So like

I said before, the parties we had were always a huge success, this one was no different. It never failed that after I'd had a few drinks and I'd smoked some weed, all my defenses seemed to come down, and I was a little weaker than before emotionally. I decided to grab a few rocks from one of my buddies, I would go visit my old girlfriend, to see if she wanted to smoke with me.

People didn't usually turn down a free high. I went to her apartment and I knocked on her door. No one answered, but I heard the television in the background. So I knocked again, louder this time, and I called out her name, "Hey, Terry it's me, Mark. Open up, I got something." Everyone knew when you say, "You've got something," what you were talking about, which is coke.

After I made it clear that it was me at the door, I heard her say, "Go away. I have company."

Now I was really hurt. She had a guy over here, and I'd only been gone for two weeks. Now I was really upset. I pleaded to please open the door, and of course she said "No, go away."

So I said, "I just want to talk to you for a minute. I don't mind if you have company." Of course, she was not going to open the door because I was being irrational at this point. I was outside kicking her front door. And this was totally out of character for me. What I failed to mention was that I'd already taken a hit myself, I was really off the deep end at this point. I was pretty much tweaking at her front door, and I was getting a little louder. Because she did have neighbors, people were starting to come out of their doors to see what was going on. Knowing Terry like I knew her, her and her new friend were probably already inside smoking crack, that was why she wouldn't let me in.

At least, that's what my mind was telling me. She threatened to call the police if I didn't go away, but I knew that wasn't true because if they were doing drugs, they were not going to call the police. So I beggedged and pleaded with her a little longer to let me in and she continued to say, "No, go away." Finally, I did. I left because if she didn't call the police; one of her neighbors would because of all the noise I was making, and I had cocaine in my pocket and I didn't need trouble. By this time, I was an emotional wreck and there was only one thing that could cure this horrible feeling, and that was another hit. I went back to my mother's house and I smoked the rest of the cocaine I had by myself. And when all the cocaine was gone, all I was left with was my broken heart. A situation that was all my fault in the first place. This was all taking place at 2:00 a.m. I was out of control. I tried to use this as my reasoning for not smoking anymore. My emotions got out of control when I was high on cocaine, and it was a horrible feeling, especially when there was nothing you could do about it but bask in your emotions. Which had you jacked up once again.

I put the pipe back on the shelf for a while and started playing basketball, jogging, and I actually joined a local band who needed a drummer. I was thinking, *This'll do it, being in a band is something I always wanted to do. Now I'm in one, I can finally put crack behind me.* Now, I was in the band, It's been two months since the last time I smoked. I was back on track. Things really turned around during these short spurts of sobriety. You think, *Okay I've got it this time.* I just need to stay busy. I couldn't let my mind be idle too long. I needed to keep busy and stay involved in lots of activities. Playing in a band was great, I was doing something I loved; I was accountable because I had to show up for practice and gigs. It was working. I started hanging out with the bandmembers and they didn't smoke crack. Staying away from my smoking buddies was working; I was again being productive. I was still a part of Zoom Productions, so I did most of the band's bookings. This worked out great because the band would play at some of the Zoom Production parties, so they turned out to be very exciting events.

The band was a fun band and we played all of the funk songs from the seventies and eighties and a lot of the current R&B music. We kept the old school music alive and there was quite a market for it. All of our gigs would sell out. Now I had Zoom Productions, I was playing in a band, and I was working a good job. Things were really cool. If I just stayed away from crack, I would be okay. So now I'd been able to put some time between my last relationship. The pain of losing Terry had subsided. The thing about me was I didn't stay single long, and I've had a few lady friends to help me keep my mind off my ex. There was one young lady who was so good to me

45

throughout my whole ordeal who'd always stood beside me through thick and thin, and I should've realized she probably was the best woman for me. Her name was Diane.

She was the one who would create all of the flyers for Zoom Productions, and now for the band. She was with me through all my relationships. We did have an intimate relationship at times, and when we got together, it was hot and heavy! She definitely knew how to please a man. She was the one responsible for creating the flyers that had our pictures on them, which were a major part in all of our parties being so successful. She would make hundreds of flyers, and I would pass them out everywhere I went, and I would hang them on every telephone pole, on every building wall, and every barbershop I would visit. It became our trademark. When people saw those beautiful flyers, they knew we were about to have another event. She always supported me and everything I did. We eventually got into somewhat of a relationship, but I would never totally commit to her, and I should have because she truly loved me. I took advantage of her love like I had done to so many other women in my past.

She really loved a brother and had no problem showing it. We would make love pretty much anywhere; she was down for it, as long as it pleased me. I remember one night I was working on the Xerox machine in her office, and it was pretty late, and we decided to go home together. She left me working on the machine and said she would be back shortly when I was finish doing my work. When I was done, I called her to let her know I was done, and I was about to get on the elevator and come down and meet her in the lobby; she said okay. I was on the Ninth floor. I had packed up all my tools and gone to the elevator to go down to the lobby to meet her. I pressed the button to call the elevator. When the elevator arrived, and the doors opened, there was Diane standing in the elevator door in a trench coat. She opened the trench coat as I was about to step into the elevator, and when she did, she was wearing a red lace bra, red thigh-high stockings, with a red lace garter belt, and red high heel pumps, and nothing else.

Remember this was late in the day, so the building was pretty much empty, that was why she was able to pull this off and not be seen by anyone else but me. What you must understand about Diane was that she was a brick house. Her body was out of this world. What she was wearing on the elevator that evening was out of this world. I stepped into the elevator and repeatedly tried to hit the close door button, which wouldn't close fast enough. When the doors did close, I immediately started to kiss her from head to toe. When the elevator started to descend, I press the emergency stop button, which turned on an alarm, which rang through the building. I quickly turned it back off and took my chances on doing as much as I could do to her before we got to the bottom floor. Thank goodness this particular elevator was an express and it didn't stop for any more riders, so I had my way until we reached the first floor.

These were the types of things Diane would do for me, like what she would do to me in a movie theater. I'm not even going to elaborate on that; she just loved her some Mark. And I let her get away. Actually, the way I was acting, I didn't deserve her; she deserved much better.

Getting back to playing in a band, there were also special favors that came with being a bandmember. I tried to stay focused and put the womanizing on the back burner a bit. Plus, this was when Diane and I would spend a lot of time together. She was my friend with benefits, and that worked out pretty good for me during these times.

6

Meeting Monique

City hasn't changed much

Now during my days of working for Xerox in downtown Baltimore, I met bunches of women—many secretaries, office managers, and the like. But at the Department of Education Building, there was this cute little security guard that used to always flirt with me whenever I would go there to service their equipment. In the beginning, I didn't pay her much attention, but I would always invite her to the Zoom Production parties we would have. Her reply would always be the same: "I'll go if you take me."

I would just laugh and say, "One day maybe."

During these times, I wasn't trying to get started with a different woman. I had just gotten out of a relationship and Diane and I were pretty cool. So I continued to always drop off a flyer when I went to her building, I would always invite her, and she would always give me the same answer: "When you're ready to take me, I'll definitely go to your party." A little time had passed, and we had a party coming up, and I figured you know what, I was going to ask Monique if she'd like to go. So I did my same routine as always.

I walked in the building. When she went to sign me in, I handed her a flyer, and I asked her if she'd like to go. And she gave me the same answer, "Are you ready to take me?"

I said "Sure!"

This was Monday, so she had all week to prepare and be ready for me to take her to her first Zoom Productions party. I was a little excited and also a little scared because I didn't know what I had gotten myself into. But there was no turning back now. I invited her and she accepted, so let's see what happens. I may have seen her one more day during that week before Friday, so I confirmed, "Are you still going to the party Friday?"

She said, "You still coming to get me?"

I said, "Yes, I am."

She said, "Yes, I will. I will be ready." Now the drive from Baltimore City to my place was thirty to forty-five minutes, and of course, after the party, I didn't plan on coming all the way back to Baltimore to drop Monique off. I made the comment when I said, "I'll come get you was I'm not going to be dropping you back off after the party," to which she replied, "No problem."

Okay she was spending the night. I didn't say this to her; I was just thinking to myself. The first time I brought Monique out to one of our parties was during the time I was still rooming with my uncle Ricky in our three-bedroom townhouse. Friday came so after work, I went to pick up Monique and she was ready, so we headed to my place. We drove down I-95 and she was amazed how far away I lived. She made the comment, "You live in the country."

To which I said, "Yep, and I love it. If you've lived in Baltimore City all your life, then Aberdeen is definitely country to you."

When she saw where I was living and the neighborhood I lived in, she fell in love. She made the comment, "This is a nice neighborhood." The neighborhood I lived in was majority White and a small percentage of Black folks lived there. Mostly everyone had two cars and children. It was a very nice community. When we got home, I allowed her to unpack. I showed her around the house and then I said, "Let's go out and take a walk so I can show you around the neighborhood." This just blew her mind that much more. As we walked, she saw kids playing and people said, "Hi" as we passed by. She was just amazed at how friendly everyone seemed to be in my neighborhood.

After our walk, we got something light to eat, and then we got dressed to go to the party. Ricky and I kept a very clean house, this to amazed her. Two men with a clean house, she was impressed. I must admit when she put on her party clothes, she looked really nice, very cute. And I had to say I was pretty sharp myself. When we arrived, all my buddies complimented us on how cute we looked as a couple as I introduced everyone to her. Of course, when we arrived, all of my Zoom buddies had jokes, but her feisty Baltimore attitude put them all in their place.

One thing about Monique was she didn't play and she wasn't a pushover. If you joke her, trust me the jokes would come right back. She had a very sharp tongue. But it was all in fun and they wound up loving her because she kept it real. So the meet-and-greet was over; now it was time to get to the party. The music was jumping and the crowd was flowing in. One thing about Monique was that she loves to dance, and she wanted to test my dancing skills immediately. Like any party, the dance floor didn't fill up in the beginning, but that didn't matter. Once she heard the music, she was ready to get on the floor. She was looking very cute and she wanted to show us country people how the city folks party.

Don't get me wrong, because I can dance a little bit myself, but Monique was ready to show these country girls in Aberdeen, "I have one of your Zoom boys on the dance floor." So she pulled me out to the floor. I was a little hesitant at first, but I let her lead me out there. Because I was not scared of the dance floor, because I could dance too. There was no lacking in my dancing moves, and Monique found this out quickly, so we began to tear up the dance floor. In the beginning, we were the only couple on the dance floor but that didn't matter to Monique. Shortly after we started, the dance floor filled up with dancers with Monique and me in the middle. When she realized I had dancing skills, she really started to cut loose, and she started to back that thing up. She was basically staking out her territory, making sure that all the women knew that he was with me, back off. We sensually danced all night long in each other's arms. It was evident that she was going to give it up that night.

Remember, when a city girl knows what she wants, they just go for it unashamedly. So after a night of partying, drinking, smoking, kissing, we went back to my place for the grand finale. Monique was a small girl, but she knew how to go. Took me a little bit by surprise, but it was okay; I hadn't done my best performance, but I let her know it only got better. It was all good with her because she was just happy to be there in my arms at my townhouse, out in the suburbs in the country, in my beautiful neighborhood, in my bed. I told her, "Tomorrow morning, after I make you breakfast, we're going to have round two. Then we're going to go for a bike ride."

She was so excited! She was like, "I've died and gone to heaven."

The next morning, we got up, watched some *Three Stooges*, and then I made her an awesome breakfast because that was my specialty. I loved making breakfast. Then we had an awesome session. I had to back up what I promised the night before and I did. We woke up to a beautiful Saturday morning. I asked her if she knew how to ride a bike and she said yes, so we went for a nice bike ride around the neighborhood. So now that we were on bikes, she really got to see how nice the neighborhood I lived in was, and she just couldn't believe it; it was so beautiful that day riding bikes and taking in all the sights as we rode. She couldn't tell me the last time she had ridden a bike.

But I said, "That's okay. I'll teach you. I'll help you sharpen your skills." And it was a little rough at first, but she soon got the hang of it. I kept her the whole weekend with me and it was a fantastic time. She enjoyed herself fully. Plus, I didn't want to drive all the way back to Baltimore until I had to go to work Monday, and that was okay with her. I told her I had children; Shelby and my second child Shaela. Since this was our first date, I thought it wouldn't be a good idea to allow her to meet them just yet, and she was cool with that. Even though she didn't really have a choice. That would come later if our relationship lasted.

I did like Monique, she was spunky and confident. My co-workers at Xerox would make fun when I told them about my weekend with Monique. They would say, "She's just the security guard at the front door. You haven't even gotten into the building yet with all the educated women." Even though they had a point because there were a lot of pretty women in the Department of Education Building. I was a little hasty just getting out of a relationship that ended because of crack. The good thing about Monique was she was fun and she just wanted to have a fun weekend. No commitments, no ties, let's just have a good time, and that was all we did. I didn't pay them any attention, and Monique was doing everything she could to sink her hooks in fast. She was not trying to let me get away. We kept talking, having lunch together, and things were moving forward. So now, it was time to see where she lived. I really wasn't ready for what I was about to see. She lived in a beat-up row house in the hood. When I saw her living conditions, I saw an opportunity.

If you know anything about row houses in Baltimore City; they've been there since the 1800s. Some of them are pretty run-down while others are pretty nice. It depends on the owners whether they took care of them or not. And some people did a pretty good job at making their row homes look nice. Most of the ones that were for rent weren't necessarily taken good care of. They were run-down and mice-and-rat infested. Did I mention roaches? You couldn't forget about the roaches. Most of the ones I'd been in had roach problems.

As Monique and I continued to date, I would just help her fix up her living conditions. If I was going to be visiting there, I couldn't stand to let it continue to be run-down. Especially after her seeing how I lived. My house was spotless because I liked cleanliness, and my Uncle, being ex-military, also liked to keep a clean house. Not to say that she was dirty, but people would just settle with the conditions of most row homes. You couldn't really do anything about the mice infestation because they had been there for decades. And since each house was connected to the other, if your neighbor had mice, you had mice. And most row homes are maybe eight units to a building all side by side. So after I would put my touch on her place, it would be much more livable. She too enjoyed what I would do to her living space. She knew if she wanted me to visit her, there had to be a certain level of cleanliness. I would always contribute to it getting to that point so everything was cool, because at first, I made it clear there was no way I was going to spend the night at her place, unless we clean things up a bit. Of course, she wanted my company overnight, so she abided to that rule. Not to sound vain, but she knew what I was used to, and that was okay with her to make it nice, especially since I would do most of the work.

To give you an idea of what I'm talking about, when I speak about the mice, there was one night when I spent the night with Monique. Don't get me wrong, I've lived in apartments that had mice, but nothing like the Baltimore City rowhouse mice. One evening after work, I took Monique out for some drinks and some dancing; after that, we went back to her place. We grabbed something to eat to take home with us because we just smoked some good weed, and we had the munchies. And Monique always had some good weed because she knew where to find it in the city. So we started to eat our food, watch some TV, do what we do, then it was time to go to sleep. As soon as we turned off the lights, I heard a crackling sound.

I asked her, "What is that?"

She said, "Oh, they're mice."

I said, "Mice?"

She said yes. So I got up and turned on the lights, and I didn't see anything. So I turned the lights back off, got back into bed, and it wasn't a minute before I heard the crackling sound again. I said, "You're kidding me. They are mice?"

Soon as we turned off the lights, they immediately attacked our leftovers.

She said, "Yes, all you have to do is tie the trash above the floor. Just hang it onto something so they can't reach it."

I couldn't believe what I was seeing or hearing because of course it was dark, and I couldn't see them. But now I was curious and I got to see what was going on when the lights go off. So I got a little flashlight, I turned the lights off, and I watched. And sure enough, the minute the lights went out, here came these little mice crawling from under the heater unit. The row houses were heated by steel heater radiators I guess you could call that, real old school. That was where they came from, the hole in the floor for the heating unit. It must've been three or four mice every time we turned out the lights that would come out of that hole. I couldn't believe it. They were so bold; as soon as the lights went off, they came right out. I think I tried three times just to watch them. Then we had to tie the food in bags and suspended them from different things in the room, just so the mice wouldn't get to them. Who was to say if they didn't come out and walk around the room and check stuff, but we didn't hear the crackling bags anymore, because there was no way I could sleep listening to the mice have their party.

As I lay in the bed, I remember thinking to myself, *What in the heck did I get myself into?* But I was a trooper so I hung in there. I had to admit, for a young Black woman with no kids living in the city, she was handling her business, so I had to give her credit for that. Some time had passed and it had been a while since I stayed at her place. I'll never forget, it was Fourth of July and we had made plans to stay in Baltimore City that weekend. By now, you could say we were in a relationship. I wasn't crazy about staying at her place, but I did out of convenience for the weekend. This particular Fourth of July, it was 90 degrees, and 90 degrees in Baltimore comes with 90 percent humidity, which makes it miserable. You had to have AC in order to survive. Of course, in the city, all they had were fans, no air-conditioning.

After our evening out from having a great time in the city, we grabbed a bite to eat, and then we came back to her place. And boy was it hot in that row house. Sweaty sex was okay, but now it was time to go to bed. We turned on fans. I believe she had two, and we lay on top of the sheets because there's no way I could get under sheets when it was that hot. Remember, I had central air-conditioning in my townhouse; I never had to deal with these types of conditions. I tried to go to sleep, but there was just no way. I couldn't; it was too hot! So I told Monique in the nicest way I could, "Baby, I'm going home. I can't take it."

Then she said, "Please don't leave. I'll cool you off."

But I said, "No, it's okay. I'll come back tomorrow."

She said, "You don't have to do that. Let me cool you off." So she went and got a wet rag with cold water and began to wipe my forehead and my chest, and she did everything she could to cool me down. Nothing was working. I was sweating like a pig, and when it was that hot, I couldn't sleep. But she continued to wipe me down with the cool rag. The whole time this was going on fireworks were being exploded right outside her window. So along with it being hot, kids were blowing off fireworks all night long. Which didn't help for falling asleep, but she continued to wipe my forehead, and as the evening temperatures started to drop, I eventually fell asleep. It was about 3:00 a.m. when I awoke. I decided to go downstairs and grab a beer. When I got downstairs and turned the corner to enter the kitchen and turned on the lights, there were full-grown rats eating on top of the kitchen table, crawling around on the kitchen floor, and more rummaging in the trash can.

As I walked closer, they ran out of the kitchen through the back door through a hole, which had been gnawed through, giving them total access to the kitchen. I counted about six rats. Each one was about a foot long. I didn't know how much more of this I could take. This was starting to get ridiculous. I returned to the room to tell Monique what I just saw. And all she said was, "Oh yeah, I meant to tell you about the rats."

I was thinking, *You meant to tell me? I could've been eaten by rats, this could've been another scene from the movie* Ben.

At this point, I really wanted to go home, but I couldn't just bail on her, so I just did my best to go to sleep and get through the night. So we fell asleep and got up the next morning to some morning sex. I remembered last night there were fireworks since it was the Fourth of July. When I got outside, again I couldn't believe what I saw. My brand-new company car was covered with fireworks remains. It was like they launched all their fireworks off the hood of my car. I could not believe it; my car had burnt marks all over it. Once again, that was what you get when you were in the hood. I guess they realized that I wasn't from there. "Too bad, homeboy, we're going to use your car to launch our fireworks." This was the last straw. I told Monique from now on we'll visit at my place and I couldn't stay overnight here, it was too dangerous. Luckily, I was able to clean off all the burn marks from their fireworks. I was really starting to question this relationship, if it was a good idea or not. I started to have my doubts. But I hung in there again and since we had been together for a while, it was time for me to meet her mother. This was a whole entirely different situation because her and her relationship with her mother was a bit strained. Her mother was a bit on the mean side, mean to Monique and mean to anybody who was in a relationship with Monique, meaning me.

But I was finding that in the inner city, most folks were a little hard when they met you at first until they got to know you, and then they lighten up a little bit. Monique's mom was a little rough around the edges, for reasons I'll find out later. But for the most part, we just distanced ourselves from her mother and only dealt with her when we had to. She wasn't horrible, she just had her ways. Monique moved again into another row house with a friend of hers who had some space in the basement, which she turned into her own apartment. And like always, I came in and cleaned it up and made it more livable. It was actually kind of nice; the only problem was the ceiling was only five feet high, so when we got inside, we had to bend down as we walked. But it was livable after we cleaned it up and it didn't have a rat problem like the last place. She only lived there for a short period of time because her friend made her move out after we had fixed it up.

We think it was for that reason that she wanted Monique to move out from the space we just made nice. The good thing was, Monique had a grandmother that needed someone to help out, so it worked out for Monique to move in with her, and she would have her own bedroom upstairs in her grandmother's row house. Since I was now a part of her life, every time she moved, I was the guy that helped her do it. But that was okay; we're a couple now, and that was what you do for your girlfriend. Plus, Grandma was sweet as can be. She did have mice, but by now, we were kind of used to that. Just made sure we elevated all our trash, didn't leave it on the floor or in the trash can, or the mice would definitely get it. So we got Monique all moved in her grandmother's house in her own bedroom.

Problem was, she had to sleep on a bunkbed, which was a twin mattress size. Good thing was, she had her own room and we had privacy because Grandma never bothered us. She was glad to have the company. I would only stay there sparingly because I didn't feel good about staying at Grandmother's house even though she loved me like I was one of her own. Now as far as the cocaine use, I was doing pretty good because I knew Monique didn't use it, so I thought this would be a great opportunity to leave it alone, or at least slow down on my crack smoking. Things were good. I was playing in a band, I got a new girlfriend, and I was working every day.

7

What's That Taste?

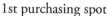

1st purchasing spot   Another crack spot in the Village

One thing different with Monique was, instead of smoking marijuana in paper, she smoked it in blunts; that was the new thing: everybody used blunt paper then. You tore open the Philly Blunt skin and filled it with marijuana. This was the new craze; no one used Ez-wider paper anymore. Everywhere you went, you would see the tobacco from the inside of a Philly Blunt on the ground because when people would tear one open, they would just dump the tobacco on the ground wherever they were. Monique's ashtray would always be filled with half-smoked blunts. If I came over and she hadn't arrived there yet, Grandma would let me go upstairs to her room to wait for her. This day was like any other. I checked her ashtray and there was a half-smoked blunt. So I picked it up and lit it. I pulled on it and tasted an all-too-familiar taste. I tasted crack. And I know crack when I taste it. So when Monique came home, I asked her.

I said, "What's in this blunt? It tastes like crack."

She denied it. She said, "There's no crack in that blunt. It's just a regular blunt with weed in it."

Now I didn't want to let her know she was talking to an expert who knows the taste of crack all too well. But I did let her know that I knew this was crack. So she finally relented and admitted that the blunt had coke in it. Now I was playing dumb, like I was interested in that feeling it gave me, like it was something new. She didn't realize that when I hit that blunt, it set off the phenomena of crave that was inside of me, and I definitely wanted another one. I passed the blunt to her and we finished it off. Now we were both craving more. She wasn't at the level of crackhead that I was and I didn't want her to know how bad I was. Of course, I had to ask her if she could get some more, and we could smoke together, and she said, "Sure!"

Just like that, all that clean time gone. I was now smoking again, just from a little taste. That was how easy it was to get off the wagon when you were talking about crack cocaine. What was so amazing was that it wasn't from smoking from a pipe, it was from picking up a halfway smoked blunt and getting the taste of crack cocaine left in a blunt, mixed with marijuana. We put our money together and she said, "I'll be right back." She didn't need a ride or anything. She just took a walk, and in fifteen minutes, she came back with more weed, more blunts, and three dimes of crack. Only in the inner city could you pull this off. This would never happen in my neighborhood, it was so easy in Baltimore to get drugs. This was so convenient, a twenty-minute walk and she was able to pick up all the party supplies we needed. This was too easy.

Of course, later that night, she made two more trips because we had both awakened that addiction. I guess it didn't matter how much you smoked, when you fed that monster, it always called you back for more, whether you wanted to or not. When it was all said and done, we had spent $100 that night. But of course, when we were done with the smoking, we had good sex, and I spent the night that night and left the next morning. Not feeling too proud of what took place. I now had to realize I had a girlfriend that also smoked crack cocaine. Even though she smoked it in blunts, it still was bad. Of course, I never let on that I preferred to smoke it in a pipe; this would be too tragic for any relationship. And maybe if we continue this way, maybe we could control it, and things would be okay. We would have to see. Deep inside I knew this was the beginning of another bad cocaine ride. It seemed just as I had gotten out of the cocaine life, Satan knew just how to slowly bring me back in.

At least I wasn't hitting the pipe. Yeah, right, for now! That was my rationalization: I was only smoking blunts; I'm not hitting the pipe. Things only go bad when you were smoking from a pipe. At least, that was what I told myself. Plus, this way, when you hit it, it didn't take you straight to the moon like smoking from the pipe does. Smoking mixed with weed kind of took the edge off, so it was not so intense. It seemed like the crave wasn't as bad. I later found out that was a big lie. I took the bait because deep down inside, I enjoyed the effects produced by cocaine, and I really did want to continue smoking it. And of course, I liked the Baltimore hookup. It was easier to get and the packages were bigger. So my thing was, as long I was putting it in, I didn't care how I did it. It now meant whenever Monique and I got together, we were going to smoke some cocaine. Of course, I was now spending more time in the city with her. I was basically back to my old tricks again. All I had to do was show up at her house after work with twenty bucks and we were good. I would just give her the money, relax in her bedroom, and wait until she came back. It was like clockwork; she always came back with all the party items.

I later found out she was going to the local corner store to purchase what we needed. This was known as the block and it was full of young kids who worked the corners. When I rode by, I could see the malay that was going down on the corners. The young kids had no respect for the crackheads that came to buy crack from them. But when Monique came, they gave her the utmost respect, basically because of how she carried herself and for the simple fact that she still looked good.

She didn't look like a worn-out crackhead, she was still pretty, and she didn't let them talk to her any kind of way. She demanded their respect and they gave it to her. Even though she was a customer, most of the crack customers were my age, in their forties and fifties, and they referred to us as the, "old heads." Monique was in her late thirties, so she didn't fit the bill as a local crackhead. All the young guys would always try to hit on her, but she knew better than that because the last thing you wanted to do was to give those young guys any ideas that they have a possibility to date you. Because at that point, they'd never leave you alone, and they would start trying to say that you needed to stop smoking this stuff and let me take care of you.

But Monique knew how to deal with them, and she kept them in their place. We were able to always get our crack from the corner store. That day came when Monique said, "You can go get it." I was totally comfortable waiting for her, but I knew it was my turn. I wasn't really worried or scared, but I didn't want to deal with the young kids because they could be obnoxious and very disrespectful because you were already looked at as a crackhead. From the beginning, you lost a bit of respect from them even though they wanted your money. I was used to buying in my town. In Aberdeen, I knew all the drug dealers, and all the drug dealers knew me. So there was never any problems or issues or concerns as long as you got your money, that was all that matters.

But again, it was that little issue of size. What you got in Baltimore didn't even compare to the small amounts they sold in Aberdeen. I just had to figure out how to purchase in the big city. But as you continued to use, you wanted more bang for your buck. So it was inevitable that I figured out how to make it work in the city. The first time I did it, Monique went with me to kind of help me out. Introduced me to the game, so to speak. And of course, I was a quick learner. The main thing you had to do was find a particular dealer to deal with and whenever you wanted to cop, you just looked for him, and that was who we would purchase from.

Of course, if he wasn't there, you had to find someone else to deal with. It was trial and error finding a person to deal with because some had big packages while others had small packages, and of course, we wanted the biggest package for our money. You also had to watch out for the burners; they were the ones that were selling fake drugs. They usually came out later, after the young boys were done. Since transactions happened fast, you didn't always have time to examine what you were buying. They would sell you sheet rock, chalk, aspirin. This was why you wanted to know who you were dealing with, because there was nothing worse than copping on the street and coming home, ready to take a hit or roll a blunt and finding out that you had been ripped off and, instead of getting coke, you got garbage. And there was no redemption; once they got your money, they were long gone. I've never been able to go back and find the person that burned me on the street. They were somewhere with my money smoking.

Sometimes, if you let the regulars know that the burners were selling on their block, they'd track them down and take care of them, making sure they didn't return. They didn't want to ruin the reputation of their block because they wanted their customers to return, so there was a level of street justice. Usually, the burner took the money he robbed from you and bought from the regular dealers on the block anyway. Ultimately, they got the money so it was a give-and-take situation. There was also a street code. If your dealer was there and he saw you purchase from someone else because maybe they had bigger rocks than he did, he would feel betrayed and would be pissed. These are some of the things I had to learn if I wanted to be able to go out on my own and purchase crack in the city.

One bad experience I had when I was trying to make a purchase on the street, I got to the corner and I saw what I thought were the guys with the dope. And that was what they said, "We got it over here!" So I walked up to him and gave them my money. Now usually, they didn't have the crack in their possession because if they get pulled up by the police, they didn't want to get busted. They normally walk to wherever they've stashed it to get your dope. This particular time, I gave him my money, he turned to go get the dope, and before I knew it, he took off running with my money. I just got ripped off. My first thought was to give chase, but I knew I couldn't catch him; you can't catch a Crackhead, they run fast, everybody knows that. Plus, they probably had others that were a part of their little scheme and it was not worth getting jumped in a dark alley in Baltimore City. Chalk it up as a loss.

Now that I thought I got the hang of this thing, I was starting to branch out and purchase in different areas from different people, just because they look like they may be dealing. Another bad experience I had was when I pulled over in my car and the dealer approached and asked me what I wanted. I told him, he left, and came back with what I thought was cocaine. I just so happened to have the money In my hand and I was just about to give it to him when he reached in my car, snatched the money out of my hand, and took off running. Again, I was burned by the streets. You may get better sizes, better quality in the city, but it did come with a price. There was always that chance of getting ripped off. Not like at home where that just didn't happen because you knew where the guy lived when you were buying in your hometown.

In the city, you didn't know them from Adam, but you took that chance time and time again. This was the cost of buying in an unfamiliar neighborhood. So when the guy snatched my money and ran, it was in his neighborhood, so he knew exactly where to run, and it was better to not even think about chasing him, and of course I didn't. So through this process, I was gaining my street knowledge, and this was important if you wanted to indulge in this cocaine game in the city. Through trials and expensive errors, I learned the streets were not your friends, and if you got a good dealer, you better stick with them. Dealers also knew that people who smoke, smoked all around the clock. You began to find dealers who deal all around the clock. So I had at least five spots that I could frequent to find cocaine at any time of the day or night.

One time, Monique and I went out in my car to get some cocaine. I parked my car and let her get out to go get it. Twenty minutes had passed and no Monique. I ventured out to find out what happened to her because twenty minutes was a long time, the process usually took fifteen minutes tops, and we were on our way back to her place to smoke. When I got around the corner where I thought she might be, I asked a few people if they had seen a young lady around here. And they were quick to say, "Yeah, she was here. She got arrested and they took her away in a police car."

My girlfriend got busted! They said 5–0 just made a swoop, and she got caught up! I couldn't believe what they were telling me. I was thinking, *What do I do now? Do I go to the police station and try to figure out how to get her out?* No, I was a crackhead so I asked the main question: "Does anybody have anything out here?"

They said, "Sure, red tops are right over there." (The color of the top of the vial the crack rocks were in was how the dealers identified their product)

I said, "Thanks!"

I copped me some red tops and I was on my way! Yeah, I know, it's just not right; your girl got locked up trying to purchase crack for the both of you, and when you find out she got popped, you get some for yourself. My reasoning was, I was already out here. I might as well buy some for myself. Now remember I was not used to copping in this environment, but I had to see what was taking her so long. My first intentions were to find out what had happened to her, but since I was right in the middle of where you could purchase it, I just asked And got lucky. I was able to purchase some in the Baltimore City open air drug market (the Hood). First time buying in the inner city and I was successful. Boy was I excited. This wasn't as hard as I thought it would be. It was like my right of passage. Monique had always urged me to try because I always put it on her to buy our drugs in the inner city.

I would always say, "It's your neighborhood and you know how to deal with these folks." I looked more like a target—someone they could take advantage of. Now that I pulled it off, I didn't have any more excuses. Monique was in jail, I was able to score, so I went home. The next day I got the call. The first thing she said was, "Did you know that I got locked up last night? Why didn't you come to at least check on me?" That was when I used the excuse of "How was I to find out where they took you? I didn't know anything about where they took a person after they locked them up. So I waited for a phone call from you." I didn't dare tell her that after I found out she was locked up, I was able to buy some crack for myself. I just said, "It's good to see you're out." We had small talk about what happened to her; she said she spent the night in jail and only got a misdemeanor charge for drug possession. Overall, she got off easy. I didn't tell her that I went out and bought some after I found out she was locked up. I told her from time to time I'd go out and try to purchase in the future.

A week later, I showed up at Grandma's house with some crack that I had purchased on my own. She was impressed. I said, "I told you I could do it." I just had to always remember the rules that you follow when buying on the streets. If you have a relationship with one dealer, you have to stick with that dealer. If you try to go to someone else because that person may have bigger rocks, that's considered a no-no! It can get you in trouble. Something about customer loyalty is big in the streets. The worst thing that could happen was you got told to not come around there anymore. If you did, it might not be a good experience. It could actually get physical because they were normally in a gang, and you didn't want to deal with the whole gang. So from time to time, I would purchase our cocaine off the streets, and Monique would also purchase as well. But after her incident, we slowed down a little bit.

By now, Monique and I were in a full-blown relationship. I had introduced her to my daughters and they they got along just fine. Yes, I did say daughters. Because on a one-night stand booty call, I went to visit my baby mama and got her pregnant, and she made my life a living hell for that. She swore that she would be in my pockets for the next eighteen years plus, because she was actually very bitter about our breakup. I never stopped being in my daughters' lives, and I always made sure their mother was taken care of. Monique didn't mind meeting the mother of my children, but the mother of my children didn't want anything to do with any other women that I was dealing with. So I did my best to keep them separate, even though my girls learned to love Monique and they always talked about her. I soon had to explain to them not to do that and they did to the best of their ability. Monique also got to meet my mother and my brothers.

She got along well with all of them; they all liked Monique because she was cool. A little rough around the edges but cool.

Since Monique was starting to be more involved in my life, it created more tension on the relationship with me and my children's mother. And since she had custody of my girls, she would use that as leverage when I would come to pick them up. Sometimes when I had weekends planned with the girls and they knew it, they were expecting me to come and pick them up. Soon as I would arrive, she would tell me, "Plans have changed. They're not going with you."

This, of course, would make the girls cry because they loved being with their daddy. I continued to always be available for my children and I would always go pick them up when their mother didn't give me a hard time. Eventually, she realized that the girls liked Monique and she was good to them, and that was really all that mattered. So raising two girls brought some normalcy to my life and my relationship with Monique. She didn't have any children of her own, so she enjoyed helping me with mine. During this time life was okay. The band was doing okay and this was good because it kept me busy. Monique loved hanging out with the band members and going to gigs to support me.

At that time, we were one of the best cover bands around. We had a very large following and our shows always sold out. So with all this positivity going on, Monique and I did our best to keep the coke smoking to a minimum. We were doing pretty good. The band members just smoked weed, drank beer, and we spent a lot of time hanging out together preparing for our gigs. We had biweekly practices. I continued to do most of the bookings and all of our advertisements. I didn't mind. I really enjoyed playing in the band, but I always knew if I wanted to make a career of this, we had to start playing original music, and we were a cover band.

One day, I was in a music store looking at some drum sets, and they had a bulletin board. On the bulletin board were advertisements for drummers needed. Mind you, at this time, I had no desire to leave the band that I was in because I was enjoying what I was doing. A few of the advertisements were for drummers needed for an original band. I thought this might be a great opportunity. So I snatched the phone number, and I kept it for a couple of days. I eventually called the number and left a voicemail message to the effect that I was a drummer, and I would like to audition. Of course, I didn't share this information with my present band members because I was sure they would be crushed. But like I said earlier, If I was going to make a go at this, I had to be in an original band, playing original music, and that was the only reason that I reached out to the ad. I was the youngest guy in the band that I was in, and if I was going to do this, now was the time because I wasn't getting any younger. This pretty much was the time to try. I had to follow my dreams.

Three days went by before I got a call. I didn't get the call, they left a message for me. When I received the message, I had mixed emotions. I didn't know whether to be excited or worried. I knew there were a lotta good drummers out there, and what if I didn't pass the audition? Then on the other side, what If I did pass the audition and they chose me, Then I'd have to tell my old band I was leaving. But I returned the call, they answered the phone, and we set up the audition. Before the audition, I had to meet with them to get a copy of their first album. These guys had already produced an album. This added to my excitement; this was exactly what I had been looking for. I met with them to pick up their CD. They were an alternative rock band and I had no problem with that. They seemed like really nice guys. They told me they were auditioning other drummers, so I had time to practice the CD before I came back for my audition. We set my audition for two weeks later. This was great because I needed the time to practice, because I wanted to be impressive when I got my chance.

I took the CD home and devoured it. I practiced all the songs as much as I could. The problem was my drums were stored where my band practiced. So now I had to tear them down, bring them home, practice, and then take them back to my band's practice location. The fellas asked me why I was doing all this. I just said I needed to practice at home. All my present band members were from my hometown; this new band was located in Baltimore in Parkville. They had an awesome practice location, in the basement of one of the gentleman's beautiful home. Everything about this new opportunity seemed to be so nice. And you could tell these guys were driven for success. From our first meet and greet, they explained to me all of the things they had planned for their success. I also shared with them that I was presently playing in a funk band, and we played pretty regularly. This was impressive to them to know that I was in a working band that was very active and playing a lot of gigs. What they liked the most was that I was playing funk music. They were actually looking for a funky drummer, and I definitely was that!

There were nine tracks on the CD I had to learn, so I had my work cut out for me. In those two weeks, I had to prepare; I really put quite the effort forward to make this thing happen. The drummer on the CD was actually a good drummer, so I knew I had to practice diligently. But it was nothing I couldn't handle. I just had to play all the music from memory, and that worked out for me because all my life I played from memory. I didn't read much music, but I could listen to a song a couple of times and get it. And that was what I did. When the day came for my audition, of course I second-guessed myself. I had doubts if I could pull it off. I was lacking confidence. But I thought, *What do I have to lose? I'm already in a band, so if it doesn't pan out, I'll just continue what I'm doing*, which helped to take some of the edge off. So I brought my drums in and got all set up, loosened up a little bit by jamming with the guys. Things seemed to be going pretty well.

Musically, these guys were good. They were excellent musicians. Plus, they knew the music because it was their own; the only variable was me. I had to show my stuff. First song, it was an easy one, so I nailed it. I could tell from the looks on their faces they were impressed. Second song was a little tougher, but it sounded good. By the third fourth, and fifth song, we were buzzing right along. By eight, nine, and ten we were jamming, and I could see they were enjoying themselves playing with me.

As I looked around the room at the guys' faces, I noticed the smiles. You could tell we started to vibe as a group, the music all came together. When we finally finished the set, we had a few beers with some conversation about how things went. They went as far as to talk about some of the previous auditions they had been through and how disappointing they were. This was comforting, but I still didn't want to get my hopes up because they still had two more drummers to audition. That kind of news took the wind out of my sails about the good time we just had. Now it was over; it was positive, but now the wait. All was cool because I was still in a band and if all else failed, that was what I'd fall back on. I really liked these guys, and I would love to be a part of this band. To be absolutely sure and ready if I got the call, I continually practiced the CD. If they called me back, I wanted to blow them away with how well I could play their music. Deep down inside, I knew I nailed it. And I thought then I was going to get the job. But of course, you couldn't be absolutely sure. It was about two weeks that went by when I got the phone call.

8

The New Band

I was chosen. I was now a member of the Unprovoked Moose Attack band. You can't imagine my excitement. It was almost like making the high school baseball team. Now I was faced with my next dilemma: How do I tell the guys, or when do I tell them? We had more gigs lined up that I had booked and I couldn't back out of my commitments to the guys. My new bandmembers were totally understanding of my situation. These guys were consummate professionals and all-around good guys. I just had to tell the fellas that I was done and that I was moving on. This wasn't easy because we were a band, a unit, and we were friends. But I knew deep down inside when I told them they would understand because they were musicians. The ultimate goal of a musician is to make it big one day. And the only way to do that is to create new music, not play someone else's music.

A couple of the guys had original tunes, but we never pursued playing original music or even played any of the original tunes at our gigs. We just played what the people wanted to hear, what they wanted to dance to, and that was why we were so popular and got so much work. However, playing in a cover band was fun and I was excited about playing in an original band. So I realized there was no easy way to do it; I just had to do it. At the next rehearsal, I decided I was going to let the guys know that I was leaving the band and I did. Initially they were a bit surprised, but they understood and they couldn't really disagree with my decision because everybody wants an opportunity to make it, and you can't do that playing other people's music, and all musicians understand that fact.

Their biggest dilemma was booking gigs because I always took care of that. They wouldn't have any problem finding a replacement drummer because the keyboard player wanted to play the drums anyway, so he fell into my spot, and they just had to find another keyboard player. Another thing was that they were no longer going to have those cool flyers to promote the gigs that I used to provide since I worked for Xerox. I let them know that I was going to stay for our last gig, which was coming up in a week.

After that, I would be leaving. I told the guys in the new band about my last gig that I had to perform at. After that, I would begin playing with them. Believe it or not, they all decided that they wanted to come see me play in my last gig with my other band. I thought that was actually a pretty cool idea. I looked forward to them coming to see me play some funk music. The only thing was these were all White guys, and the club we were playing in was all Black people. They didn't mind; they said they still wanted to come. I said, "Okay, it's next Friday."

None of them had ever been to my neck of the woods, but they all made arrangements to come support me. If it was okay with them, it was okay with me. I let them know it was a Black club and they were cool with that. They showed up with their girlfriends and actually had a good time. They were drinking and dancing with the brothers. Of course, I welcomed them when I saw them come in the club; this probably was an indicator for my band to know these gentlemen were my new band members. I noticed my bandmembers observing the out-of-place White couples that came to our Black club. It was a little awkward at first. My girlfriend Monique knew all the funk bandmembers and their girlfriends. They all sat together, and we all hung out together. Monique knew the new bandmembers were coming, but she never got a chance to meet them.

As the evening continued and my new associates were sticking out like sore thumbs, my bandmembers asked me if that was my new band. Of course I said yes; those were my new band members. I introduced them to each other, and it was pretty cool; my bandmembers were very cordial because we were all musicians first. This also solidified the decision they made to choose me as their new drummer because they got to see me in action. Our crowd loved us because we were good, and the Moose Attack guys got to see me in my element. So after it was all over, I thanked the guys for coming out. They said they had a great time and they looked forward to me playing drums in their band.

Rehearsal was Monday, so I said, "See you at rehearsal." I wasn't sure if my original band members felt like I had betrayed them because there were a few short lines I had received from a few of them. Nothing outrageous, but I sensed a little bit of hostility. Like I was ending a good thing. But I couldn't be concerned with that because it was all about the music and the opportunity I was given. Monday rolled around and I was excited about my new endeavor. I continued to practice the CD throughout the weekend. All day at work, all I could think about was going to practice with my new band. I was confident in my ability because I had put in a lot of time that Saturday and Sunday on the CD.

I had directions to get to their practice facility. It was in a neighborhood I had never been to; the neighborhood was majority White, filled with beautiful homes. The home we practiced in was owned by the leader of the band, Scott. Scott had lost both of his parents to premature illnesses, so he had inherited this wonderful home that we were able to use. The home had a completely finished club basement, which was perfect for us to practice in and just enough to be able to relax in. This was all new to me. We have plenty of space; of course it was safe for keeping our equipment, and they had all types of equipment for recording purposes and listening purposes. These guys were lacking nothing. The music style was an alternative rock type of music, which was popular during these times and their music fit right in. It had a rock feel, which was perfect for me because as a kid in the sixties, seventies—that was all I listened to. That was a time in my life when I listened to rock 'n' roll music on the radio all the time. And when I started to play drums, I learned everything by ear, I wasn't able to read music, so I picked up on their music real fast.

The good thing was we gelled as a group very fast. Their intentions were to have a rock 'n' roll feel, with a funk bottom. That was why they acquired a Black bassist and a Black drummer, me. To provide that funky feel and we really were a funky group. Scott had a degree in music, so he was able to read and write music, and play saxophone and keyboards, and he was our lead vocalist. Some more good news was that they already had a gig booked to break me in. I thought this was great. I didn't have to book all the gigs like I did for my previous group. We worked hard to prepare for that gig and it was in two weeks!

I have to say that I was a little nervous because this was a whole new world for me with the new genre of music and new crowd. I was ready for the challenge. The drummer they had before me was a good drummer and there was one song on the CD I was having a little trouble with. I could pull it off but I was striving for perfection. So the day of the gig arrived and of course, we got there early to get everything set up and have a few beers because that was the norm in the rock 'n' roll world. A couple of cold ones always relaxes me anyway, so by the time it was ready to start, we were ready to go; we were feeling it. And wouldn't you know, the drummer who played on their CD was there. He was a cool brother. We met, and he wished me well. He never intended on staying in the band; he was only there to help them with the recording process. I guess you could say he was actually a studio drummer because his skills were tight. But now it was time for me to step into that spot as the new drummer for Unprovoked Moose Attack.

It wasn't a large club; it was fairly small, but there was a capacity crowd. All their friends were excited about seeing the new drummer and seeing the band play live. The club had an awesome sound system, which was a plus. We did our sound check and we knew it was going to be a great night. I counted off the first song and we were off to the races. When we were done, the crowd went wild—success! We went right into the next song after the applause. Every once in a while, I would glimpse over and see their old drummer checking me out. Giving me the nod that "Hey, you sound pretty good!" Actually, I knew it because we practiced hard before this gig to be totally prepared.

By the time we got to song 3, 4, 5 to end the first set, it was no question that we definitely had a good sound and the crowd enjoyed every minute of it. When the set was through and we were taking a break, the guys were slapping high-fives saying, "Great job, Mark!" We looked around for the old drummer and he was nowhere to be found. The guys exclaimed, "We think you ran him off the way you were playing tonight."

I didn't think that was the case, but I took the compliment in stride. All I did was play the parts that he created exactly like he played them, with my flavor on them. But I could now breathe a sigh of relief, knowing that the guys were happy with the decision to choose me as their drummer. That was only the beginning because these guys were hungry to be successful in the music game. We stayed busy and everybody had a part in our success. All types of doors started to open from gigging every weekend, to traveling to New York frequently, and spending a lot of time in the studio recording our own music. One of our recordings actually got played on the radio. (Of course, we called the radio station multiple times requesting our song to be played). We finally got signed to a small independent label. We even appeared on a local morning show. Everything that I looked forward to was actually happening. This is why you get into music, for the opportunity of maybe being famous one day. And we could see our dream actually taking shape.

It was so refreshing to see a group of young guys with all the same ambition. We knocked on doors, sent out demos, toured up and down the East Coast, played on college campuses, and built a college following. If you could build a college following, you could pretty much write your own ticket. After signing our first record deal, which wasn't the greatest record deal, but it was a deal nonetheless, they paid for our recording time in the studio and we got to use studios that professional artist used. Shortly after that, we had to hire an entertainment attorney. Our attorney also worked for the Gin Blossoms, which was an already established group with hit records. So we got to go see them perform in stadiums, from a backstage perspective. It was hard to believe that our music career was actually moving to another level, one which none of us had ever experienced, or even believed could happen.

With all this going on, I had a new reason to leave the crack pipe alone. My life was on a new trajectory and I was trying my best to stay on it. The only thing we did in the band was drink and smoked weed, so we were able to manage our partying, and these guys were not to be distracted. No one really did it to excess, but on occasion, Monique and I would go and purchase a little cocaine after some of the gigs for a little celebration. I guess as time went on, I was starting to get a little comfortable with my position in the band. I never stopped working hard, making all the practices, and doing my best as a member, but I started to get a little too comfortable.

Once I brought some cocaine with me to New York to one of our gigs. New York gigs were usually overnight. When we were done playing, the one guy I knew who had tried cocaine before, I offered him a hit off of the crack pipe, and the crack did what it does. He loved the high and when it was gone, he wanted more. But the only difference between him and I was that he was he was okay with saying "That's enough, I'm done," but I wanted to see if I could find some more. I couldn't find any because we were in New York and I wasn't familiar with those streets, and of course, it was too risky. the weird thing was, I was almost willing to try.

After a while, I came to my senses and I said, "That's the last time I'll ever try to share smoking crack with my bandmember." That was truly a mistake. Heaven forbid they find out about my crack problem. I also really felt bad about turning a bandmember on to a hit off of a crack pipe. I guess misery loves company. The realization of what I just did gave me reason to put smoking on hold again, especially with a group member. I could see how smoking was starting to affect my playing with my new band and these guys worked so hard for success. I can't blow this opportunity. So I got refocused on playing with my band, and being a positive member.

At the rate we were working, there was really a possibility for success with these guys. The future was looking good. I was not smoking now, and my job was going pretty good with Xerox; It was just that I Had a girlfriend that continued to smoke. Monique was a little more controlled when it came to smoking crack because she would only smoke it rolled up in a blunt; she knew nothing about the crack pipe. Me, on the other hand, preferred smoking it from the pipe. I didn't dare let her know this. When we were together, I smoked it the way she smokes it, rolled up in a blunt. This was just as bad because it sets off the phenomenon of craving just as if you smoked it out of a pipe. When we were together, we did it her way.

Since we were both getting high together, I was spending more time with her in Baltimore City because That was where the good drugs were. So now instead of me sending her out to get it, I went out to make the purchases because I was trained; I knew how to do it on my own. We both had spots we would frequent because they were nearby, and it was just easier to get it and get back to Monique's house. On the corner was the liquor store. It was a one-stop shop. We could get the crack, the blunts, and also some liquor. Jack Daniels was what we drank with Coca-Cola.

Remember, we were buying this cocaine from a bunch of kids who were selling on this particular corner. This was called; "The Block". The problem was, once they got to know you on The Block, and they knew you were going to spend a decent amount of money; everybody wanted to get to you first. When my car would pull up, eight kids would run straight toward my car, shouting the names that they gave their drugs. Red Tops, Black Bags, I got those Fat Dimes, I got them Nickels! It was crazy! Of course, eight kids running up to your car made you stick out like a sore thumb because the kids could care less. If the police were anywhere around and saw this happening, they would immediately pull you over because the kids would run, and you were stuck sitting in your car.

So I learned quickly to just keep driving and go around the block, park my car, and walk back so they could serve me. When they saw me walking up, they would still ambush me because they were all trying to sell their drugs, and they knew I was spending good money. They tried to do this to Monique as well but she knew how to shut it down. She would just point out who she wanted to purchase from and the rest would just back off. A little street respect. Street purchasing had its own advantages and its drawbacks. You just had to learn how to roll with it. Now, as I continued to use this method to get my drugs, you knew it was just a matter of time before karma comes a knocking.

9

Getting Busted

1ˢᵗ arrest Carey St. sign   1ˢᵗ arrest/Thrown to the ground

I'll never forget the first time I got busted purchasing crack off the streets. It was during a workday. I decided to go get a rock on my lunch break. I went to the same place where the kids would bum rush me. This particular day, there weren't a lot of kids out; the corner was pretty much empty except for one guy. In this world, you had to read the signs. Usually, when the corner or the block was empty, it was because the police had run everybody off earlier. Of course, I had no way of knowing that. There was one guy still there, or maybe he had returned—again, I didn't know. I was just happy to see someone that

Calhoun st. arrest   steps of Calhoun arrest

I recognized whom I could purchase from. There was just something eerie about this particular day, but I ignored that feeling and walked toward the guy and gave him the sign of how much I wanted. We made the handoff, cash for crack, and I turned and walked the opposite direction and he did the same.

Success! At least that was what I thought! I had my drugs, I put them in my pocket, and now I was walking to my car at a little faster pace than before, probably because of the sheer excitement that I was about to get high. Before I could get to my car, a police car pulled up right beside me and said, "Stop right there!"

I did exactly what he told me to do and he jumped out of his car and asked me, "What are you doing out here? You just bought some coke from that guy, didn't you?"

I gave the only answer that I could give, "No, sir!"

To which he replied, "Hands on top of your head!"

I immediately obliged. I said, "What seems to be the problem, Officer."

He said, "Just shut up and keep your hands on top of your head!"

I was thinking in my mind, *I'm going to jail, right in the middle of the workday. How in the world am I going to get out of this? I'll lose my job.* Of course, that was when to myself I called on God, *Lord, please get me out of this. I promise I'll never do it again!* I failed to mention that he had already picked up the guy I had purchased my crack from, and he was sitting in the backseat of the police car. I wasn't going to tell on the guy, but I was sure the police officer already knew what had happened and who was involved. He was basically trying to put it all together so he could take us to jail. He rummaged through my pockets and found my two dimes of crack. The strange thing was, even though he found the cocaine, he never put handcuffs on me; he just threw me in the backseat of his car next to the guy I had bought the coke from.

As soon as I got in the car, the guy asked me if the cop found the cocaine. I said yes. He asked me if I told the cop that I got it from him and I told him no; I didn't snitch him out. So now we were sitting in the back of the cop car, my dealer and me. The police officer started driving around the neighborhood, very erratically bumping over curbs and driving through alleys. He would stop the car, jump out, look in places where dealers may stash their packages because that was a common practice. No one liked to keep their cocaine on them while they were selling it, so there were little nooks and crannies where they stored it before they sold it to us addicts.

When he didn't find anything, he jumped back in the car and started driving around again, turning hard corners, rolling us around in the backseat of his car trying to find a stash. The backseat of a police car is not a comfortable place; there are no see cushions—it's just hard plastic. And the way he was driving us around, he wanted us to feel every bump and curve. What I later realized was since all I had were two dimes, he was trying to find a stash to pin on me so when he arrested me, the charge would be for a greater amount than I had. When he didn't find anything, he pulled the car over and told the young guy I bought it from to, "get out of here and I better not see you around here again!"

I was still in the backseat of his car, thinking, *I'm going to jail, this is it!* Remember this was the middle of my workday and I had on a trench coat with a shirt and tie and hard shoes. I didn't look like a crackhead. Then the cop opened the door and told me to get out! And since I didn't have any handcuffs on, I got out. I didn't have a clue what was about to happen, but I was thinking, if he let that guy go, and he already had my cocaine, maybe he'd let me go too! So I was standing on the sidewalk, looking as sad as I possibly could because I was truly sad that day. All I thought was my career was over. Then the cop asked me a question, he said, "Man, you really like this stuff? You really like this stuff?"

I couldn't bring myself to give him an answer. What was I going to say "Yeah, I like it?" I couldn't say no because I had it in my pocket; I had just purchased it. I knew his question was rhetorical. I knew he didn't want an answer; he was just trying to make a point. He was teaching me one of life's many lessons. But this was the kicker! He said, "If you like this stuff so much, tilt your head back!" Naturally I was thinking what in the world was going on. But I didn't hesitate; I tilted my head back. He said, "Now open your mouth!" Again, I followed his orders, and I opened my mouth wide!

When I did this, he tore open my packages of crack, poured them in my mouth, and said, "Now chew it up!"

So that was what I did; with my head back, I chewed up all the rocks he had dumped in my mouth. Just from the taste of it, I knew it was real good coke. Once I chewed it up, he told me, "Now get your ass out of here, and if I see you back around this place, I'm going to lock your ass up!"

I didn't realize at that moment, but God had answered my prayer; I was free to go. What a relief. I could actually go back to work. Remember, I said the coke was good. It was so good my mouth was totally numb from chewing it up, and since I had to swallow it, five minutes later, I had to pull my car over so I could throw up my guts. A small price to pay for dodging jail. Rather than think about how good God was to me, all I could think *man that was some good coke, what a waste.* I was able to go back to work and finish my day.

Of course, I didn't share that with Monique either. She wasn't crazy about me not sharing with her, especially when I was buying it in her neighborhood because I bought it from the spot right around the corner from where she lived. Now that I had my first fling with the police and I was able to walk away, it almost emboldened me. It did scare me straight and convinced me to take a little break for fear of running into the same policeman again. God was watching over me. I truly thanked God for protecting me and keeping me safe during my brushes with the police while dealing in the drug culture. But it wasn't enough to make me stop.

I continued to go out and purchase on my own, and like anything else, the more you do it, the better you get at it. I got more and more confident at purchasing in the Baltimore City open air drug market. I started to pick up on the signs of how to locate where the good dope was. I started to get more and more connections as I ventured out. You must always remember, no matter how good you think you are at copping, if you increase the number of times, you go out and cop, you also increase your chances of getting busted. A couple of months had passed since my last run-in with the law. That time I got Off Scott-free! In Baltimore City, there were a lot of corner stores. These were houses that had been converted into stores. There was a small area about nine by nine feet, a big glass window that separated the patrons from the store owners, and the owners were always Asian folks. Everything you wished to purchase was behind the glass, so you had to point out what you wanted and the people behind the glass got it for you, put it in a turnstile after you had placed your money in the turnstile, and that was how you got your goods.

The dealers hung out in their stores, and the Asians hated them because they sold their crack in their stores. They would alert the police to this activity, so the police knew about what went on. That was one thing about the Asians, they opened up their stores right in the middle of the hood, and this was what came with the territory, but they still fought against it and tried to stop it. For buying crack, it was kind of convenient because you didn't have to be outside in the open when you purchased your drugs. I had just finished a day of work and I was buying some cocaine in this particular store. School had just let out, so the store was full of kids, plus the drug dealers. My dealer was inside the store and I bought fifteen nickels from him.

That was fifteen small glass vials about two inches long, stuffed in my pocket.

The police were nowhere in sight, but they randomly came through the stores to try to stop this activity. Now, mind you, I just got off work, so again I have on my trench coat and a tie, I was in a store full of kids buying cakes and candy. I stuck out like a sore thumb. I did nothing to alert the police, but just the fact that I was in there made them suspicious. So as I was trying to walk out of the store, the police Officer said, "Excuse me, sir, could you come here for minute?"

At that same moment, he grabbed me by my arm and started to direct me out of the store. I was thinking, *Oh my goodness! Nowhere to run, nowhere to hide.* When he got me out of the store, I reached into my pocket, grabbed all fifteen of the nickels I had just purchased, and I threw them up in the air! With this, the police officer immediately threw me to the ground and put his knee in my back and said, "Don't you move!" Now other policemen were coming to the scene, the kids in the store started to scatter. We actually had a crime scene! I didn't know where this next part came from, but I started to say with the cop's knee in my back, "Thank you, Jesus! Thank you, Jesus, Thank you, Jesus!" All I knew to do was to call on the name of Jesus, and I did it over and over again. When the police that had his knee in my back heard this, he said, "Don't call on Jesus now!"

But I continued to do it. I couldn't tell you why, but that was what I did. Maybe it was my way of repenting for the mess I was in. Looks like I chose a fine time to repent while the policeman's knee was in my back. These policemen were pretty mean to me because they had just caught a drug user in the middle of a purchase at a store around a bunch of kids. I was caught and I was guilty. But for some reason, the same police officer that brutally threw me to the ground after he heard what I was saying started to say, "Don't worry, sir, everything will be all right. You just stay calm."

It was like his whole attitude changed toward me and he started to treat me with respect. I couldn't understand why, other than it had to be Jesus. They put the handcuffs on me and the police officer started to search and gather as many of the vials that I just threw in the air that they could find. This time, I wasn't as lucky as the last time. I was going to jail. And of the fifteen nickels I had thrown in the air, they had found ten. So apparently, there were some happy crackheads in the crowd. The police officer that arrested me was still being kind to me, but he still took me to jail to be processed.

This was a first and I had no idea what was about to happen to me. The only good thing was this was a Friday night so it was the weekend. Maybe there was a possibility of me getting through this process and being released before Monday to make it to work. When we arrived at the police station, of course I was very remorseful and totally respectful to the police officers. The same cop that told me not to call on Jesus all of a sudden, he started to be really nice; he reassured me that everything was going to be okay and he offered to buy me a soda. Police officers just didn't do that for criminals. This assured me that God was working on my behalf and I even got a sense of peace during this whole process. Because in the beginning, I was terrified I was getting locked up, and I had no clue what was about to happen to me. I'd driven by the Baltimore City Jail facility many times. I'd even worked on equipment inside the building because they use Xerox copiers, I'd serviced them before, but never have I been an inmate.

My Mind was telling me that I was going to run into someone that I'd met in a professional capacity. The good thing was that they took me to one of their field offices, not to the Baltimore City Jail, which looked like an old-style English castle, with big gates and barbed wire fences all around it. Just the look of it was scary. So when we finally got to the field office and they started to process me in, they told me what the charges against me would be. Here was when God let me know that he was in charge. Remember I threw the vials in the air, fifteen of them. The police only found ten, which means my charges were misdemeanor charges. If they would have found eleven or more, it would have been a felony. I definitely called that a God shot. He was caring for me before I really knew Him. I found this all out later after I had to start dealing with the criminal justice system, and after I had to get a public defender because of course, I couldn't afford a lawyer.

So while I was laying on the ground, with the cop's knee in my back calling on Jesus, he was there through the whole process, and I didn't even know it until later. Now it was time to go through the booking process. I got my mugshot and fingerprinted, and now the waiting—oh, the waiting was the worst. Before you ever went to a cell, you were sitting in a room on a hard chair with ten to twenty others who had also been arrested and who were being processed in. All you could do was to wait your turn. The police doing this are in no hurry. They were on the clock, and they were just waiting for this shift to end. You were not a priority, you were just another criminal. You would be amazed of the flow of people who were constantly being brought in. People were committing crimes continuously and the police are out there locking them up. This experience also allowed me to realize how tough a police officer's job really is. I was sitting there trying to be as respectful as possible, some of the people brought in were drunk, high on drugs, and just downright unruly, giving the police officers a hard time.

This was routine for many of the people the police locked up. Some are locked up over and over again. When they showed up, the police officers called them by name and said things like "You're back already. I knew you would be back. You love us so much you didn't want to stay away too long." I couldn't believe what I was seeing, but I just sat there quietly and observed. I was all processed in, and it was time to be led to my cell. There were five other guys that were with me going to the cell. I thought I would have my own cell, but what I found out was we were going to the holding tank. Inside the holding tank there were already twenty guys laying all over the floor, sitting on the benches that were there, and just laying all over the place. You actually had to walk over people to find a place to sit down. Of course, there were no benches to sit on and the room was filled to its capacity; all the benches were taken, so I had to find room some-where on the floor to sit down.

Since this was my first time, I was hesitant to talk to anyone. But after you sat there for a while, people started asking, "What are you in for?" I was just watching others start to entertain conversa-tions about their charges. But everyone seemed to be helpful when it came to talking about why you were there and what the possibilities were of you getting out. At first, I just listened, and then I got the nerve up to start a conversation with one of the guys sitting around me. I told him what happened, I told him how much drugs they found on me, and I let him know that this was my first time.

With all that information, he told me, "No problem, you'll be out of here tonight!" For a moment, I was overjoyed at what he just said to me because I thought for sure I was going to be spending some time in jail. So now I had more questions. Like "Who do I talk to, to arrange getting out of here?" And they all said, "You have to wait to see the commissioner." We all got a chance to talk to the commissioner. Naturally, I wanted to know when I got to talk to the commissioner. A few of the inmates started to shout to the guard, "When's the commissioner coming?" And this was about 6:00 p.m., so they answereded, "The commissioner will be in at 11:00 p.m.," which turned into 12:00 a.m., which then went to 2:00 a.m., then they said 3:00 a.m. Now I was wondering if this was just something they told the inmates, or did they really not know when the commissioner would arrive? I thought it was just a head game that they played with the inmates to keep us in suspense. Because at 6:00 a.m., we finally got the message from the guard that the commissioner was here. One by one, we got to see the commissioner to find out what type of charges we would be facing and whether or not we will be serving more time. Even though the jailhouse lawyer gave me good news, I was still worried about what might happen once I got my chance to talk to the commissioner.

I think fifteen guys went before me to speak to the commissioner. I didn't get to speak to the commissioner until 8:00 a.m. I spent a very uncomfortable night in the holding cell. But believe it or not, it wasn't as bad as I thought it was going to be. People were just minding their own business, waiting to talk to the commissioner. No one gave anyone else a hassle, no fights or arguments, just waiting. It amazed me that a lot of the people that were in the holding cell slept the whole evening like they were home in bed. I didn't sleep a wink. It wasn't that I was worried; it was just that there was no way that I could sleep on a hard cement floor with a bunch of men laying around snoring and calling for the commissioner all night.

Okay, It was finally my turn to talk to the commissioner. What a relief when they finally called my name. The guard came to the cell, opened it, and summoned me to follow him. I was never so happy to hear my name called. Strange as it may seem, the few acquaintances I had met in the holding cell gave me the thumbs-up when I got up to leave. It was a reassurance that things were going to be okay. And I needed that. So the guard led me through the jail to another bench and told me to have a seat. I waited another ten minutes before I was led to the Office of the Commissioner. He sat behind a glass wall; I sat in a chair on the other side. There was a small window with a slot where we talked to one another through. It didn't take as long as I thought it would. He reviewed my charges, told me what I was guilty of, gave me my court date to return, and told me I was now being released on my own recognizance. I had no clue what that meant; all I knew was I could finally leave. I was free to go. This was very important because the guys in the holding tank said, "If you don't get released by the commissioner today, you'll be going to City Jail. Where we were was just a temporary holding facility, it's where they keep you until they decide whether or not you're going to the big house, and that's real jail where you're probably going to spend some time."

Where I was arrested, my car was around the corner. The precinct they took me to was two miles away. I didn't have any problem walking all the way back to where my car was parked. This gave me time to think about what just happened and my experience of being locked up behind crack cocaine. I got back to my car. I thank God it was still there and no one had bothered it. I didn't go to see Monique. I just went home and I didn't tell anyone about my experience. Monique couldn't know because I didn't want her to know I was out there buying crack without her because then she could've given me the "I told you so" or "That's what you get." A week went by, and I was pretty much scared straight.

After that, there was no way I was going to go buy anymore cocaine in Baltimore City. At least that was a normal person would do. Saturday rolled around and I went to visit Monique in the city, and of course, she has some cocaine to smoke, so we chilled and partied a little bit together. Again I didn't tell her about what happened to me a week ago. After we finished, I decided to go home, but since I got that feeling started, I decided to stop by one of the spots I frequented and picked up just one more rock to take home. This was about 11:00 p.m. Not a lot going on in the streets. I got to my spot and I saw that they were sitting out on the front step, which means they were in business, the store was open.

So I parked my car around the corner, my usual routine, and I walked back to the house where the guys were sitting outside. I asked them for two dimes of crack; they said, "Hold up a second" because they had to go inside the house to get it. I waited on the step with the guy who was the lookout. A couple minutes went by and they brought me out my dimes. At the same time I was sitting on the step, there was a van stopped at the traffic light right at the intersection. I didn't pay it any mind because the light was red, but I seemed to notice just for a minute when the guy came out the door with my cocaine, the light had turned green for the van to proceed, but the van just sat there.

As soon as he put the coke in my hand, the van pulled up in front of the house where I was standing and police jumped out of every door saying "Freeze!"

One week later, busted again. I was so ashamed I didn't even bother calling on Jesus this time; there was no way he was going to get me out of this again. They told me to put my hands above my head and I obliged. Then they commenced going through my pockets, and of course, they found my crack. While all this was happening, the people I just purchased from ran back into their house. Did you think the police knocked on the door and asked them to come out? Of course not! They got who they wanted: the buyer not the dealer. They put the cuffs on me and put me in the van and took me back to the precinct. The one I had just visited one week ago.

Again, I went through the booking process for another drug possession charge. Once again, I was put back in the holding tank with another fifteen to twenty guys who also had been arrested that day. Again, we sat all night and waited on the commissioner. This time, I knew I was going to get some time in jail. I called on the expertise of my fellow inmates, but strange enough, when I shared that this had happened to me a week ago, and already I was back again for the same charge to see the commissioner again, they told me, "You're going to get out tonight or at least in the morning." Now I was thinking, two times in a row and they were just going to release me? These guys seemed to know better than me how this whole drug game works. It was apparent that my crime was somewhat petty in comparison to what goes on in the city streets. They'd just run me through and release me with another court date. My biggest problem would be when I faced the judge, and he sees that I was a repeat offender. That was why it might be a good idea for me to get a real lawyer.

But of course, I still didn't have any money to afford a lawyer, so I'd still have to depend on a public defender. I hadn't been to court for my first drug charge, and I'd already gotten my second. After I went through the booking process and I was put in my holding cell again, my hope was that I didn't have to see the same commissioner. Because I knew he'd throw the book at me this time. After an uncomfortable night in the holding tank, 8:00 a.m. arrived, and I was sitting in front of the commissioner, a different commissioner. But he did have the record of my previous arrest, and again, he released me on my own recognizance. I was ecstatic, but a little worried because this was strike two, and I wasn't sure what to think might happen to me. So again, I walked back to my car to find that it was okay, and again I drove home not bothering to go by Monique's house. Besides, it was early in the morning, and again I didn't sleep one wink in the holding tank.

I went home and got some rest and tried not to dwell on what I just went through because my court date for the first arrest was coming up in a couple of days. I tried my best to put together some sober days. I didn't know what to expect, but I couldn't have drugs in my system when I went to court; at least that was what I was thinking. This was all new to me, but I relied on the information I got from the guys I got locked up with. They said this would be just a slap on the hand; I'd probably just get probation. So the date arrived and I got to court late. I was running around trying to find out what room my trial was happening in because remember, I'm new at this and I didn't know where to go. But I found the list posted that had my name on it and the courtroom I was to go to.

By the time I got there, it was over. I was running around trying to find out what I could do to have a retrial because at this point, I was told by the clerk that a warrant was put out for my arrest since I didn't show up for the trial. Of course, now I was freaking out! I was able to find out what I could do to remedy my situation. I was told to go back to the clerk's office, let them know I was late, and they gave me a retrial date! I just dodged another bullet! Smoking crack, I just couldn't seem to get it together.

10

Drug Testing

After it was all said and done, I had my trial with a public defender. Since it was my first and second offense, I was able to get one-year probation with drug testing. Maybe this was just what I needed because now I had to stay clean and give urine samples for a whole year. I had two weeks before my first visit to give a urine sample. During these two weeks, I got high because I was sure they expected me to give them dirty urine, then after that, I could start trying to clean myself up. So that was what I did.

After you gave urine samples, the following week, they gave you the bad news that you've tested positive for cocaine. Of course, they understood that they were dealing with drug addicts and we have addiction problems. So after that, they explained to me that they expected me to stop smoking crack or there would be consequences. So a week later, I came back and gave another sample. Apparently, they could see the levels of cocaine that were in your urine and they did notice a slight improvement. They explained the next time I showed up, they didn't want to see any cocaine in my sample. Now I was a little concerned because I had to give a concerted effort to stop smoking crack. It sounded easy, but it was not because I was realizing that I really did have a problem.

I came up with the bright idea to find some clean urine from someone who didn't smoke crack. I can't remember who I got it from but I was able to get some clean urine, put it in a jar, and I had it with me ready for my next drug test. Actually, one of my friends told me he went through the same process and he was able to trick the person that administered the test by giving them someone else's urine. He told me that I had to keep it warm because if it was cold, they would know. So before I went to give them my urine sample, I put the urine that I was going to give in a ziplock bag and stuck it between my legs right under my nuts so it would stay warm. The only thing that was holding this ziplock bag of urine in place was my underwear. I was trying to keep my legs together because at any moment, it could fall down my pant leg and I would be done.

When the officer gave me the cup to pee in, she told me to go into the bathroom and get a sample for her. I did. I made it into the bathroom without the ziplock baggie falling out. It was a little tough to maneuver once I got in the bathroom because I was also a little nervous. I was able to unzip the baggie, pour the pee in the cup, come back, and give it to the officer. I thought I was home free. A week later, when I returned for my next urine test, the officer said, "We will be doing a supervised analysis of you this time." I was caught. I guess the urine that I gave them wasn't warm enough, so they knew what I had done, and the next time I did my Drug test, it had to be supervised, whatever that meant. But I would soon find out, because the following week when I returned for my next drug test, there was also a man with my probation officer. She told me, "Officer Smith will be going in the bathroom with you when you give your urine sample today." It was now total humiliation, but I brought it on myself.

And yes, when I walked into the bathroom and pulled my penis out to pee in the cup, Officer Smith stood right beside me and looked at the whole procedure. I had my penis in my hand, peeing in a cup, and this man was standing right next to me watching. Unbelievable! But this was what I did to myself. I managed to get through the procedure and still my urine came up dirty because I hadn't been abstaining like I should have. All of this was taking place right at the last two months of my year on probation. I was actually almost done if I could just stay clean. Through the course of my year, I was able to put together some clean time, which would be followed again by a dirty urine test.

After this last failed test, my probation officer said If I didn't pass the next test, I'd be violating my probation, and I'd have to go back before the judge. It was time get serious, so I put a concerted effort into remaining clean. I took some supplements to help clean up my urine, and I just stopped smoking cocaine. Too much was on the line and I needed to stop playing games with my life. A week passed by with no smoking at all. I reported to my probation officer to give my urine test. Of course, it was supervised so Officer Smith again was standing right next to me watching me urinate in a cup. I was feeling pretty confident because I did all I had to do to pass this time. I only had one month of probation time left. If I passed this test, it was over, and I was through with the courts, and I could go back to living a normal life.

One week later, I got a call from my probation officer, and she said, "Congratulations, Mr. Barnes, you passed and you're done. We will be sending your paperwork to you in the mail to acknowledge that you've satisfied your probation requirements." What a relief, now it was really time to party. After it was all said and done, all they really wanted was consecutive negative urine results. I would have been done with probation long ago, but I couldn't put together consecutive negative tests. I would always slip up and use, and they would always catch me with dirty urine. I had to get past probation because I couldn't let it affect my job. Through the whole process of probation, I was able to maintain my job with Xerox, the company was never aware of what I was going through. This process did slow down my using and I was able to continue being a functional addict. But I did continue to use with Monique or by myself. I was well versed on how to buy crack in the streets of Baltimore, thanks to Monique. So whenever I felt like it, I would either ride into the city to just get some for me, or I would go visit Monique and we would get some together. As I delved deeper into the city streets, I started to find a lot more dealers that I could purchase from. Since people smoked crack all around the clock, there were places to purchase at different times all around the clock.

After work between 5:00 p.m. and 10:00 p.m., you just went to the street corners and saw the young boys selling. From 11:00 p.m.

to 2:00 a.m. the places were a little more out of the way. It might be an abandoned building that they had opened up for business. It might be in an alley behind the buildings. The later it was the sketchier the places were. There was one spot that I always would frequent from 3:00 a.m. to 5:00 a.m. It was located in the woods.

You had to walk into the woods off the beaten path and start asking for the blue topped crack vials. And sure enough, someone would answer your call and say; "Blue Tops over here". You would follow him still deeper into the woods and eventually you would come upon a group of guys dishing out the coke. Sometimes there would be a couple of people lined up in the woods ahead of you, and as scary as it was, they would serve you crack in the woods. It actually was a reliable spot to go and purchase from because the guys would always be there In the woods, waiting for customers at the wee hours of the morning.

The only problem was leaving the woods. When you exited the woods, you didn't know what was waiting for you because they wouldn't let you exit the same way you came in. Then you had to walk back to your car with cocaine in your possession. So even though it was a pretty cool spot to cop, it had its drawbacks. Luckily, I was never busted coming out of there, but there were times when I got into the woods, people in that area would say; "The Blue Tops got busted". So the police were onto what was going on in the woods and eventually caught up with them and put an end to a great spot.

As you see, getting drugs in Baltimore City was an amazing task, and each dealer stuck to his time schedule. So if you showed up at the 3:00 to 5:00 a.m. spot at 6:00 a.m., because you knew they had the good stuff, someone would be there, but it wouldn't be the regular guys and you ran the risk of getting burned. The crack smokers would capitalize on the dealer's clientele by being in the woods knowing stragglers would show up already high just looking for some more and sell them anything from crushed up aspirin, to pieces of sheetrock crushed up to look like crack cocaine. All people who use crack know that when you set off the phenomenon of craving and you're geeking, you have to have more, and they know the dealer's customers will be returning to purchase more, so they lie and wait for them.

Of course in the woods, there was no way you could verify if you got real drugs or not, so you had to be on time because when the dealers were done, they left, and you were on your own. During the daytime, the young dealers were so aware of how crackheads crave more after the first hit, they would go out on the block with a hand-ful of vials of crack while the buyers were all standing around, the dealers would throw the vials straight up in the air. This would cause a frenzy, and all the crackheads would grab for free vials of crack. How ingenious because when they took their freebie and went and smoked it, twenty minutes later, they were back to spend their money. It worked every time. These guys were young entrepreneurs, and they knew how to make their money at the expense of the crackheads. The only way around dealing with this type of activity was to get the phone number of the person you dealt with. They would just rather deal with you on the streets, but if you spent considerable amount of money, then you had a chance at getting your dealer's name and number. Then you could just call him and arrange meeting them somewhere and purchase it. That was the way I prefer to do it, and I was able to get a few of my dealer's phone numbers and also, you never wanted to have "short money". Which means If you wanted to get a $20 piece, but you only have $18, that was short money.

The dealers hated it, but they never passed up a sale. They may tell you, "Don't come back unless you have my $20", but when you were on crack, you didn't always have the full amount of money to purchase, but you wanted to get high and nine times out of ten, the dealers wouldn't turn you down. The bad part about purchasing on the street was a lot of times, you would be out in the open purchas-ing, and the dealers would make us stand in a single file line. They would have us have our money ready and ready means to have it folded in a small square with the number or the denomination show-ing. It was truly a sight to behold. Crackheads lined up single file eager to purchase some rocks. And we did exactly what the dealers told us to do, we were very obedient.

One time I witnessed a young guy go up to some people who were pushing in line. This particular line was to purchase heroin; that wasn't my thing, but the line formed near the crack line. The young guy walked up to the two people who were pushing each other, who were much older than he was, punched one guy straight in the face and knocked him down on his butt. When he got up, all he said was "Sorry man, he was pushing me". And the dealer said, "Get your money ready, or I'm not going to serve you."

He didn't make any fuss about getting punched in the face, he just wanted his heroin. This was one of the many reasons that I never wanted to try using heroin. They treated the crack users bad, but they treated the heroin users worse because they knew the people on heroin would get sick if they didn't get more. This process was to make as many sales as possible in a short amount of time and get out of there. It was effective, and just as soon as they were done with one line, another line started to form. This happened in broad daylight.

I preferred making my purchases after the sun went down just to be a little more discreet and to not be seen by the police. One night I was out on the prowl looking for crack in the inner streets of Baltimore City, and I saw a bunch of lights and TV camera crews. They were filming an episode of *The Wire*. I thought to myself while they are filming *The Wire*, I was living *The Wire*. How ironic! They could turn these cameras around and start filming me, and it would be a real-life episode of the drug culture in Baltimore City streets. My drug use seemed to grow more and more, as well as Monique's. She, too, was using more than she did before. Money started to get short, so we had to get creative on how to get more money. We started to borrow money from Monique's family members and at first it was easy because no one knew it was for drugs, but as time went on and we continued to borrow, they started to get skeptical and lend to us less and less.

Since we both had jobs, we would always pay back our debts. Then it got to a point when they lent us money, we would have to pay it back with interest. But we didn't mind; we took it anyway and paid it back with the interest they asked because we just wanted to get high. One thing about Monique's family members, even though we always needed to borrow money, they never asked us if we had a problem. I guess they gave us the benefit of the doubt as long as we repaid our debts and we made sure that we did it in a timely manner.

Now you would think with all the positivity that I had with my band members and the love for music that we all shared along with the goal to one day be successful, you would think I would be able to stop using crack. Those days, I couldn't understand why I should stop because we worked hard, we practiced a lot, and the band was moving forward as a unit. We got opportunities I had never experienced before, like being a guest band on a local TV morning news show and we had a single that actually got played on local radio. Of course, all the band members and our friends continuously called and requested our song to be played on the radio and it finally was.

And this was also enough to keep me somewhat focused on being a successful band member and to leave the pipe alone. All the guys in the band drank beer and a couple of us smoked weed. So we all still got a buzz on something from time to time. Since a lot of the gigs we played were in bars, after we would finish, the patrons would treat us to beers and then we would smoke a little bit of weed. If I got too buzzed that night, my mind would tell me that it would be a good time to buy some crack. Sometimes I did, sometimes I didn't, but I knew this was a problem that I had to get ahold of if I were to continue to be in the band and keep my problem a secret. Believe me, I tried to stop, but I would always seem to get the itch, and when I got the itch, I would scratch it. And instead of getting it under control like I wanted to, more and more it started to control me.

The guys started to get their suspicions that something was wrong with me. They called a meeting on a Saturday afternoon. It wasn't for practice, it was just to talk. I wasn't suspicious because we had these types of meetings once in a while. So I showed up. The guys had beers already there and they offered me a beer. We sat around the table and they asked me if everything was okay. I knew this was an intervention. This was before the TV show about interventions was ever invented. The guys didn't really know how to address what they knew was going on, so they just left it open for me to be honest, and I wasn't. I merely said everything was fine, I had a few issues with my baby's mother, but other than that, things were good, and they pretty much left it at that. But I knew inside they were worried about me and more so worried about the success of the band.

I had been late to a few practices, and I had also been late to a few gigs, which was a definite No! No! The guys liked to be early at all of our appearances, so showing up late was a red flag, especially since I had never been late before. Then we had studio time slotted to do some recording, and I didn't make it. I got stuck on a cocaine binge and couldn't show up to record at the studio, which the record label paid for. So now, I was costing them money, and the label told the guys they should be looking for a new drummer. But since we also had a friendship, the guys pushed back and said, "We'll talk to him." Again, the guys pulled me aside and explained to me that I needed to get it together because the label was a little upset with my actions. And of course, again I said, "I apologize" and "I'll do better". Knowing that I was wrong, and the truth probably would have set me free at that point, I couldn't tell the truth because I was deeper in my addiction than I even realized. I would try, and I would have moments of doing better, and everybody would be happy again, and then I would fall again, and the fall would always be worse.

11

Missed the Gig

Then I did the unforgivable: I didn't show up for a booked gig. I was at Monique's house and we were both smoking crack. She was smoking blunts, and by this time, I was putting it on a soda can and smoking rocks off the can in front of her. She was actually disgusted to see me sink to this level, but my addiction had me in its grips. The guys were calling me repeatedly, begging me to show up for the gig. I would just listen to the voicemail messages and I continued doing what I was doing, even though every time I listened to the messages, I felt horrible, but I just couldn't stop.

One of the messages they left said they had set my drums up for me and all I had to do was show up. I could hear the desperation in their voices every time they left a message, but that one was the ultimate. And you can't explain that to someone who doesn't smoke. So finally, the calls stopped coming because it had gotten to be around midnight the guys realized that the drummer was a no-show. I knew then that was the last straw; the next conversation I would be having with the band would be my termination. And I knew it was all my fault. When Monique saw that I had missed a gig because of smoking crack cocaine, she looked at me in a totally different way. She never smoked off the pipe, so she didn't really understand what I was going through, and for her, when it was gone, she just went to sleep while sometimes I went out looking for more.

But this time, I was disgusted with myself, so when it was all gone, I too decided to crash at Monique's house. This was Friday night, and we had a big gig that we had been planning for a month in New York. It was probably one of our biggest gigs to date and some record label reps were planning to be there; plus, we chartered two buses of fans that were going to New York with us, so it was a big event. All the tickets were sold out for the bus trip to New York to see us play live. Now I was still sure my days with the band were over after what I had just done. I guess they didn't have my replacement ready, and we had to make a good showing. I didn't know for sure; my replacement might have been on the bus. Before waking up Saturday morning to call the guys to apologize for not showing up to the gig Friday night, there was a knock at Monique's door at eight o'clock in the morning, and guess who it was.

It was Scott, the leader of the band. He didn't jump down my throat. He didn't fuss about me not showing up Friday night; he just said, "I'm staying with you all day. I'm not letting you out of my sight so you might as well prepare to be hanging with me all day."

It was kind of funny, but I understood; no way was I going to blow what was going to be one of our biggest gigs. There was too much riding on this, and they couldn't afford for me to miss this gig. Deep down, I felt so crappy, but I tried to shake it off and prepare for the night. So Scott followed me around all day on Saturday. He followed me to my house and waited for me to shower and get dressed. Now I didn't want to be a problem, so I said, "Hey, Scott, let's go to your house, and I'll just hang with you for the rest of the day, and you don't have to follow me around."

When I look back, these guys were so good to me, and I was such a knucklehead. So when it came time to get on the bus, all the fans showed up. We had free beer on the bus for everyone who bought a ticket to come see us play in New York the very next day. It was an all-around great time. We partied the whole way. It was so sad I let my addiction ruin another relationship, one that could have changed my life, all for another hit on the pipe. The trip to New York was a three-hour ride.

At first, all I could think was everybody knew that the drummer didn't show up for last night's gig. But that was just in my mind. But when you think about it, all our fans followed us around to the local gigs, so I knew half of the people on the bus were at last night's gig.

My feelings were probably correct; I looked like a total butt-hole. I didn't think about it; I just drank some beer and enjoyed the ride to New York. Monique was also on the bus with me, so we just had a good time. The guys hired someone to videotape the whole trip to New York, sort of like a documentary because the guys were trying to move the band to another level, and that was one more tool they used to get the name and our events into hands of those that would be interested in helping us.

Videotaping the band's trip to New York was a great idea, but that was a videotape I never got to see. Since I knew this was my last gig, I made sure I hammed it up when I got off the bus because the videographer was videotaping everyone as we departed the bus in New York. He gave everyone a chance to make a comment or talk about the bus ride, talk about the upcoming concert, or to just show their excitement. When I stepped off the bus, and it was my turn to make my statement to the video camera, I looked right into the camera and said, "This is probably going to be my last concert, so let's go in here and Rock this joint!" talk about being prophetic.

We had a great show, our friends had a great time, everybody got drunk, and slept on the bus all the way back home from New York. And the next day, the guys called me and said, "Mark, sorry to tell you this, but we gotta let you go. Come pick up your drum set." I already knew this was going to happen; I was prepared. One more bridge that I had burned due to my use of crack cocaine. When I arrived to pick up my drum set, it was kind of a solemn moment, but the guys were cordial as I expected them to be. I, too, was sorry for my actions and gave my apologies which they accepted, as they helped me for the last time to load my drum set back into my car. We said our goodbyes and that was the last time I had spoken to the guys in fifteen years. I did see the band members on Facebook, so I reached out with friend request, and they all accepted my friend request, which was very cool, and we've had some light communications through Facebook postings.

Of course, they continued on with a new and actually better drummer. I was able to see a few YouTube videos that they had posted of live performances with the new drummer. It was cool to see the guys still active and performing because they deserve every success that they might achieve, but ultimately, the dreams of stardom never did materialize. From what I gather from Facebook postings, they all married and started families.

For some crazy reason, I think one day we will play together again. A while ago, I had a dream of us playing together on a great big stage in front of thousands of people. The dream seemed so real that the next day when I went to rehearsal in utter excitement, I shared the dream with the guys. I told them we were going to be famous because I had a dream that was so real, I could actually see the crowd that we were playing for. Of course, they just laughed and said, "That sounds good!" I never mentioned it again, and while I was with the band that dream never came true, but you never know what God is up to. Now that I was no longer in the band, I had more time to party since I had less responsibilities. That had never been a good thing for me; I needed to stay busy. Every time drugs caused a major loss in my life, I would come to a realization that maybe it would be a good time to stop and get my life together. So I would at least stop using cocaine, but I would always smoke marijuana and drink, not always to excess but I would drink till I got a nice buzz.

If I took it too far or if I drank too much, a hit off the crack pipe was just around the corner. Therefore I tried my best to control my drinking and smoking. One of the good things about me was when I stopped or slowed down my drug use, I would always go right back to the gym and start working out or playing basketball or jogging. So I never really looked like a crackhead because I could always get back in shape quickly. Along with this, I was also a better dad. Didn't want to forget that.

Things were looking good. I was looking better; I still maintained my job, so I wasn't broke. It was funny every time I stopped getting high, my life started to get better, opportunities started to present themselves. If I could only stay stopped. I also started to visit my brother's church a little more frequently. Maybe God was helping me stay sober; all I knew was, I was starting to put together some actual clean time. I was slowing down on all of my vices—drinking, smoking, and definitely crack smoking.

12

❧

New House

One Sunday at church, the pastor preached a sermon about how God could bless you with a new house if you asked him. So the pastor told everyone who had recently purchased a new home to come up to the front of the church and stand on one side of the stage. Then he said everyone who would like to have a house to come up front and stand on the other side of the stage. I wanted a house, so I went up to the front and stood on the stage. Now he told everyone who had already received a new home to stretch their hands toward the people who would like to receive a new home, and he told the people who wanted to receive a new home to lift up their hands and receive the prayers from the people who had already received new homes.

I stood there with my hands outstretched, crying like a baby to receive my new home. I didn't know if it was going to work, but what did I have to lose? It was maybe about three months that had passed when my brother called me and asked if I wanted to purchase his home because he was about to purchase another home. I couldn't believe it; God was working already. Already He had opened the door for me to buy my own home. I had only stopped smoking for three months, and already God was opening doors. I knew it had to be God because it didn't take any time for the finances to go through, the loan to be approved, and for the whole transaction to happen.

In the book of Deuteronomy 6:11, it talks about how God will give you homes you didn't buy, filled with all the good things you didn't provide. That was me because when my brother sold me the house, it was fully furnished and it had a pool table in the basement.

I just couldn't believe how God would still bless a crackhead like me. Since I started to attend the church more, I decided to join the church and give my life to Christ. I joined the church band and got to play the drums. I couldn't believe God was just restoring everything that I had lost through my drug use.

God was showing me what he would do with just a little bit of obedience because I was far from being an obedient son, I was just a baby in Christ, and he was pouring out blessings in my life. I had watched God turn my brother and his wife's life around because they, too, suffered with crack addiction. It seemed like as soon as they joined the church, their whole life changed. They had asked me to come visit their church for some time, but I had always turned them down. I still wanted to party. The real reason was cocaine had not beat me up enough yet.

After eviction notices, electricity getting turned off, phone getting turned off, and getting car repos, you finally get tired of being sick and tired, and you realize there has to be a better way. I remember once when my phone service was about to be turned off, and I needed my phone because I had a job and kids. This was before everyone had cell phones, I was on the phone pleading with the phone company representative to allow me to keep it on. She saw all of my bad history of not paying my bills on time, so I didn't have a leg to stand on. As I spoke with the lady, out of the clear blue sky, she said, "I don't know what's going on, Mr. Barnes, because I could see your service was always being disconnected, but I want to pray right now for you. Whatever is going on in your life, I ask God to intervene and turn it around in Jesus's name. Amen!"

At this point, I was crying uncontrollably. I knew God was using her to speak to me, and she allowed me to keep my phone on. One of the many times God showed up even when I didn't ask. Getting kicked out of the band was my proverbial last straw. God had been speaking to me for a long time prior to this because I couldn't stop watching TV evangelist even though I wouldn't go to church, I loved watching preachers on TV all the time. When I finally decided to go to my brother's church, I had already been familiar with listening to preachers. Before I had given my life to Christ at the altar of the church, many times I prayed the Salvation Prayer with TV evangelists. I've laid my hands on the TV screen with Benny Hinn. I've prayed the sinner's prayer with Joyce Myers. I had one minister send me some miracle water so I could anoint my forehead with it, and I've been convicted by the preaching of John Hagee! But I've never darkened the doorway of a church until now. It took what it took.

I was really enjoying going to church. I attended every Sunday plus Wednesday night Bible studies. If there was a visiting preacher at our church, I was there. When the men's group had activities, I was a part of them. My life was looking up. My brother was so excited about me joining the church in the beginning, he and my sister-in-law would come pick me up every Sunday and treat me to breakfast. It didn't take long before I made sure I got to church on my own since I took part in so many of the church activities.

As far as I was concerned, I was done with crack cocaine. Just like God did for my brother and my sister-in-law, he had done it for me. He took the taste of cocaine out of my mouth. I kept praying, and I kept watching television evangelist TV shows with an occasional beer and a joint every once in a while. Apparently, I wasn't broken yet. I had not reached my rock bottom yet. It always seemed when things were starting to get good, I started to get lazy and forgetful. And I couldn't forget peer pressure because I still hung around the same crowd that still partied and smoked. But I thought I would be fine if I just stayed away from the crack cocaine, I could still party with my friends.

After all God had done for me, I slowly started to turn back to my old ways, slowly going back to my old habits. Since I now was a homeowner, when I would run into financial problems, my mother would always bail me out; she never wanted to see me suffer since I had the kids living with me in our new home. She wouldn't let me lose my car or have the lights turned off. She didn't understand that in order for me to get better, I had to reach my rock bottom. She enabled me to stay afloat, which probably wasn't the best thing for me. My short periods of sobriety always seemed to be followed by relapse. My brothers were annoyed with my mother continuing to help me out of all my problems. Her helping me was easy to hide at first, but like everything else, it came to the light. Since my mother had money running her own business, she would just help me out with some quick cash. Mom was on top of her finances, and she kept notes of every time she gave me money.

The last time she showed me just how much I had borrowed over the years. It was over $15,000. I felt bad about the financial strain I had put on my mother, but even that wasn't enough to make me stop. Because sure enough, I had started to smoke again. Again, I hit the pipe. I wasn't the only brother in her pocket because two of my other brothers were struggling too with their finances, but I couldn't use that as my excuse. We weren't the best sons, but Mom loved us all unconditionally, and she would bail us all out from time to time.

I did eventually get out of her pocket, but it took a while. I was doing so good I must have had three or four months of clean time. My finances were back in order, and I was able to save up a little bit of money. It seemed like once I stopped, it didn't take long to get things back in order, but it also didn't take long to ruin things once I took another hit. Monique and I were taking a little break from seeing each other. I couldn't blame my relapses on her, but whenever she would give me a call, she would be high because I could hear it in her voice, and I had no defenses to keep me from going to see her. Part of me wanted to see her, and part of me knew if I went to Baltimore, I was going to be able to smoke. So we had gotten back together and started right back with our old habits. And of course, the money quickly ran out. We got right back into borrowing money from her relatives, me borrowing money from my mother, aside from me spending all my money from working. How could we come up with money since we didn't steal, and the borrowing thing was starting to get pretty old. Because her family was starting to get suspicious of our constant borrowing, we knew we had to stop.

13

Hacking for Dollars

hacking spot   Penn ave.

Monique came up with the idea, since I had a car, why don't we just hack for money? The cab drivers in the inner city didn't always pick up Black folks. And if you called for a cab on the phone, they didn't always show. So in Baltimore City, people preferred to just catch a hack. A hack was someone who didn't have a license to pick up riders, but rode around the city looking for people flagging one down. It was just a two-finger wave like you would see in New York City to hail a cab.

In Baltimore, you did the same thing to hail a hack. It was so prevalent in Baltimore City that you could make a lot of money doing this,

Poplar Grove

and a lot of People did. If you rode around the city, you would see people everywhere trying to get a hack, but there were certain things you had to be aware of because it was a risky business; it was illegal, and some of the people that you may pick up could possibly give you a hard time or maybe not even pay you. One common rule was to stay away from the young kids because they were good for ripping you off. Jumping out of your car and just running away without paying you a dime. A perfect customer to pick up for a hack would be a middle age or older woman. Usually, all they needed was a ride, and they always paid well. Preferably, you just wanted one rider. There was nothing worse than having a car full of people, who wanted to go to all different locations that could be problematic. If you saw a young person by him or herself, that could be good or bad. I had one situation where there was one guy standing on the corner; he was a younger guy, but I was a little desperate because I had already been smoking. So when I pulled over to pick him up, I always asked for the money upfront when dealing with a youngster. He opened my door and three more of his buddies ran from around the corner, and they all jumped in my car. I was had, and they took advantage of my services for at least an hour and never paid me. That truly was one of my bad experiences.

But getting back to Monique and me when we first started out, I let her drive, and it didn't take five minutes before we picked someone up. Of course, she had the eye for who and who not to pick up because she herself always used hacks to get around Baltimore City. We picked up a woman and took her where she wanted to go, and she gave us $5. Wow! That was easy, so we continued. Before you knew it, we had $30 from hacking, in just thirty minutes. Then we went and got some cocaine. That was when I realized this was pretty easy; when the money got low, either she or I could get in my car and go make some quick money hacking, and we did that for a while.

The thing about hacking was, people were looking for hacks all around the clock—anytime of the morning, noon, or night. Of course, at nighttime, it was a lot easier to be taken advantage of, so you really had to be aware of who you were picking up. When you've decided to pick someone up because you thought they were going to be trustworthy in paying you, and you've asked for the money upfront, which I always did, if they responded with, "I got you, don't worry. I got you," those were the worst three words you wanted to hear because that pretty much means you were about to be taken.

And as they were telling you that they got your money but not giving you anything, they started with directions, like "Make a left here, go straight, three blocks, make another right." Then you asked again, "I need my money upfront," and they replied with "Don't worry about it, I got you." You just picked up a bad hack.

The bad part was, what you were doing was illegal, and they knew it. You couldn't really make them get out of your car, and they probably wouldn't without giving you a hard time, so the best thing you could do at this point was just take them where they gotta go and get them out of your car. This had happened to me several times, but what you got to do after you'd gotten them out of your car was immediately look for another one. Because the law of averages would work in your favor if you have large numbers of hacks that you picked up. Not everybody in the city was a rip-off. I would say 80 percent of the people I picked up paid, and some paid very well. This was all to purchase more drugs anyway, so you didn't need a whole lot of money; you just needed enough to put a little bit of gas in your tank and enough to buy another rock of crack cocaine.

In the beginning, I was leery about going out hacking, so I would give Monique the car and she would go out and do it, and she didn't even have a driver's license. But I didn't care. I gave her my car and I waited. Of course, I was on pins and needles waiting because it did take a while. I was worried sick because two hours had passed, and she still hadn't come back. The minute I heard her pull up, all my worrying had ceased especially when she walked in the door with crack in her hands. Mission completed! She was successful and that was all that mattered.

This was what we did when we ran out of money: Monique went hacking. She got tired of this and said, "Why don't you go out and do it? You know how to do it." I knew how. I just didn't want to. I didn't want to deal with the inner-city people in my car and me asking for money. It just didn't feel right. But that didn't last long because after I did it a couple times, I became an immediate pro. I started hacking all the time. I was hacking when we were together. I was even hacking on my own when she didn't know anything about it. It was like I was hooked on hacking. No matter how much money I made, it always went back to the dope man for more crack. I had some nights when I made $100. That was how much crack hacking I did. Hacking had a level of excitement that came with it. You were riding around the streets of Baltimore City.

The best days to do it were Fridays, Saturdays, and Sundays. The weekends were always good times to make money. People were going out to nightclubs, to bars, and to just hang out so everybody needed a ride, and the hacker was the best way to get there. If I was home in Aberdeen getting high and I ran out of money, I would jump in my car, drive to Baltimore, and start hacking. It became an obsession because it was so easy to do. The problem was, it took a toll on my car, and I didn't always have the money to fix things that needed to be fixed. The competition was also great in Baltimore. There were many times when I would see someone giving the hack sign, and I would have to make a U-turn to get to them, and before I could, someone would've already picked them up. I have many hacking stories because I was out there doing it for quite a while.

Like the one guy I picked up while he was on his cell phone. I kept asking him for the money, and he kept saying, "One minute, I'm on the phone". Of course, he told me where to go, and again, I said I need the money upfront, to which he replied, "One minute, I'm on the phone." His destination was Lexington Market, and we were almost there. So again, I asked him, "I need my money."

Then he said, "Pull over," and I did. And he just got out of my car and walked into the crowd. All I could say was, "Oh well," and go find another hack. One time I picked up a guy, he was a nice guy with a lot of conversation, which was a red flag. When they were too nice and they had a lot to say, it was usually because they were about to burn you. I took this guy on a twenty-mile journey, and he talked the whole way. He promised to give me $20.

At that point, I started to worry because when they make big promises, it was usually a lie. So we got to a truck stop, and he told me wait right here. "I'll be right back."

I must've waited thirty minutes, and he never showed up. Burned again! So I learned to be a little more careful when it came to picking up people. I learned not to pick up people after I'd taken a hit because I was a little more desperate at that point, and I just wanted to hurry up and make some more money to buy another rock. I also learned to just leave young kids alone, they were not worth it and more times than not they were just going to string you along and take advantage of you. Once, I picked up some young kids after school. They paid me upfront which was good, and they wanted to go to McDonalds, so I said no problem, because they had already paid me. We went to McDonalds and we went through the drive-in window. They got all their food. Now I was taking them to wherever they had to go, and they were eating in my car, which I hated, but at this point, I didn't have a lot of choice. The worst part of the whole ride was when these kids finished eating their food, they threw their trash out of my window! I couldn't believe it. I told them they didn't have to do that. I'd throw it away, but it was too late. Empty wrappers and bags and cups right out of the window in the middle of the street. Thank God the police didn't see it because I would have definitely been pulled over.

That was the problem with the young kids, they just didn't care. This was my worst hacking experience ever. It was a beautiful sunny day, normally during the day you didn't have too many problems with the people you hack for. It was a young lady who was looking for a hack, so I thought, *Great, I'll pick her up.* So I pulled over to get her, and when she got in, I asked her for the money upfront, and she said, "I got you." I immediately thought, *Oh no!* But I had hope she seemed like a nice young lady. Then she asked me to pull over for just a second, and three more people got in my car. Now I was worried. Again, I asked for the money upfront and this time they gave me $3, and they said they'll give me more when they got to their destination. So I thought, *Okay that's fair.* In the back of my mind, I was thinking, *This isn't going to be good.* But I was hoping for the best, so they asked me to go to a liquor store, and I said sure.

Then they asked if I could purchase their beer for them. I said, "No problem", I'll do that. So when I got out of the car, I took my keys. I hated leaving people in my car while I was not there, but one of them was going in the liquor store with me to show me which beer they wanted, so I was thinking, *Okay this will be all right.* Then they asked if I could leave the keys with them because there was a song on the radio that they wanted to hear. I didn't know why, but right then, I should have known better, but I said okay. I turned the radio back on so they could hear their song. I walked into the store with the one guy who was with all these girls. He was going to show me which beer to purchase, and we were standing in line together. All of a sudden, I started noticing that he started to ease out of the store. So I asked, "Where are you going?" Before I knew it, he took off running, so I took off running after him. Of course, he was young, so he was running like a track star. There was no way I was going to keep up with him. So I let him go. I turned back to get my car, and it was gone. They took my car! Unbelievable! I've not been paid before, but I had never been carjacked by a hack.

Now I had to call the police and report my car stolen. The policeman showed up, and of course, he asked me, "How did they steal your car? Did they break your window?" I had to say no. I told him that I must have I dropped my keys, and someone found them. When I came out of the store, my car was gone. This was the worst! But that was what I get for being out there in those streets up to no good. When I told the police officer my story, I could see the doubt in his face. He knew most car thieves don't have the keys to the cars they steal. I guess the look on my face wasn't very convincing to the officer either. I had to stick to my story so that the police officer would file a stolen car report, and they would be on the lookout for my car.

The officer filed the report, and I was relieved to know that the police department was looking for my car. Now I was faced with my next dilemma. I didn't have a ride to anywhere. I asked the police officer if he could give me a ride to the west side of Baltimore, back to my girlfriend's house. He replied that he was not allowed to let me ride in his car, and that there was nothing he could do. I was on my own, but he was kind enough to give me $5 so that I could catch the bus. I finally got on the bus, and since I didn't ride buses regularly, I didn't have a clue on how to get to Monique's house using public transportation. Each bus that pulled over, I had to ask the bus driver which bus to use to get to the west side of Baltimore City. Bus drivers were usually very friendly and they gave me all the information I needed to get where I had to go. On the bus ride to Monique's, I was trying to figure out what I was going to tell her; how in the heck did I lose my car? She was street smart, and I couldn't just feed her any story and expect her to believe me, so I realized that I might as well just tell her the truth, that I was out hacking, and I must have dropped my keys walking into a store because when I left the store, my car was gone. Okay, not quite the truth, but when you're a crackhead, lying comes easy for you.

At that point, I couldn't just tell her how stupid I was by leaving my keys in my car with a bunch of kids I was giving a ride to.

That would just raise a lot more questions that I just wasn't ready to answer. I reached Monique's house and gave her my sob story. She kind of believed me; she was a little sympathetic, but now I had to figure out how to get back home to my house thirty miles away. We called on our favorite aunt who was willing to give me a ride home. I was able to give her some money for gas because it was a thirty-minute ride each way. I was truly grateful because after that experience, I was dejected, and I no longer had a car. I had to give credit to the Baltimore City Police Department because they were able to find my car two days later. When they called me, I had to go to the city and pick up my car. They actually caught the guy who I chased out of the store driving my car. He was arrested for car theft.

When I finally got to my car, the whole interior of my car was covered with graffiti. They had written all the names of their friends, their gangs, their girlfriends, boyfriends and street names. My car looked like a ghetto billboard. It was done with a black magic marker, so there was no way of getting it out. I had full coverage, and the car was reported stolen, so I was able to file a claim and have it repaired. But for one week, I had to ride around with my car like that. Of course, everyone who got in my car asked me, "What in the heck happened to your car?"

And every time I had to come up with some crazy answer. I always explained that my car got stolen and this was how it was when I got it back. Again, there was no way I could tell the truth about what really happened to my car, especially to my local friends and buddies from my hometown. I would never be able to live that down. This was what happened to me in Baltimore City, and no one knew what I was going through in Baltimore City because when I was home, I was the normal Mark; it wasn't until I crossed that city line that I turned into the crackhead Mark.

For the longest time, I lived two lives. I kept them separate from my family and friends, what was going on at home verses when I went to Baltimore. Eventually, I had to appear in court to testify against the guy they caught driving my car. He got probation and that was that. The case was over. I was okay with that because if it wasn't for my stupidity, none of this would have happened, and he, like me, just made some mistakes, so probation was enough. Plus I got my car back, and there was no damage other than the graffiti, which I had fixed. You might think this was a good-enough lesson to teach me to stop hacking in my car, but it wasn't, I continued to hack because the money I made hacking, seemed to outweigh the problems it caused, and when the get high money ran out, I could always make more as long as I had my car. It was just one more lesson on who and who not to pick up while hacking. Hacking had a level of excitement that came with it because you got to meet so many different people. The good ones outweighed the bad ones on any given day.

I've picked up gay men on occasion, and they always paid, and sometimes they even tipped. They would always hit on me. These were the days during the height of the AIDS epidemic. I was curious why they hit on me, not knowing me from the man on the moon, and I would ask them, "How do you know I don't have AIDS?" Even though I was smoking crack, I was in pretty decent shape, and they would tell me that there was no way I had AIDS because I was big and had muscles. And I would ask them, "That's your only criteria? I'm big and have muscles so you automatically assume that I don't have AIDS?" I would tell them that was pretty risky. But I must admit I did enjoy conversing with all types of people that I gave rides to in my car.

I once picked up a guy who had just gotten out of prison. He shared a little bit about his story, and we had a good talk. This guy seemed like a totally straight man; I had no reason to believe that he was gay. Then out of nowhere he said, "Every once in a while, it's cool to suck dick! Sometimes you want some pussy, sometimes you want to suck a dick!" Naturally, I was in shock, but I had to remain cool, and I replied, "Whatever floats your boat!" Inside I was saying, *What in the world is going on in jail?*

Thank God I don't know, but I had to get this guy out of my car because I didn't know where his mind was right now. Like I said earlier, you met all kinds in this hacking game. No matter which way the conversation went, you had to remain cool. Some people were very comfortable saying whatever was on their mind. Yes, hacking allowed me to meet all types of people. It also allowed me to continue to make money to keep smoking crack. Twice, I watched the sun rise and set three times. Meaning, I stayed in a car hacking for three days. I would hack just enough to make some money to buy some crack. I would go buy it, sit in my car and smoke it, then start hacking again. So I stayed up and didn't sleep for three days. When my car got stolen, and I didn't have a car to drive. My mother let me borrow her car. Her car was in much nicer condition than mine. She had a Honda Civic; it was perfect for hacking because it was good on gas and in good shape with low mileage. If she would have had any idea of what I was going to use it for, she would have never let me borrow it.

At first, I had no intention on using her car that way because she was good enough to let me use it, but somewhere, somehow, I was able to take a hit at home, which set off the obsession. Then there was no control, I was on my way to Baltimore City to do what I knew how to do, and that was to hack up some more money. My mother had just gotten her oil changed at the three-thousand-mile interval. So it was running great. I used her car to hack for three days in a row. Again, I watched the sun rise and set three times.

By the third day, my mother was calling me, asking when I was going to bring her car back. My intentions were to keep it until she asked for it back. When she called, I told her I was done, and I'd be bringing it back today. Of course, when I brought it back, she checked her odometer to find out that I had put three thousand miles on her car in three days. I had driven three thousand miles in three days in a ten-mile radius—hacking! She had to have her oil replaced again, and she had to have her brakes adjusted because I had driven the heck out of her car. Needless to say, she never let me borrow it again! Another bridge burned! My mother never questioned why or what I did, but she did tell my brothers, and they made sure that I wasn't able to drive my mother's car again. Like everything else while smoking crack, hacking also took a bad turn.

It was a beautiful Friday. I was out hacking to make some money. This particular day I had money, I just felt like going out and doing some hacking. It was almost like a second job that I actually enjoyed, especially during the day. Now since I was pretty good at it and I knew what to look for, I was now hacking for pleasure. I haven't even taken a hit of crack. Payday Fridays, you could make a lot of money hacking. So far, I've had a few good fares, and it looks like it was going to be a pretty good day to make some extra money. North Avenue was one of the busier streets, and there were lots of fares to get. I saw a potential customer giving the hack sign, so I turned around and pulled up in front of him, and he asked me if I was hacking, to which I reply, "Yes, I am. Do you need a ride?"

And he replied, "No, that's okay." Now why was this guy giving the hack sign, and when I pulled over to give him a ride, he asked me if I was hacking. When I said yes, he said, "No that's okay"? The answer to that, I was about to find out shortly. As soon as I pulled off, I heard the chirp of a police siren, and police cars surrounded on every side, told me, "Hands on the steering wheel."

I was getting busted for hacking. When the police officer walked up to my car, he asked me, "Are you out here hacking?"

And I said, "No, Officer."

Then the guy that I just offered a ride walked up and said "Yes, you are, you just offered me a ride."

I just put my head down and realized that I was going to jail. Not only that, but I was also going to have my car towed. They had set up a sting that day to catch hackers. The only good thing about this bust was that they caught a bunch of us and put us all in a large van in handcuffs. They towed our cars, and they took us all to the police station to charge us with our offense. Then they immediately released us. We were able to get our cars back immediately with a slap on the wrist. Do you think this was enough to make me stop hacking? Absolutely not! I chalked it up as a lesson on how to be a better hacker, and which signs to look out for while hacking. I was getting my street knowledge with all these bad experiences to smoke crack. Unbelievable! Now you can imagine with all this driving, it was taking a major toll on my car. But I couldn't say that I was keeping up on all the maintenance needed to keep it riding in tiptop condition. All my money was going to purchase more cocaine.

14

The Dirty Ant

I was driving an old Nova. Not the cool kind or the classic kind; it was a little economy kind, maybe 1990-ish. My daughters called it the Dirty Ant. It was very inexpensive to maintain, it didn't burn a lot of gas, and it had four doors. So it was perfect for hacking, if I would have only taken better care of it. All the driving that I did in the city wore the brakes down, and I never had them replaced; even though they were squeaking, I continued to drive on them. That's right! I didn't have money to buy new brake pads because I needed money to continue to buy more rocks. My brakes continued to wear down. They wore down so far the brake pads finally just fell out. Now the caliper was pressing against the rotor. This was making a horrendous sound. Did I stop and get more pads? Absolutely not! As long as the car would stop, I could continue to drive it, and that was what I did. So now I had metal against metal.

At night, while driving down the highway, people riding next to me would point at my front wheels because sparks would be shooting out of the wheel well because the caliper was pressing against the rotor, steel against steel. All I had to do was pump my brakes, and the caliper would release from touching the rotor and the sparks would stop, and I would continue down the highway. Was this crazy or what? And that was not all. Since the caliper was pressing against the rotor, one side of the rotor wore away. If you didn't know, the rotor has two sides, since one side was gone the caliper was pressing against what is called the fan blades between the two rotor pads, this made a clunking sound. The teeth of the rotor fan against the caliper made such a noise, some people once they got in my car and heard it would ask me if my car was okay. Of course, I would say "Sure, it's fine!" Some would continue to ride, others would say, "Let me out at the next corner."

I was hacking on a Saturday with my brakes in this horrendous condition. I remember being in the middle of downtown Baltimore; it was a beautiful hot day, people were everywhere, and as I pulled up to the crowded intersection to stop at the traffic light, the people on the corner waiting to cross the street heard *clunk! Clunk! Clunk! Clunk!* I stopped right in front of them, and all eyes were on my car. I had all the windows down, so I could hear all the gasp of the people who heard my brakes make that noise as I came to a stop. One gentleman from the crowd looked at me and said, "Man, you need to leave that shit alone!"

Even the people on the overcrowded corner of this Baltimore City street knew that a crackhead had just pulled up in front of them. I couldn't wait for that light to turn green so I could leave. Talk about the humiliation! Still not enough to make me stop. Needless to say, the maintenance of my car took a backseat to my addiction. Again and again, riders would hear the sound my brakes made and ask if my car was okay. I would always say that my car was fine because the last thing I wanted to do was lose the fare. Even though a couple of times I have bumped into the back of other cars because I couldn't come to a complete stop in time. Lucky for me, no one ever gave me a hard time about tapping their bumpers. I had actually mastered how to use my parking brake to bring my car to a complete stop, so now, not only were my front brakes gone, but because I was using my parking brake to bring the car to a stop, I was also wearing out my rear brakes. If I kept this up, I wouldn't have any brakes at all.

Once I was on I-95 going about sixty miles an hour and traffic was moving at a fair pace with a little slowing. I tried my best to keep my distance between me and the car ahead of me. The traffic started to pick up, and we started to get back up to the normal speed limit when all of a sudden, people started putting on their brakes, and all I saw ahead of me were brake lights. I immediately started to put on my brakes and pull my parking brake lever. Did everything I could to stop before I hit the car ahead of me, which was coming toward me faster than I thought. I was faced with a dilemma; do I run smack into the back of the car ahead of me, or do I veer off to the right and broadside the car to the right of me.

I decided the latter, and I just veered off to the right and crashed right into the car on my right side. Of course, the driver was in total shock because I literally ran right into the side of her door which in turn, made her veer off to the shoulder. I immediately pulled over behind her and apologized for my actions. No one was hurt because the decision I made was the best because if I would have run into the car ahead of me at sixty miles an hour, all kind of craziness could have happened. She had a big dent in the side of her door caused by me, and I gave her my insurance information because at the time, I actually had car insurance, full coverage. She was able to get her car fixed. This was just one more of the many times that crack cocaine put me in a dilemma that could have actually been a lot worse.

Thank God she was able to get her car fixed, but of course, I just kept the dent I put in my car. Now, let's get back to hacking. One day, I picked up a White girl in the city. I was sure I would not have any problems with her. She looked nice and harmless, but she did look a little sketchy. It was rare that you see White women looking for hacks in Baltimore City. When I picked her up, I asked her to pay upfront, which she did immediately. This was a good sign. So she told me where she wanted to go, and while driving, we struck up a conversation. She told me she used to be a Bel-Air City police officer who got hooked on crack cocaine and lost her job, and now she prostitutes in the streets of Baltimore City. And I thought I had it bad. This was during the time when I owned a home in Bel-Air. I gave her my address, and she knew exactly where I lived. I told her that I also smoked crack cocaine.

After I told her that, she asked me if I knew where to get some because that was what she was out looking for. Of course, I knew exactly where to get some, so we put our money together (my hacking money and her trick money) and bought some rocks. Now I usually smoke in my car because I didn't have anywhere to go to smoke it while in the city because when I was smoking from the pipe, I couldn't share that with Monique, plus we were taking a break from each other anyway. She offered to let me go back to her place and we could smoke together. This was a great idea. Now don't get me wrong; I have never done anything with the crackheads or prostitutes in the city, but she didn't look bad, and yes, the thought did cross my mind. But at this time, all I was concerned with was smoking crack.

We got to her place, it was halfway decent, and we chilled out and smoked some crack together. The only problem was, an occasional trick would knock on her door and she would have to accommodate them. I didn't mind at all; she just told me to wait in another room until she was done, and then we could continue smoking, and she would have more money that we could use to buy more crack because I had the car. I almost felt like her pimp. Overall, she was pretty cool. Even though she was prostituting herself, she kept her head about her. She wasn't whacked out; she was down to earth.

Since I knew where she lived, every once in a while, when I would buy some crack, I would just go knock on her door, and if she was there, I would smoke with her. We actually became, I guess you could say, friends. Once she realized how laid-back I was, she looked forward to me stopping by. She didn't geek and I didn't geek, so we partied together a couple of times. It was so ironic that we both came from the same town to do our dirt in Baltimore City. I have to be honest, from time to time she would offer me sex, and I was a little vulnerable because I hadn't seen Monique in a while.

For me, one line that I refused to cross was sex with someone off the streets. There was no way I was going to put my penis in a prostitute. Even with a rubber, it was out of the question. But her giving me a blowjob, now that was a different story, and you know what they say about White girls when it comes to giving head. One day, we were both getting high together, and I said what the heck, so I let her give me some head. And it was great! Now I was sitting there rock-hard and she asked me if she could ride it. I said no way! Call me crazy, but I just couldn't do it. Again, that was one line I couldn't cross. Actually, when I look back on it all, I never thought that I would have any sexual dealings with a prostitute, but again, when you were smoking crack, you managed to do a lot of your nevers.

As time went on, we became good friends, and I asked her if she would like to come and hang out at my house in Bel-Air? My only intentions were to get her out of the city for a little while and to just take a break. It wasn't sexual, I was just trying to remind her of how and where she used to live. Maybe it would be a reality smack for her. I knew we would need party supplies, and this particular time, I had plenty of money, so I bought what I thought would be more than enough crack. I convinced her to go, and she was cool with it. So we got on the highway and while driving, we took a couple of hits just to get in the right frame of mind. This was going to be a relaxing smoke session. On the ride to my house, things were going great; she seemed to be excited about getting away from the city for a day or two.

So we got to my place and go down in my fully furnished basement. We smoked a little; she gave me a little more head. We were having a great time. We got some drinks. I was thinking this was going to be a nice little getaway for the both of us. We finished smoking all the crack, and we still got some alcohol, so I figured we would just relax here and have a few drinks, take a shower, and go to bed. Nobody was knocking on the door for her to pull a trick; she could actually put her work on hold.

For a minute, I have gotten her out of that environment. I thought she would appreciate that. Oh, how wrong I was. No sooner had we started to relax for a minute; she sat up in the bed and said, "I want to go back to Baltimore!"

I said, "Are you kidding?" I thought we were having a good time. I thought you would like to take a breather for a minute." But she said, "No, I want to go home."

That was when I realized what I had heard so many times before: "You can't be Captain Save-a-Ho!" A Ho was going to be a ho no matter what; she was missing the attraction of prostituting in the city, just like I missed the attraction of hacking or buying crack in the city; it was just an attraction. I couldn't believe it, and I realized it when we got back to the city, when she saw men standing on the corners or on the streets, she gave them that prostitution look, the look that means "I'm available." She started rolling down my windows and hollering at the men on the streets to which I said, "Please roll my window back up. You can do all of that soon enough." That was when I said, "I got to get this chick out of my car!" The valuable lesson that I learned that day was, "You can take a ho out of the city, but you can't take the ho out of the girl". That was the end of that relationship.

At least I never tried to pull her out of her environment again. People are going to be who they are, and there's nothing you can do to change them until they're ready to change. I learned that lesson the hard way. It was just that I saw something good in her, and I thought just a little nudge in the right direction would be enough to bring her back. There I go playing God. Only God can change people. Not me. And it was not like I didn't need some changing myself.

Actually, this experience did open me up to another side of this crack world, and that was messing with crackhead females. When you buy crack, the crackhead females were always standing around watching, and if they see you buy a lot, they always asked if they could go with you. And normally, I would always walk away. Now, If they didn't look half bad, and I was not in any hurry, and yes, I was single again, so I would invite one of them back to my car. It would just be a quick blowjob and me giving her a nickel then sending her on her way. I didn't do it all the time, just once in a while. Just one more of my nevers. I got blowjobs in doorways, while driving my car, behind trees in the woods. These women didn't always look bad, some of them were downright cute, they were just caught up in their addiction, and they did whatever they had to do to get another hit.

One story I will never forget. I hooked up with this girl while buying my crack. She invited me back to her place, which wound up being an abandoned building that she moved into. She actually had furniture in this place, but it didn't have any electric or running water. When we got to her place, we went upstairs, and we started to smoke in the attic of the abandoned house. She actually had it fixed up pretty nice. So while we were smoking, she knew what was next, so she started to take off her clothes. Now this was in the winter in Baltimore, so it was pretty cold outside. She was dressed in three layers of clothes like a typical homeless person. She had to peel off these layers of clothes to finally get naked. Now remember, I was not having sex. I just wanted to get my dick sucked. So when she finally got out of her clothes, she had a body out of this world. I mean her skin was smooth and brown, and she had perfect breasts, with big brown nipples. Her body was so nice I had to comment. I told her, "You would never know how fine you are under all those clothes that you wear." To which she just smiled and said, "Thank you." Then she told me her story.

Remember every crackhead has a story; we didn't just start out as crackheads. She used to be a cocktail waitress and a burlesque dancer in the elite night clubs of Washington, DC. She actually had newspaper clippings of her in her costumes dancing. She danced professionally until she met up with crack cocaine which changed her life like it did to so many of us. I was in awe. But that explained why her body was in such perfect shape. She kept it covered up so the men in the streets that she dealt with wouldn't take advantage of her because she looked like a homeless person until she came out of her clothes. She also shared how they used to snort coke back in those days while she was dancing, and once crack hit the scene, everything went south. That was the beginning of the end. And that was the same story for so many of us.

I was intrigued by her story, and now it was time for us to engage in a little bit of sexual escapades. After seeing how fine her body was, you would think that maybe I would want to have sex with her. Absolutely not! Even though I was surprised by her story and she was fine as could be, I still wasn't going to put my penis inside of anyone who was on crack that I just met on the street. So she did her thing, and I moved on, promising to come by and see her maybe another day. I actually did stop by a few times to try and hook up with her, but she was never there when I would visit. I guess she was off to the next abandoned building. By this time, I was pretty much back into my addiction.

15

Robbed at Gunpoint

I was spending a lot more time in the city than in my beautiful town-house in Bel-Air. As I continued to hack for money and purchase crack in the streets of Baltimore City, I also continued to run across crazy situations. Monique and I spent less time together because visiting her meant I would have to share my crack with her. No Monique meant more for me.

One of the breaking points for me and Monique's getting high together was the day I told her, "I'll be right back, I'm going to get some coke", to which she replied, "Okay, see you when you get back." This particular time was during the day. So I got to the dope spot and there was already a line forming. I got in line and I had my money in my hand ready because that was how the dope dealers liked it: you got to have your money ready so you could make a quick transaction, crack for cash. When I finally got to the front of the line to be served, I handed the money to the dope dealer, he handed me my crack, and as soon as I put it in my pocket, some guy ran up to the dope dealer with a gun. He banged me in the forehead with the handle of the gun and told the dope dealer, "You know what this is, give me all your cash and your drugs."

The dope dealer was getting robbed right in front of me. When the guy hit me in the forehead with the butt of the gun, it split my head open and I was immediately bleeding profusely. Since his attention was on the dealer, I ran to my car with dope in my pocket. At this point, I was terrified and nervous, my hands were shaking, and I was trying to put the keys in the ignition to start my car so I could get out of there. Blood was running down my face as I was trying to start my car. I found some napkins in my car to put on my forehead to slow down the bleeding. Believe it or not, through all of this, I was still excited because I made it out with my crack. I finally got my car started and I headed to Monique's house still bleeding. Trying to clean myself up as best I could because by this time I had blood all over my face and clothes.

When I got to Monique's bedroom and she saw the blood all over me, she immediately showed concern and asked, "What happened?" So I told her what happened, and she was very upset but glad that I was okay. She also asked if I was able to get the crack. Now, normally, I would be a little concerned that all she was worried about was if I had the crack or not, but after an experience like that, I, too, needed a hit. Monique cleaned up my wounds and put a bandage on my head. The bleeding finally stopped and then, we were able to sit down and smoke some crack together. I relayed the story to her one more time, telling her all the details and how close I came to being shot, because there was nothing keeping him from shooting me as I ran off to my car. But thank God he didn't.

Once again, God was taking care of me when I didn't even realize it. When I would take a hit off of the crack pipe, my wound would start to bleed again because the hit would make my heart race, and I started to get a slight headache because the whole incident had my blood pressure high. I have never experienced anything like this before in my life. I don't think I'd ever been that close to a gun before either. After going through all of that, I haven't even gotten to the worst part yet. Monique bandaged me up, tended to all my wounds, and we sat down and smoked together. When we had finished smoking all the crack I had bought, I figured since I had been through so much trauma, I would be able to relax with her at her place.

That wasn't the case because right after we smoked the last hit, I started to get comfortable, and she told me, "Sorry, you have to go home."

I said, "But I'm tired and I want to just relax."

To which she replied, "Sorry, you have to go home. I'm staying here by myself tonight." I was utterly dejected and rejected, and I felt terribly used. She only wanted me for the crack, not for the company. At that point, I knew the only thing we had in common was smoking crack, and since I loved her, I had to test my theory a couple more times. I would ask her if I could come visit, and she would ask me if I had any crack. If I had crack, she would allow me to come over; if I didn't, she was busy. She would always tell me of the good sex we would have once I arrived with the crack, which always proved to be a lie because she knew after one hit, I wouldn't want to have sex anyway; I would just want to smoke the crack. She played me like a fiddle, and I went for it for quite a while.

At this stage in the game, we both had problems smoking crack, and there was no way we were going to be able to solve them as a couple; we had to do our own thing. So the occasions that we got together became more and more rare. Now my trips to Baltimore City were only about me being on a mission, to get more crack, and I was happy with smoking by myself. I still had a job, barely, so I still got a paycheck. I kind of paid bills so I managed to keep a roof over my children's heads. The crazy thing about my addiction was, I didn't get high every weekend, or every day; it was those binges that would get me, and I would just get stuck. I would be held hostage in the city for days, hacking day after day unable to break free and go home.

When you were stuck in your car hacking for days without a break. You could always stop somewhere and go pee, but when it came to relieving your bowels, that was not always so easy. I would be holding back bowel movements for days, trying my best to keep my legs together so nothing slipped out. Then of course there was the occasional fart that you couldn't avoid. Day one and day two, I was okay but by day three, when I released a fart that wasn't the only thing that came out. A little bit of poop came out too. While sitting in my car, I didn't realize how bad it was because I was high on coke; it was hot outside, and my mind was on the mission of getting more hacks. There were times when I finally would get home, and I would take off my underwear and they would be really soiled with poop. I would just throw them in the trash, and immediately take a shower to wash all the residual poop out of my butt crack; it was awful.

There were times that I smelled so bad, the people that I would pick up to give a ride would ask me to pull over a block or two prior to their stop. I would Ask them, "Isn't your stop a block up the street?" They would answer, "That's okay, just let me out here." And for a while I didn't realize that I was the reason why they would get out prematurely. I didn't realize that my whole car at times smelled like poop, because when you were riding around in it, you actually got used to it. That reminds me of one time when I was on a three-day binge, riding around picking people up for three days in a row. The first day everything was okay; second day I had to pass gas more.

By the third day, I needed to sit on the toilet and relieve myself, but of course riding around, there was nowhere I could go to do that, and I wasn't going to do it outside; I was not homeless you know. If you added that I was making good money and I had a steady flow of rides, there was no way I was going to stop to try to find a toilet. As I had been farting, and I knew stuff was slipping out of my butt crack, but as long as I kept finding people to pick up, I continued to hack.

After a while, it dried up anyway. I must admit that I could feel that awful sticky feeling between my butt crack. I knew something was going on there, but I just ignored it. When I think back to those days, I'm amazed that I could sink to that level. This was day three; a warm summer day, I had made a considerable amount of money hacking. Now it was time to go buy my party supplies. I needed a box of blunts and a glass pipe. I bought my crack from a dealer who was outside so there was no problem with that. Now I needed to go into a store to purchase my glass pipe and my blunts; this was when things got a little hairy. I walked into one of the local stores; you know, like the one I explained where I got busted, the small area where all the kids congregated to buy their candy and soda.

So I went in the store and I was standing in line, and there were kids in the store with me. We were all standing in line. Behind me there were three other kids. I was standing there minding my business waiting for my turn to be served when I heard, "Do you smell that? That smells like *shit*! I think that's Unc. Unc smells like *shit*!"

Kids didn't care who heard what they said, and I realized that I did smell like shit! All I know was I had to get out of there as quick as I could, but before I left, I still had to get my blunts. The kids continued on with their comments and their snickering, and I just stood there there and acted like I didn't hear them. If I would have left the line and tried to just walk away, then they would've unloaded on me, and I would've been one big joke, the old crackhead standing in line smelling like *shit*! Once again, total humiliation! The sad part was, like there was an even sadder part; they kind of knew me because I was a regular, and I always frequented the area to purchase my crack and my party supplies. So even though I walked away, they knew who I was, and I would be back again.

Once you were known as one of the local crackheads, you pretty much lost all respect in the neighborhood, but as long as you came back and spent money, they didn't care. There was a lot of others who were worse off than me. That was the only hope that I held on to there were others worse than me. The problem was no matter how bad you humiliated yourself, if that area had the good crack, you always came back. The trick was, I would always park my car a couple of blocks away from where they actually sold the crack, because if something went down, you didn't want your car to be connected to it, because they would tow your car as well as take you to jail. Even that system could backfire on you. Like the time I found a good spot. I parked my car around the corner, and I was walking a block or two to go purchase my crack. As I was walking to the spot, just before I got there, a police car pulled up beside me. The officer got out of the car and asked me where I was going I told him, "I'm walking to my car."

He asked me, "Where is your car?" I pointed and I said, "Right over there." Then The cop told me that I needed to leave the area because there were a lotof people walking around here buying crack. I told the officer, "I'm leaving right now, thank you." Since that was a close call, I got in my car and I left that area because there was always somewhere else I could go to purchase. When a spot gets hot, you just had to go to another spot. That was one more of those lessons that you learned when you purchased on the streets. A spot could be hot right now, and if you came back later when it cooled down, it'd be okay to purchase. I just used this opportunity to go out and raise a little bit more money hacking. Then I'd come back a little later and try it again because this was a spot that had good coke. A couple of hours passed and I came back to try again. I parked my car and I'm walking to the spot. As I got near the spot, two young guys approached me and they asked me, "What did you tell the cop that you were talking to earlier today?"

I told them exactly what I said that he asked me where my car was and I pointed to it, and I walked to my car. They said, "No, you didn't. You pointed us out!"

I said, "No, I didn't. I was pointing at my car." All of a sudden, one of them just hauled off and punched me in the jaw. I was in shape, so I was able to take his punch. I just rolled off and backed away and asked, "What was that for?"

They said, "You ratted us out to the cops," which was something I would never do. What happened was, the cops set me up to mess with the guys selling the crack. They had lied to the boys about what I really said. It was just one of those lessons I learned. The police could be cruddy too. Turning the dealers against the buyers on purpose. So now they thought I was a snitch, so I can't come around here anymore to buy crack. But if you waited long enough, all situations died down and returned back to normal. Ultimately, It was all about the money. As I dove deeper into this world of smoking crack, my world was starting to fall apart. My production on the job was starting to suffer, my numbers were starting to be seriously affected. Everything in Xerox was based on your numbers; that was how they graded your performance and my numbers were tanking. I was starting to show up for the job later and later. I could hide this a little by going directly to an account rather than showing up at the office where all the other techs would congregate before we went out into the field. Since I couldn't get there in time, I would just go to my first account. They wouldn't mind they just wanted to see a tech there working on their machine. One thing I couldn't hide was the fact that we would occasionally have breakfast meetings at a local restaurant. And I loved to eat so I was known as the guy who would always order a big breakfast before we started the meetings.

As time went on, I would show up at the meeting after an all-night smoking affair. And no one has an appetite after smoking crack all night. I would get to the breakfast meeting and not order any breakfast. This truly was a red flag, and they would ask me why I wasn't having any breakfast, and I would just have to give them the; "Well, I'm not hungry today". Which was a lie because I just smoked crack the night before and I didn't have an appetite. It was a terrible feeling because I was jittery, my skin was moist from a light sheen of sweat, and I could barely talk. An ominous warning. But this was before I was armed with some facts about my addiction, I was just caught up in the middle of it and I didn't have a clue. It was really starting to affect my job and it was getting harder and harder to hide it.

These were the times when I learned to hate the sound of chirping birds in the morning. When I was smoking at night into the wee hours of the morning, the birds always started their chirping at the same time and all that told me was, I did it again. I smoked all night long. Thirty minutes after the birds started to chirp, the sun would begin to rise. And that was a horrible feeling because usually about that time, all the coke was gone, and I was left with that terrible demoralizing feeling that I had spent all my money, I didn't get any sleep, and I had to start to prepare for work. These things you only learnt when you sit up all night and smoked crack. Birds start to wake up every morning at the exact same time, between 5:00 and 6:00 a.m., they begin to sing their songs. It's like clockwork: they are never late, they never start too early, they're always right on time. I guess they answer to God's alarm clock. What was strange was, while you were smoking, you didn't think about any bills you had to pay; you don't think about the job you had to go to the next day, but the minute you blew the smoke out from the last hit, all those realities came flooding back into your mind. You were immediately reminded of the bills that must be paid with the money you just spent; You also remembered the customer that you promised you would be there first thing the next morning, and it was 6:00 a.m., and it was an hour away, and you had to take a shower and get out of the door, park your car, and get to that account.

It was like a nightmare, and it all flooded your mind after the last hit. I knew that it was nothing but Satan reminding you how you blew it again. It was almost as if he was laughing at you because he tricked you into buying the lie. I could just take one hit and put the pipe down. I was never able to pull that off no matter how many times he convinced me that I could. The strange thing was, about halfway through the day, I was finally able to shake off that feeling, and the obsession to do another hit finally subsides.

As the end of the workday came near, I would actually be thinking about how I could get some more money to do it all over again. That was the insanity. I knew it was nothing but God that gave me relief from the night before, and after that relief, if someone would show up with a free hit, I would be willing to start it all over again without a dime in my pocket. So I tried my best to abstain during the week, after the crazy weekend. The one thing that kept me from starting all over usually was because I didn't have a dime to my name, and I was exhausted, and I needed to get some sleep. I had to remind myself of the night before when I didn't sleep at all because for some strange reason, I got a burst of energy after work, and I almost feel like I could do it again.

But the minute I sat down and put on a movie, I immediately crashed out. Somewhere between the ride home and having dinner with the girls, I got a moment of clarity and realized that I needed to get some sleep, and then the body shut down. Now I was relishing in the thought, I got paid every Friday, and if I could just get through the week, payday was a couple of days away, for the cycle to begin again. But who knows, maybe I'd make it through this weekend coming up? That was one good thing about being in the band and being involved with my brothers from Zoom Productions was because those activities would also keep me on the straight and narrow. I couldn't have an idle mind; it was definitely the playground of the devil.

When I had important activities coming up, that kept me from doing the wrong thing on the weekends, I didn't blow my brains out. I was truly a functional addict, but when that urge came on, or Monique called and I had money in my pocket, I would more times than not answer that call. If Monique would call me and invite me to come over with the promise of some good sex, even though we were on the outs, I would take a chance and go visit her. It usually never turned out like she made it sound on the telephone. Later, I realized it wasn't the love for her; it was the love for the drugs. She would always make it sound so sexy. She knew just how to get me to Baltimore. It took a while before I finally figured it out and stopped running to the city every time she called.

In the beginning, we did get high and then have good sex. But toward the end, it never seemed to work out that way. I would go all the way to Baltimore, spend all my money, and we wouldn't do anything but smoke until the money was all gone. Then she would tell me I had to leave. She was so cold. Once again, I would be left with that feeling that I just got used.

By this time, I faced the realization that I wasn't the only man in her life. I should have gotten a hint when I went all the way to her house, her boyfriend was just leaving as I was arriving, and she gave him a goodbye kiss right in front of me. All I could do was just stand there and wait till they were done. Because she was going to smoke some coke with me, he just got all the loving. It was crazy! It was so bad at one point that I used to drive her to her ex-boyfriend's shop because he used to give her money. Sometimes I would have to wait for at least half an hour before she would come out with the money. No one was in the shop but those two and I didn't care what happened. I just patiently waited until they were done doing whatever they were doing as long as she came out with some money and she always did. These were the depths you sank to when you were chasing after a hit.

From time to time, I would question her about what was taking so long, but she would just get an attitude and Say, "Nothing! Stop asking questions!" And I would do just that; I would stop asking questions because all that was important right now was we were about to go buy some more crack. So I sat there and waited for what seemed like an eternity. My eyes fixed on the door waiting for it to open. The door opened and here she came. She seemed to have a little bit more pep in her step as she returned to the car. The long wait didn't seem so long after all, she had money and we were on our way. I know, crazy, right!

This relationship was pretty much out of control, the only common denominator was crack. She and I had moved on to dating other people, but if one of us had some dope, we would call the other and hook up. Even though we both dated other people, we were both smart enough not to date someone who also used crack, nor did we let anyone we were talking to know about our crack issue. That would definitely be a dealbreaker for anyone who didn't use. Deep inside, we were both trying to break free from our addiction, but it had us in its grips, and part of it we enjoyed, but the other part was tragic. Even though I tried to stay away from her, if I would take a hit by myself, my defenses would weaken, and I would reach out to her to see if she either had some or wanted to try and get some. Sometimes when I went to Baltimore on my own to purchase some crack, I would ride by her house and look at her window to see if the light was on. Everything in me wanted to give her a call, but I didn't want to get bad news.

At this point, you could say I was actually stalking her because I would sometimes sit in front of her house in my car for an hour or more trying to decide whether to call her or not. If the light wasn't on and she wasn't at home, I would sit and wait until she arrived. And more times than not, when she came home, she would be with some dude, ending a date. I would wait until she got out of her date's car. Sometimes I would actually see her lean over and give the guy a good-night kiss. But I still patiently waited until she got inside the house, and then I would go to a phone booth because I didn't have a cell phone. I would call her and say, "I'm out front. Can I come in?" The only insurance I had of getting in was to also say that I had crack too. She would open the door and let me in, and I didn't dare talk about where she was, or what she was doing that night. I was just glad that I was able to come inside and smoke with her.

When I look back to those days, I always say to myself, "What in the heck was I thinking about to put myself through such torture?" It amazes me to this day how vulnerable I was when I was under the influence. I had no defense. There were so many nights from parking my car somewhere near the front of her house, that I was starting to get recognized by the young kids in the neighborhood. They knew my car.

One night, as I sat in my car waiting for Monique to get home, a group of young kids walked by my car and shouted, "STALKER!" This was probably twelve o'clock at night, but I didn't care. I just shrank down in my seat and tried not to be seen, but of course, it was too late. One more embarrassing episode. I knew somehow, some-way I needed to break away from this crazy relationship, which really wasn't a relationship at all; it was just me acting like an out-of-control fool. I knew we were no good for each other. The thing that was so baffling was, I might stay away from her for a week, or sometimes even two. All it would take was one hit off the pipe, or one phone call from her with that sound in her voice that I recognized. I could tell she had been smoking, and I would run right back to the city.

Church was another way for me to escape the grips of my addiction. I would attend church to keep my mind occupied on something other than Monique and crack. The pastor would allow me to sit in with the choir and play drums because he knew I was a good drummer, and he would offer that opportunity to me. But for some reason, I would always slip up and go MIA. I would have a week maybe two of sobriety, enjoying life clean and sober. But even in a sober state of mind, I would make a decision to go take another hit and put all the progress behind me. I also had friends in my hometown that would stop by and offer to smoke with me. This too made it hard to keep clean. It always seemed when I was doing good, someone would visit or call with an invite to get high. I never said no. What would start in Aberdeen would always end up in Baltimore City.

16

Weird Tweakers

Alley purchase · Behind the shed buy

One night, I got to Baltimore, got some good hacks, and ran into this brother who invited me over to his place to smoke. You took a chance when meeting smokers; some would be a little weird and some would be cool. This particular gentleman was one of my cool hacks, I thought. He asked me if I knew where to get some crack. Everyone knew the hackers knew where all the good spots were because we were driving people around who were usually out looking for drugs. So I took him to one of my many spots.

By this time, I had raised some money myself, so he bought some, and I bought some too. Then we went back to his place to smoke. I always preferred not to smoke in my car if at all possible to avoid the risk of getting caught by the police. So we were at his place getting high. He had a fairly decent house, and I was able to relax while smoking because he seemed pretty cool. Finally, kicking back and relaxing while smoking he walked out of the room. I figured he was going to the bathroom because he said he would be right back. I had just taken a big ol' hit off of the pipe and my head was zooming! The next thing I hear was a clanging that must've lasted for ten seconds. It was so loud, it actually made me jump out of the chair I was sitting in. Naturally, I went to see what just happened, and the guy was kneeling on the floor in front of a pile of tools that he had just dumped out of his toolbox. I asked him if he had dropped them. He said, "No, I'm counting my tools. I think some of them are missing." That was when thought to myself, *Unbelievable, this guy is crazy.* But that was his tweak! I had never seen anyone tweak quite like that before. I had seen people peek through curtains for long periods of time. I had seen people pick crumbs out of carpet that they thought were pieces of crack. But I had never seen anyone dump out a toolbox full of tools.

For the next twenty minutes, I had to listen to this guy count each tool as he placed them back into the toolbox one by one. Now you might think that that was crazy. After he had finished putting all the tools back into the box, he sat back down and took another hit off the pipe. Then he disappeared again around the corner for a minute or two, and then once again, I heard that loud clanging sound that again lasted for about ten to fifteen seconds. This fool dumped all of his tools out of the box, back onto the floor again. This time, I couldn't bring myself to ask any questions. I just knew it was time to leave. So while he sat there and began to pick up all of his tools again, I told him, "Hey, man, I have to go, see you later!" He was blowing my high. There was no way I could sit there with him and relax and enjoy my high, knowing that at any moment, I would hear that sound of him dumping tools on the floor again. That was too much to deal with. Like I said before, I have seen a lot of different people tweak, but the toolbox guy takes the cake.

Another time I gave someone a ride, he wanted to go get some crack. So again, I took him to a spot where he and I purchased. He invited me back to his place to sit down and smoke. Everybody seemed cool when you first meet them, but you never know what you were going to get after they take that first hit. When we got to his place, it was a typical run-down row house that he was squatting in. No electricity, no running water, it was just a row house full of stuff he had moved into. It did have a few comfortable chairs and tables that we could sit at and smoke.

When you were trying to keep from smoking your crack outside, you didn't need much. So we sat down and started to enjoy our rocks, and everything seemed to be okay, he seemed to be pretty cool. We got to the last of our crack. He smoked his last, and I smoked my last. Now we were sitting there looking stupid because we wished we had more. We were both stuck in the phenomena of crave. Then this guy started to look around in the crevices of chairs and under tables.

I was thinking, *What is he looking for?* Then he asked me, "Did you take my rock?"

I answered him, "No, we both smoked all that we had." But he insisted and he asked again, "Did you take my rock?" Again, I answered, "No, we finished smoking all that we had. It's all gone." He said, "I had one more piece sitting right here on the table."

Again, I told him, "It's all gone. We smoked all that we had."

Now I was starting to worry. What was this guy thinking because a lot of people will steal your rocks if you don't keep your eyes on your stash. One thing I don't do is steal. Since now he was accusing me of stealing his rocks, I started to help him look for what I knew wasn't there. I was also realizing this guy was just tweaking and it was time for me to go. So as our search came up empty, I told him, "I told you, it's gone." I could tell he was still not convinced; he still had his doubts. This nut thought I stole from him. I had to now figure out how to get out the door because the more I tried to leave, the more he'd think I was leaving with his crack. The one thing I didn't do was misplace my crack. I always knew how much I had and where it was

137

After we stopped searching and I was ready to walk out the door, this fool reached under the cushions of his couch and pulled out a thirteen-inch knife with a serrated edge. A large hunting knife. While he had it in his hand, he said, "I know I had another hit". He was not necessarily threatening me, but just the fact that he pulled out a knife was a threat enough. I couldn't say I wasn't scared, but I knew I had to think fast. With the knife in his hand, he asked the question, "Did you take my hit?"

And again, I said, "No, I did not. I don't steal man. We smoked it." By this time, my high was blown, and I had to figure out how to get out of this guy's house. So I came up with a great idea. I said, "Look, dude, I'll go out and do some more hacking and get some more money. I'll buy some more crack, and I'll come back and smoke it with you. Just give me an hour or two, and I'll come right back."

I was very surprised when he said, "You promise?"

I told him, "Yes, I'll be back!"

He was good with me returning with some more crack. Of course, when I got out of his door, there was no way I was ever coming back. That was one promise I couldn't wait to break. Luckily, I never saw him again. Even if I would have seen him again, it probably wouldn't have been a problem, because we only acted weird like that when we were tweaking. Thinking about him as I walked these streets, I saw that there were so many different reactions people had after taking a hit off the crack pipe.

One time I picked up a female and she wanted to go find some crack. So I took her to find some, and we both bought some. This chick loved to give head after she took a hit. And she said she'd love to do it to me right after she took a hit. So I obliged her and she really enjoyed doing it, and I really enjoyed having it done to me. While she was doing me, she told me to take a hit while she did her thing. I couldn't believe it, I found a girl that loved doing what most men love having done to them, getting some head while taking a hit off the crack pipe. It was like a dream come true. It was always more fun to smoke with females than it was to smoke with men. As I explained, many people have different ways that they tweak when they take a hit! I must admit that I was guilty of this tweaking phenomenon. My tweak was a little bit more subdued and sometimes easier to deal with.

After I'd taken a full pull and I started to hear bells ringing in my ears, all of a sudden, my hearing got super sensitive. It felt like someone turned the volume of life up to ten! I started to hear everything; I even heard things that were not there. My mind starts to fill in the blanks where there should be silence; It added sounds. If there was a television on, I needed to turn the volume down. If music was playing, I needed to turn it off. If someone was talking too loudly, I couldn't always ask them to be quiet, I wished they would. The nerve-racking part about it was I knew that I was tweaking, but I couldn't do anything about it. I couldn't just shut it off. If I was alone in my room, I heard sounds coming through the walls, and the sounds were always of someone having sex. I could be in a house all by myself, and I'd still hear sexual sounds coming through the walls. If I'm alone, I'll have my ear pressed against the wall so that I could hear everything going on in the next room, even if nothing was going on in the next room.

I sat there with my ear pressed against the wall for twenty minutes before, thinking that I was hearing something. It was brutal. It would come to a point where I would just have to make myself stop. Even though everything in me wanted to press my ear back against the wall. I've been pressed against the wall so long sometimes that I would start to get cramps. Then I would have to stop. It was amazing how the mind can play tricks on you when under the influence of crack. Naturally, if I was in mixed company, I had to control my urges to do these things. But the urge was still there, and I wanted to answer the call of my tweak, but I just had to sometimes sit there and try my best to ignore it. There had been times when in mixed company, I would go into the bathroom and put my ear against the wall and listen, pretending to be using the bathroom. Of course, it was only so long you could stay in someone's bathroom before they start to get suspicious. It was pure insanity. But you can't control it while you're high. The crack game is tough. My other tweak was also based on paranoia. This is a common tweak among many crack users. We all fear that someone is coming to get us. Whether it be the police, or just someone in general visiting.

I remember one winter snowstorm, I was in my house all by myself smoking crack. The snow had accumulated to about a foot. It was late at night, so there was no one outside. But I just knew someone was coming to my front door. I sat at my front door pressed against the peephole looking out into the snow, waiting for someone to walk up to my front door. I know it must've been forty-five minutes that I sat pressed against the peephole watching and waiting for someone to walk up to my door. Only one person came trudging through the snow and walked right past my door during the whole forty-five minutes I sat there watching. My feet and hands started to cramp up from being in that position for so long. My mind told me that someone had tipped off the police, and they were coming to bust me.

Now, I know it was just Satan planting thoughts in my mind since I was in such a vulnerable state being high on crack. All this did was make it hard to relax and enjoy your high. You were in such a heightened state of paranoia you couldn't relax. Your mind was constantly racing with all types of crazy thoughts. These episodes of tweaking were just evidence that my addiction was reaching new levels. The one common tweak that I'd seen many times before, but I didn't have was the crawling around on the floor looking for crumbs of crack. I'd seen so many people exhibit this behavior, but a hit never affected me that way. I would look at folks doing it, and ask them, "what are you looking for?" And they would answer, "I think I dropped a piece of coke somewhere". And they would continue to search no matter how ridiculous they looked. Once again caught up in the grips of crackish behavior. This type of behavior always started when all the crack was gone.

At that point, you wanted another hit, and you were convinced that if you searched long enough on the floor, you would find one, and you never did. The main problem with this was after searching on the floor for a possible crumb of crack, they would find all types of debris, dirt, or trash. Then they would put it on the pipe, light it, and try to smoke it. Depending on what it was, it would sometimes create a horrible smell. Even if it didn't resemble cocaine, they would put it on the pipe. It could be anything and the minute you smelled it you knew, and everyone around you knew, that you had just put some trash into the pipe and lit it.

I would have to say that 98 percent of the time what some-one found in the carpet was not coke. This drug really took you through many changes physically and mentally. If you were weak mentally when these tweaks would manifest, there would be nothing you could do about it no matter where you were or what the cir-cumstances were, you were in its control. I do recall one of my own tweaks that I'm not proud of. When my crack was all gone, I remem-bered how the residue coated the inside of your mouth from so much smoking. I took a butter knife and scraped all the residue out of my mouth. It was actually a sizable amount, so I figured I could cook it and bring it back to a rock. I tried, but I had no success.

After I had realized what I'd done, I just felt horrible. I can't criticize the people who pick in the carpets because we all have our own skeletons. I thought that I would never share that, but I guess it needed to be told. So if someone else has tried this, now they know they're not the only one. When the monkey is on your back, and the crack is all gone, we will do all types of crazy things to keep the party going. I didn't always get stuck in the city, sometimes I would get high in my hometown. I had a few people I could purchase from in Aberdeen. It was just so much cheaper in the city, and you got more for your money.

Of course, there was no drama purchasing at home because you knew who your dealer was, and he knew you. In the city, you just blended into the crowd; in my hometown, you stuck out like a sore thumb. When I purchased at home, I would get in my car and drive to the Susquehanna state park. I would ride around that park sometimes for hours. I wouldn't get out of my car and sit at a park bench because I was too paranoid. If a car was behind me, I would become super paranoid. Sometimes I would pull over and let them pass; other times, I would make a turn, hoping they didn't. Every once in a while, a park ranger would be behind me. This would make me extremely paranoid because I'd already taken a hit, and I was sprung. I would just exit the park. This area was full of long winding roads with no traffic lights. I was able to just drive and smoke. This was how I used to wear my cars out. They always needed some type of maintenance because I stayed behind the wheel smoking crack. Once, there was a major snowstorm in the forecast. They were calling for four feet of snow. The snow had begun to fall, but I needed groceries and crack to prepare to be shut-in.

I got to the grocery store which was full of people trying to get last-minute items. I managed to purchase food for the next four or five days. The snow was coming down harder and harder, and it was starting to accumulate on the streets, making driving difficult. I called my dealer to arrange picking up a large amount of crack. My dealer said he was also getting bombarded with calls from people trying to get enough crack to get through the storm. That's right, having crack was just as important as having food. Go figure. There was now a foot of snow on the ground, driving was almost impossible, but I've been driving in the snow all my life, so I know exactly how to do it. I met my man and got my crack. He told me he was all over the place making sales. There was so much money to be made that day, and he wasn't about to miss any of it.

Now the snow was about two feet deep. The streets were starting to clear because everyone was now at home. I was the fool out driving, trying to find cocaine. Putting my life on the line just so I could have some crack to smoke. Driving now was so treacherous that I had to keep my car in the tracks of the car ahead of me. If I made one wrong turn, I'd be stuck in the snow miles from my home. Traffic was now starting to slow down; it was starting to get backed up. Even though I was fifteen minutes from my house, the ride was taking forty-five minutes. The traffic was slowing and it was bumper to bumper. There were cars on the side of the road that had already gotten stuck. I was still trudging along, getting closer and closer to my house. Now, there were no longer tracks that I could drive in, so I had to create my own. I was getting closer and closer to home, but I was also worried because the possibility of me getting stuck still lingers. If I stopped for any reason, I would not be able to continue and I would be stuck. I had to keep my momentum going forward.

My car started to sway to the right then to the left. I recovered and got back in the middle of the street.

The snow was coming down so hard I could barely see. The windshield wipers couldn't keep up with the falling snow. I could barely see through my front window. Thank God I knew where I was going, or I would have been lost. I finally saw my turn into my neighborhood. Ignoring all stop signs, I pushed forward and turned into my court. My parking space was filled with snow, but my momentum allowed me to slide right into my parking space. Thank God I had two parking spaces because I slid into them both sideways, and I was now parked. I made it home. Now I had to carry bags of groceries into my house through three feet of snow.

Actually, that was the easy part because the drive home was quite a feat. After all of that, I could really use a hit. When I got in the house, I didn't even put the groceries away before I put a hit on the pipe. I was home alone, you would think this was an excellent time to get high. I bought plenty of alcoholic drinks and I had plenty of crack. Since they were calling for four feet of snow, with the possibility of eight-foot snowdrifts, I wouldn't be going anywhere for quite some time. I started my party of one that day, and then day turned into night. As I looked out the window, the snow had already reached three feet eight inches and it was continuing to fall without ceasing. I continued to smoke, and the higher I got, the more paranoid I got. Then those sounds of people having sex in my head.

I only had one neighbor adjoined to my house, so it had to be them. I pressed my ear against the wall to hear a little better. This did not make any difference because the sound was all in my mind. I continued to keep my ear pressed against the wall for at least half an hour. It was like I couldn't move. I was now tweaking! This was the day I wrote about earlier when paranoia was so strong, I knew someone was coming to my house, but it was all in my mind. The snow outside was so deep, and the hour was so late now that there was no way anyone was outside in these elements. I was supposed to be enjoying myself, no one home with me, a blizzard outside, and no one could visit. This was the perfect opportunity for staying home and relaxing while getting high off of crack. I was supposed to be enjoying myself, having a good time. I was miserable because I couldn't seem to shake the paranoia. I heard sounds the whole time I was smoking. Staring through the peephole four hours until my body started to cramp. This was not my idea of having fun, but I couldn't seem to stop. My mind was telling me, someone was coming, so I had to stand there and watch until they show up. No one ever did. If someone did walk in front of my door, the shock of it would probably give me a heart attack. When I was finally able to tear myself away from the peephole, I made myself a stiff drink so I could try to go the other way, to come down just a little bit. Return to some sort of reality.

I had to escape this paranoia and possibly fall asleep. That didn't happen until three or four in the morning. I was up practically all night long. I woke up the next morning feeling somewhat depressed about the previous day. I looked out of my window to see the results of the blizzard. There was four feet of snow outside. All the cars in the parking lot were completely covered with snow. This was the view from my second-floor window looking down at the parking lot. I went to my front door to go outside. When I pushed on the front door, it was completely blocked with snow. There was an eight-foot snowdrift blocking my front door. So I had to push through in order to allow the front door to swing completely open. I was still faced with a wall of white snow. The snow was so white, it was blinding with the sun's reflection bouncing off of it. It was beautiful. The snow was deep on the streets, there was no way we would be able to move our cars.

This actually was a good thing because now I couldn't go out and buy anymore crack. I was trapped in my house, and I had plenty of food. My children were with their grandmother, so everything was okay. I was going to get a much-needed break from smoking crack. I knew if I could get out I would head to Baltimore City. But with this snowstorm, that was absolutely out of the question. I made a fresh pot of coffee, and I cooked me a big breakfast because I was starving since I hadn't eaten in a day. When you smoke crack, you don't eat. Now that I'd eaten and I felt much better, it was time to tackle shoveling my walkway and digging out my car.

After a crazy night of smoking crack and dealing with the paranoia. It felt good to do normal stuff like shoveling snow with my neighbors. We were able to get it done. I dug a path to my car. Along the path were five-foot walls of snow on each side. It literally was a path. Then I dug my car out, which was completely covered with snow. You couldn't even see the roof of my car. We still couldn't go anywhere because all the streets were covered with snow. If you know anything about snow, it's easier to shovel freshly fallen snow. The last thing you want to do is to let it freeze overnight, then try to shovel it the next day. That's nearly impossible.

Now that our cars were all dug out, we had to wait for the snowplows to clear the streets. This would take a few days because the snow fall was so deep. Since the snowfall was so severe, all businesses were closed. No one could go to work or leave their houses for any reason. It was mandatory to keep the streets clear. This actually was much needed for me. I needed to sit home and think about what I was doing, and how I was going to get my drug problem under control. So I sat home and thought about my life, and what my next move was going to be. Something had to change. When my mind was clear, I was able to think about positive things, and not about doing drugs. I spent most of my time watching TV evangelist and reading my Bible. Deep down inside, I wanted to stop. I just didn't know how to pull it off. I would just say, God used a snowstorm to get my attention and allow me a moment of clarity to see what I was doing with my life. I got the same moments when the money ran out and bills were due. I could tell more and more God was starting to pull at my heartstrings. I was starting to pay more attention to God nudging me to change my life around.

I couldn't understand why, but I had this urge to watch religious TV programs. It seemed I just couldn't get enough of watching them. I was a big fan of TBN. I watched all the time. Especially when I had been on a crack binge and spent all of my money and was down in the dumps, I would watch it. Whoever was on the show preaching, I felt they would preach directly to my issues. The words they spoke ministered to my situation. It was like God speaking directly to me. I would be totally convicted by what was said. This didn't stop me from getting high, but it was really starting to get my attention. I would watch a bunch of different pastors.

At the time, Benny Hinn was one of my favorites. If I had been up all-night smoking, I'd turn on the TV and turn to TBN, and there he would be. Preaching a sermon about being a slave to drug addiction. And that would get my attention because I knew he was speaking to me. At the end of the broadcast, he would say, "Let me pray for you." He would face his palms toward the camera and tell you to put your hands on the TV screen right against his palms, and then he would pray.

I couldn't tell you how many times I put my hands on my TV screen for him to pray for me. Many nights I was stuck in my addiction and at all-time lows, crying out to God to help me once again because I had fallen and answered the call to go get some more crack. I couldn't understand why I would always return to smoking. Sometimes I would have a whole week of sobriety and then stone-cold sober. I would make a conscious decision to go and get high. I knew I had a problem; I just didn't know what the answer was. I didn't smoke day in and day out, I always took breaks from getting high to take care of my business. I was juggling a job and being a dad; also, I had positive extracurricular activities. But more and more, crack was pushing them aside.

17

✎

Prayed for Healing

One time, I knew without a shadow of a doubt, God used Benny Hinn to show himself strong and available to me. I hadn't even been smoking this week, and this was one of the times that Monique was staying at my house. She had a terrible toothache and she had it for some time. She was asleep in my bed. By now, everyone knew about my TBN obsession.

While Monique slept, I watched TBN. Benny Hinn was on this particular time. Even while Monique slept, I could hear her moan in agony from the pain of her tooth. I kid you not, while he was preaching about laying hands on the sick and they would recover, I heard him say that I, too, could lay hands on the sick and they would recover. When I heard him say that I thought to myself, *Could I do it? Would God use me to heal her sick tooth?* I could be wrong, but I thought I could feel God speaking to me about praying for Monique's tooth. I heard him say, "Go ahead and pray for her." I said, "Okay, God, but can I finish watching Benny?" I thought I heard him say okay. So when Benny was done, it was time for me to be obedient and do what I thought I heard God told me to do.

Monique was still asleep, but I knew once I laid my hands on her, she was going to wake up and ask me, "What the heck are you doing?" I was going to do it anyway. I wouldn't press hard on her and maybe she wouldn't wake up. So I laid my hands on her and I began to pray. I quietly asked God to heal Monique's tooth. Then I heard God say, "Pray, but I want you to pray out loud." I was a little fearful, but I did it. I started to pray out loud with my eyes closed. I asked

God to heal her tooth totally. I wasn't sure why I asked him to totally heal her, but I did. I asked God for a few more things and then I said, "Amen". When I opened my eyes, she never woke up. That was a relief. I did not want her to wake up and see me laying hands on her and praying for her.

I must admit I was a little apprehensive, but I wanted to see if God would do it. Her tooth was giving her a rough time. I purposely thought God let her stay asleep for me. I was new at this praying for people thing, so I wanted to go unknown my first time. It was between me and God and Monique. Now I wanted to know if my prayers worked. She was still asleep and I didn't want to bother her. It was an hour later before she woke up and I was right there by the bedside to ask her about her tooth. She was still a little groggy when she woke up, but I asked her if her tooth was better. She said, "What do you mean is my tooth better?"

I said, "The one that's bothering you, check to see if it still hurts."

She felt around in her mouth with her tongue and she said it seemed to feel okay. So I said, "Really push on it. Let me know if it still hurts or not." She said it felt fine. That wasn't good enough for me because she could've been just saying that to get me to leave her alone because I was standing there practically looking down her throat to find out if my prayer worked. That's when I told her that I had prayed for her. "I prayed for a total healing of your tooth, and I need to know the results. So I'll check back with you later to see if you're really healed. I want you to keep messing with it to find out if it's really okay."

Since I was new at the praying, I really wanted to know if God would use me to heal someone through my prayer. Even though she just brushed me off, I was still going to check on her progress. I told her that God said he would heal her if I prayed, and since I did, "I need you to let me know if it worked!" She pushed on her tooth again with her tongue, then she wiggled it with her finger, and she said she didn't feel any pain. I was not 100 percent sure, but I also think God told me to tell her that she needed to also let people know that she had been healed. She had to share her testimony with others that I prayed for her, and God healed her. This would be how she would keep her healing. I told her what God spoke to me. I didn't know if she followed the directions, but as far as I knew, her tooth remained healed. I wasn't really walking with God, but I think he gave me a taste of what I could have if I was to follow Him. It was like he was giving me a sample of his goodness.

I continued watching the religious television shows, but I still wasn't finished smoking crack. It seemed like the more I mixed the two, the more I would be convicted every time I picked the pipe up. I wasn't even sure if I was actually saved. I prayed the sinner's prayer with so many TV evangelist, so many times I thought I was saved, but I really wasn't sure because I couldn't stop smoking crack. I wasn't a churchgoer, even though my brother invited me many times. He and my sister-in-law dealt with addiction as well. They, too, used to be crack smokers. When they gave their lives to Jesus Christ, they immediately stopped smoking and never smoked again. In the back of my mind, I always thought that maybe if I gave my life to Christ, he would help me stop smoking crack too. I just wasn't ready to make that full commitment.

When my brother and sister joined the church, they were all the way in. My brother played the trumpet in the worship band and my sister worked the video cameras. So I thought if I joined, I would have to be all in, be a part of some ministry, maybe start playing the drums in the church, but I would have to dedicate my time to some type of ministry. I just wasn't ready for that. I only turned to God when my situation was desperate, I was in trouble, or my lights were about to be turned off. That was when I called on God.

Once my phone service was about to be disconnected and this wasn't the first time that I was about to lose my phone service. Many times, I got to the last day before they would shut off my service. It would come down to me making the phone call and speaking with a representative to see if I could convince them to allow me to keep my phone on. I needed the telephone because I didn't have a cell phone and my kids might want to call a friend, or their schools may call. Also don't forget, how was I going to call my dope dealers and arrange to pick up crack! The phone necessary. I had to keep the phone on.

Since I couldn't control my drug habit and I hardly ever paid my bills on time, this was a recurring event. I woke up early Saturday morning so I could call the phone company and be at the head of the line waiting to talk to a representative. I got through to customer service to explain my plight. I was connected to a young woman. She was very kind and courteous. I started to explain to her that I'd been having some problems and even though this was my third time being late, "Could you please give me until next Wednesday, I promise to pay the bill in full". The representative replied with, "Mr. Barnes you've been late quite a bit, and normally, we wouldn't give you any more chances. We would have to cut off your services, but I'm going to give you another chance." I was elated and couldn't thank her enough, then she said, "Mr. Barnes we aren't supposed to do this, but God is leading me to pray for you".

At this point, I wasn't sure what I was hearing from the phone company representative, but I didn't say a word because she was allowing me to keep my service on. Then she went in hard! She said, "Father God, we thank you right now for Mark. I don't know what has control over him, but I command it to be loosed right now in the name of Jesus! Whether it be drugs, alcohol, or whatever it is, I command it to release your son right now!" By now I was crying like a baby. How did she know! She kept it short and sweet, and when she was done, she said thank you and "Is there anything else I can help you with?" I could barely thank her through my tears, but I did, and she hung up. What just happened? A phone representative just prayed a powerful prayer for me speaking directly to my issue of drug addiction.

At that point, I knew God was speaking to me. She prayed with such power and conviction that it broke me. I sat on the edge of my bed trying to wrap my head around what just happened. Yes, I got to keep my phone service on, but I also had this anointed prayer prayed over me from a phone company representative. How often did that happen? When God is trying to get your attention, He could use anybody He wanted anytime He wanted. One more time God showed up for me in a mighty way. Now this wasn't the straw that broke the camel's back, but it was indeed another piece of the straw because slowly something inside me was changing. I hadn't realized yet that I could live life without using drugs, but I had done drugs for so long, that was all I knew, but I was getting tired and my life wasn't getting any better.

I guess I just haven't reached my rock bottom, yet it seemed right after a God moment. Satan was quick to come in with a good party situation. I would get a call from a friend who just got hooked up with some good drugs. They would invite me to come over and get high with them. It never failed. I would always accept; I couldn't say no. When I would partake, it always ended bad. If it started out free, I would always eventually go into my pockets and spend all the money I had. This was actually the game that other users used. They will turn you on to what they've bought because they knew eventually, you would spend your money and repay the favor. It's the oldest trick in the book. I could only remember one time when I came out on top while buying some crack. It happened just one time over eighteen years of smoking.

I pulled up to the spot to purchase some crack. The dealers were standing on the corner. I recognized one of them, so I flagged him to get in my car. This was happening at night, so it was okay for him to jump into my car to make the sale. He was sitting on the passenger side. I wanted three dimes. He reached into his pocket to get them for me. He was fumbling around in his pocket because apparently, he had a lot more in his pocket, and he just wanted to pull out what I asked for—no more, no less. He finally pulled out my three dimes and handed them to me. I handed him $30 and he was on his way. I immediately pulled off because I got what I wanted, and you didn't want to hang around the spot too long. You wanted to get in and get out as quick as possible. I drove off to find a nice quiet spot where I could take a hit. I glanced down in the seat where he was sitting and I noticed three white packs. Remember it was dark outside and I couldn't believe what I was seeing. I turned on my interior light and noticed three more dimes sitting in my seat.

While rummaging around in his pocket, he pulled out three dimes, and they fell in my seat. It was like Christmas. I had never in all my years of smoking got over like that. In addiction, we called that a good night. I didn't return to that spot for a while. It wasn't like he would know he lost his coke in my car because they got in and out of so many cars through the course of the night, but I didn't want to take that chance. I finally got a win, and I enjoyed it. I did notice from that point on, every time a dealer jumped into my car to serve me, they would always look back at the seat cushion to make sure nothing fell out of their pockets.

Even a good night like that when you came out on top getting more crack than you anticipated ultimately ended in depression when the crack was all gone. When you win, you still lose. I couldn't call this time an actual win because I still paid for what I got. A maintenance man was doing the landscaping with the weed wacker in front of my apartment. While trimming the grass, it exposed a package of cocaine that must have been left by a dealer because sometimes they stuck their coke in the grass and pulled it out when they have a sale. A dealer must have forgotten where he put it and left it there. The maintenance person knew I smoked, so he brought it to me and asked me if I wanted to buy it. Of course I said "Sure!" Because it was worth a lot more than he was asking.

With my last little bit of money I had, I bought it from him. The problem was I didn't have all the money he was asking, so I had to get it on loan and pay him the rest later. He was cool with that because he knew where I lived, and he knew I was good for it. Once again, I was in debt because of crack cocaine. I was buying it even when I didn't have money to buy it. I just couldn't let a good deal get away. When he left, I cooked it up and took a big hit, and it was good! It made the bells ring! I was home all by myself and I was sprung! Twenty minutes later, the guy came back just to ask me if it was any good. Remember, it was left outside and from the looks of the package, it had been outside for a while. I was so high I couldn't answer the door; plus, I could barely speak. If I would have opened the door, he would have seen me geeking, and I couldn't let him see me like that. So I never answered the door, even though he knew I was in there.

Actually, me not answering the door told him everything he needed to know. Once again, I was stuck! Once it was all smoked up, I was left with the depressing thought that I now owed him money. Money that I didn't have. Later that week on Friday, he showed up on time to get his money. I always paid my crack debts. It was bad when Friday showed up, and you already owed money for crack that you had already smoked. So now I was starting out behind the eight ball. All my friends that sold crack to me, never had a problem loaning or fronting it to me because they knew I would always pay. I guess I had good crack credit. My crack addiction was very expensive and I progressively got more and more out of control.

As I got more into financial trouble, I seemed to feel the need to bring God into my world as a fix, at least a temporary fix. There were incidents when God miraculously intervened in my bad situations. Soon as I was delivered out of whatever trouble I got myself into, I quickly forgot who brought me out of them. When God would answer my cry for help, it was always clear that It was Him because the way I got out was miraculous. It was never something that I could say I did. Like the phone incident that I spoke of earlier. It was evident that was the hand of God. Even the time I was out smoking and hacking, stuck in that vicious cycle. In the middle of it, I just prayed, "God, please let me go home!"

As I drove around the city looking for potential riders, I just couldn't break free because if I saw another person looking for a ride, I would pick them up and continue in the cycle of hacking for money. Then I would go buy more crack. But I knew if I could just work my way east and start heading in the direction of my home, I would continue that way, possibly break free from the grips of the city, and finally go home. I also had to make enough money to put gas in my tank to even reach my home. I always rode around with my gas tank on E. Soon as I made enough money to buy a rock, that was what I did. And when I made enough money to put a couple of dollars in my gas tank, that was what I did. There was no such thing as filler up, a quarter tank, or a half tank. No, it was always a couple of dollars. It seemed like all the people that I would pick up, all needed rides to the west side of the city, which was where all the dope spots where I would buy my crack.

My mind wanted to go home, but my body kept wanting more crack. I couldn't figure out what was going on, I was trying to break free, but I just couldn't get to the east side of Baltimore. This was when the miraculous happened. It was 11:00 p.m., and it was getting later by the minute. I just finished a hit, and then I said my prayer. My tank was on E, and I really needed to find a hack quickly before I ran out of gas. While driving, I saw a hack.

At first glance, it looked like it was going to be a good one. I pulled over and asked, "Where are you going?"

He said, "I just got off work, and I'll give you $10 if you take me to East Baltimore!"

It took everything in me to keep it together because I knew God had just answered my prayer. I was practically in tears. I didn't know then, but I knew His presence was all over me. So the gentleman got in my car, he was a very nice guy, and we had great conversation all the way to his house where I dropped him off. I would be lying if I didn't say that everything in me wanted to take that $10 and go right back into the city to buy some more crack. I mean, a $10 ride was a good lick. I could put $3 in the tank, get another hack going west, and easily have enough to buy some more crack. That was what my mind told me to do right after God blessed me with the opportunity to get out of the city. There was no way I was going to throw God's blessing right back in his face. My mind could be my worst enemy, but I knew that was nobody but the devil, and I decided to take my butt home. I fought this battle many times. The thing was, when God miraculously got you out of trouble, and then like a dog returning to its vomit, you went back to the trouble you were delivered out of. I have found that the butt beating you got the next time was always worse.

Another time I was driving All night, I asked God to help me break free and go home. And He did. This time, I didn't have the $10 hack to get to the eastside. I said, *God, I don't have any gas but if you get me home, I'll leave the city right now!* Mind you, I lived thirty miles from the city and I was on the west side. So this time, I was going to drive home strictly by faith. I was going to trust God that he was going to get me home with my gas tank on E, without any hack money.

As I made my way through the city, I kept looking for a hack, but there was none. I finally got to the interstate, I-95, still on E. I never paid so much attention to my gas needle then this particular night. As I drove, my eyes went from the highway to the gas needle, hoping that it didn't move below the empty line. You know, how sometimes the needle can fluctuate and rise above the E line, like there's more gas in the tank than you realize. Not this time, it stayed on E, and it did not move. It actually dropped a little below E, and I thought at any moment my car was about to cut off. I continued to drive and pray. "Lord, please let me make it home!" You know I watch a lot of TBN. I also listened to a lot of Christian radio. I tuned into a radio ministry because I really needed a word from God that everything was going to be okay. You know, like a right-now word!

At that very moment, I remembered that I still had a crack pipe in the car, or maybe that was God telling me that I still had a crack pipe in the car. So I immediately threw it out the window with any other paraphernalia I might have in the car. I heard it crash on the street. Now I was not even looking at the needle, all I was looking at is the highway, looking for my exit.

At this point, my prayer was, "God, I'm in your hands." Can you believe that I had the nerve to even blame it on God, like it was His fault that I was in this situation in the first place? That was how ungrateful I could be at times. But if I do run out of gas, I didn't want to run out on the highway. They'd tow my car if it was sitting on the side of the highway. Finally, I approached my exit. I put on my signal to get off the highway. I still lived three miles from the exit and my tank had been on E for quite some time. I was now driving totally on faith, or should I say on fumes. If I stopped, I'd just get out of the car and deal with the situation, but I was hoping that God would take me all the way home.

As I continued driving, I was getting closer and closer to my home. At this point, I didn't even care If I ran out of gas, I could

155

almost walk home, but my car continued on. I finally made that last turn into my block. I pulled up in front of my house, I turned off the car, and I immediately started crying. God had done it again. I didn't dare turn my car back on just to check because I didn't want to know if it would start again, I'd deal with that tomorrow morning. You would think when God comes through for me like this, it would be enough to make me change my ways for good. I knew it was a miracle because I knew my car. I had run out of gas before.

When my gas needle was in that particular position, it was just a matter of time before the car would stop totally out of gas. The next morning, when I came out to start my car, it immediately stopped right after I started it. You would think this miracle would be enough to really get my attention and lead me to changing my ways? Nope! Maybe two weeks later, I found myself in the same situation.

I was in Baltimore, high on crack, out of gas, and trying to get home. So what was I going to do? I knew; I'd say a prayer and ask God to please, one more time, get me home. Once again, the gas needle was just a little bit above E. I might have enough to get home, but if not, God would do the rest and get me home. I started my trek out of the city with my eyes constantly going from the windshield to the gas needle. *Come on, God!* I got through the city to the east side. The needle bouncing on the E ever so gently. I got to I-95, the main stretch. I was praying to God for his divine help. I, again, threw away my pipe and any other paraphernalia out of the window. My glass pipe crashed on the highway. See God, I mean it this time! Ten miles in it happened. My engine sputtered and all the lights on my dash flickered on. I drifted over to the shoulder and my car died.

I started begging God. Oh no Lord, don't let this happen to me. Like it was God's fault, and I had nothing to do with it. Of course, I tried starting it up. Maybe God was just messing with me to teach me a lesson. But to no avail; I was out of gas. The needle was in the same place it was two weeks ago when I made it all the way home. Now, what was I going to do? This time was a little different and to be totally honest, I did have a little bit of crack left in my pocket. Maybe God was holding that against me. I didn't know. Anyhow, I was faced with a decision. I couldn't sit here and wait for the police

156

because I got dope in my pockets, and you know I was not going to just throw it away. It was at least a dime of crack. So there were woods on both sides of the highway. I knew if I walked deep enough into the woods on the eastbound side, I would eventually run into homes.

So I started walking. I was getting deeper into the woods, and all I could think about was the crack in my pocket and wouldn't you know, even though I didn't have a pipe, lo and behold, there was an empty Coke can. If you've been smoking as long as I have, you've resorted to using a soda can as a pipe every once in a while. Perfect! So in the middle of the woods, I converted the can into a pipe. Did I mention I also had a blunt in case of an emergency? In order for this to work, smoking with the can, I needed ashes. It's like a scene from *Mission Impossible*, making this crack pipe in the middle of the woods.

Once it was completed, I put a big rock on my contraption, and took a big full pull. When I blew out the smoke, I was immediately transformed into space. The crack was excellent! Remember when you take a big hit, all of your senses are heightened. I kid you not, when I say I heard every cricket, bird, bat and bug. I heard people talking, cars driving on the highway, deer walking through the woods, and I heard everything like someone had turned the volume up to ten! Then the paranoia kicked in. I knew that someone was chasing me in the woods; every time I looked around to see who it was, there was no one. Taking a hit in the woods was a big mistake. I had to continue on; I had to get out of these woods before I went crazy. I was in the middle of the woods, hearing all kind of sounds, looking every which way to see who or what I could see.

Of course, I saw no one. Just think if I did see somebody in the middle of the woods, I would have probably had a stroke. I continued to walk, and I saw the light of some houses. There were not many houses here because the people who lived in the woods, lived there for privacy, and these were big homes. You know, people who had money. I looked for the house with the most lights on and I walked toward it. I stopped for a minute to calm my nerves because I didn't want to approach someone's front door looking crazy. I was still a little geeked up from the hit I just took. Plus, I didn't want to look too scary. A Black man walking up to your door from the middle of the woods wasn't a good look. I needed help. I didn't want to scare anybody. And I really didn't want anyone to call the police because I knew I would go directly to jail without a second thought.

At this point, I didn't have much of a choice. I had already walked a mile into the woods. I approached the door of the house I selected. I could see there was a little bit of life inside because there were lights on at 11:00 p.m. *Well, here goes nothing.* Left with no choice, and an abandoned car on the highway, I knocked on the door. More lights started to come on and a man opened the door. I immediately began to explain my plight in desperation hoping he'd listen and possibly help.

"Sir, please forgive me for disturbing you at this late hour, but I've run out of gas on the highway."

Without hesitation, he smiled and said, "No problem. I have a gas tank full of gas and you can have it." I was in shock! Again, I knew it was nothing but my Heavenly Father reaching down to help his son in need. It was like the guy knew I was coming.

After all the drama I created to get to this point, my problem was solved in an instant. The guy said, "Keep the gas can. It's okay."

Maybe from the looks of me, he thought this wouldn't be the last time I'd be in this predicament and in need of a gas can. I thanked him and gave him a few "God Bless Yous", and I was on my way back through the woods to my car. Being that I'm not a hiker, when I finally got back through the woods and to the highway. I resurfaced out of the woods a quarter mile from my car's location. So now I was walking down the highway with a gas can back to my car. Nonetheless, I made it. I had blown it again and I was going to be in big trouble. God, once again, rescued me out of my mess. When I finally got home, all I could do was fall on my knees and thank God for getting me out of one more of my trials. Once again, these types of miraculous events made me stop and reflect on the goodness of God. So I usually took a break from getting high when God was so good to me. I got back into watching my TV evangelists, and I started reading a little bit of God's word. But the reality of it all was, I still haven't reached my bottom. So I eventually fell back into my old habits.

18

Putting the Job on the Line

It was now starting to affect being productive on my job and paying bills was getting tougher and tougher. Instead of working a full day, I'd go in for a couple of hours, knockout a few service calls, and then go right back home to smoke. As my productivity on my job started to waver, they moved my territory from Baltimore to DC. I think they were sending a message. They were making the job a little more uncomfortable for me to be productive and it was a tough commute every morning to DC. Since they couldn't fire me, it seemed they were making it hard for me to hold on to my job. I remember one morning I was on my way to work in Washington, DC. I had to drive right by downtown Baltimore on the way to DC.

While on my way, my turn signal came on and I was on the exit ramp heading right into downtown to the hood to get some coke. It was like I couldn't stop my hand from putting on the signal, nor could I stop my hands from turning off the highway. Once I was heading to the hood, there was only one thing left to do and that was to find some crack. What just happened? Just like that my mind switched from going to work to going on a mission.

At Xerox, we had two-way radios and my boss could call me at any time. And sure enough, my boss came over the radio, looking for me, asking me to reply. "Mark, could you come back? Mark, come back please." Everything in me wanted to pick up the radio and reply, but what was I going to say? That day, the radio weighed fifty pounds. So I just listened to his request and never answered. Then finally I just turned the radio off so I wouldn't have to listen to his calls. I had totally blown it! This was insubordination at its highest. I had never done anything like this on my job before. I was crossing lines I'd never crossed before. I guess this meant I didn't want my job anymore, I've traded my job for smoking crack. I'm sure that part of the reason was because this was payday Friday, and all I could think about was getting high, and got plenty of money to do just that. I still had to think about what I was going to say Monday morning when I called my boss. All I could think about right now was a hit. That was the answer to all my problems.

After God had got me out of so much junk, I still created another mess and jumped in headfirst. Back to the vomit. I tried not to think about the Monday morning meeting with my boss. It made getting high pretty tough, but I got high anyway. The weekend was pretty much the same routine, getting high and spending my whole check on drugs. I spent Sunday relaxing, watching sports knowing that Monday morning I would be called into my boss's office, since I didn't show up or call in on Friday. My secret wasn't really out on the job, but my performance was really suffering.

When I was called into the office, I just gave an excuse of being really sick and not able to make it in. I think by now, I was already on some type of probation, and all I had to do was get on the ball and work a little harder and get back in good graces with my boss. Overall, I was well liked on the job, so once I turned it around with a few good weeks of hard work, my problem became a non-issue. That would hold up for a month or two, but I just couldn't keep it up. I'd be doing so good because of the pressure I was under on the job, then I would go to the bar with my work buddies after work on Friday or go to the club Saturday night. Whether it was alcohol or women, I would put myself into a situation where a hit of crack would be a great idea right then. Then it was off to the races. If my get high session went from Sunday into Monday morning, that meant it was going to be a rough day at work. It was the birds. If I was smoking Sunday night and I started hearing the birds, it was too late; I did it again. Another all-nighter. No chance for getting any rest. Now I had to try and start coming down so I could prepare for work. Of course, I was going to be late, and this was starting to be a recognized pattern with me and Monday mornings. I would be in trouble if I called in sick.

By this point, I am actually getting tired of the vicious cycle. I heard somewhere that if you admitted you have a problem with drugs and alcohol before they just fired you from poor performance, then they had to get you some help. Here I go again. I missed too much work and I didn't show up at a customer's site that I was scheduled to be at. Now my boss wanted to talk to me. The thing about my boss was, she wasn't prepared for what I was about to share. I was probably going to get another slap on the wrist and be sent on my way.

When I went into her office, I was so done with my continued drug addiction. When she asked me what my problem was, I just spilled it and said, "I have a drug problem!" When I said it, I could tell by the look on her face, that wasn't what she was expecting me to say. Then with stuttering lips, she replied, "Excuse me, what did you say?"

So I repeated it, "I have a drug problem!" Even for a Black woman, her face went flush. She backed her chair away from her desk and excused herself and left me in the office by myself. She needed to go out and get reinforcements because I knew this was her first time dealing with an employee with a drug problem. When she returned, she had her manager and her manager's manager with her. The jig is up! They now had to refer to the Xerox handbooks. *How do we deal with an employee on crack?* I knew of one of my coworkers; he was an older gentleman and he too had a cocaine addiction problem. I spoke with him about it a couple of times because he openly talked about his addiction on the job. Everyone knew about it, he went away and got help and returned to the job. He'd been working drug-free on the job for the last seven years and he was doing fine. Now, they had to figure out what to do with a real crackhead! I didn't think the handbooks had been updated to handle this type of situation. The gentleman I spoke of was sent away to an inpatient rehabilitation program. So when he finally came out, he was able to continue working for Xerox. Now, It was the young Black guy's turn. The cool thing was after we all sat in my boss's office, I was allowed to share my story. I was pretty calm.

As I explained my dilemma, I was able to cry some real tears because it actually was a very emotional moment. I had been with Xerox for eighteen years, so there was a real relationship built, and they could see I sincerely wanted some help. They told me to go home and take the rest of the day off. You can bet this was cool with me; I needed some sleep. And they told me to come back in two days so they could gather their data and figure out what company procedure was. I went home for the next two days and had time to think. Now the truth was out and I had to face the results of my actions. To me, it was a big relief. I actually had a sense of peace because the weight I was carrying was now lifted off my shoulders. During these times, crack was creating so much destruction in the workplace that companies were being more supportive to employees who were dealing with it, by offering counseling and treatment options.

When I returned to work, I'd find out how they were going to help me. Now I didn't mention that I had a few company vehicle situations that may be considered while reviewing my work history. Incident #1. I ran my company vehicle up on the median of the highway high as a kite. This destroyed the undercarriage and punctured the oil pan. I told them that I had ran over something on the highway that I wasn't able to avoid. Incident #2, which gave me my company nickname, Engine Killer. I drove for six months and never got the oil changed. One day while driving for work the engine seized up. When they towed it to the service station to be repaired, they reported back to my boss that the van was totally out of oil, which caused it to lock up. I probably could have gotten fired for that, but I was able to skate by and keep my job. I just had to deal with my new nickname, Engine Killer. Again, I dodged another bullet. Each one of these circumstances were caused by my addiction. I wasn't able to drive in the first case and in the second case, I wasn't able to take care of my company car maintenance due to my crack use. Now after my admission, they were probably able to put it all together and see that my problem progressively got worse and it had been going on for quite some time.

The day came for me to face the music, but I must say I was ready. The two days off they gave me, I took advantage of and stayed totally clean. I was trying my best to prepare for whatever was about to come my way. Plus, I was thinking that they might take a urine sample, who knows, but it turned out to be pretty productive. I walked into my boss's office that Thursday morning and there, sitting with my boss, was her boss and an HR representative of course. They explained that they were understanding of my situation and that they were going to try to be as helpful as possible. They offered me an outpatient drug rehabilitation program. While in the program, I would receive full pay and the program would last for thirty days. Me, knowing how bad I was, asked if there was an inpatient program available. I knew I needed to be locked away. I also remembered that the last employee that went away for a program had inpatient rehabilitation. They explained to me that due to the changes in the company benefits program, they no longer offered inpatient rehabilitation. Already I had my doubts if I would be able to complete a program that wasn't going to lock me away. When they explained this to me, I was sad, but it wasn't like I had much choice; so I accepted it and they gave me the details of when and where I was to report. I must say I was a bit relieved because I was finally going to get some help.

Monday morning, I was to report to the rehab facility. Wouldn't you know it, it was located in Baltimore City, five blocks from where I go to cop my crack. This couldn't be good, but I was going to make the best of it; plus, my career was on the line. In my class were all inner-city addicts. I kept an open mind because I did want to get better. I'd never been to a real recovery program, so I didn't know what to expect. I was in a classroom atmosphere and I thought that I was pretty smart, so I should do okay here. Remember I worked for Xerox; all these people were junkies from the streets of Baltimore with court-ordered rehab. I was already feeling a little better than.

Mistake number one. Now this was an all-day classroom session with lunch breaks and everything, just like school. It was very interesting being in class with these folks from the inner-city learning about addiction, raising hands, and asking questions. I kind of enjoyed it. Here was the problem, at the end of the first day of class, all of my fellow students had to report back to their dorms and get ready for dinner while I got into my car and I got to go home. I was in rehab with a bunch of inpatient people and I was the only one who actually got to go home.

When I walked out of that door at first I felt good, I was out of class, and I got to go home and eat some dinner. When I started to drive through the city and passed all my drug spots, I felt an anxiety that was overwhelming. I knew being in an outpatient situation wasn't a good idea for me. I kept thinking about the stuff I learned that day. How no matter what, I could not drink or use. I remained focused and made it home. I had to return the next day, and the next, and the next. Could I remain clean through this process? I really didn't have any choice. If I completed this program, I'd have a clean slate and I would have to be given another chance on the job. So I continued.

The classes were very interesting even though they were ghetto fabulous. Most of the people in my class weren't there because they wanted to learn about their addictions; most were court-ordered by a judge, and these classes were just a slap on the wrist. Most would be right back to their drug of choice once finished with the program. Me, I had to be successful, I had to keep my job, my career, a roof over me and my children's heads. A lot was on the line. A week went by and I was getting the hang of this thing. *Yeah, I can do this.* The class portion was actually easy. The hard part was, at the end of the day when all my classmates went to their dorm rooms, I was free to go home. This seemed to give me a sense of arrogance, like I was not as bad as those people; my problem was not as bad as theirs.

Looking back, it was definitely pride, and you know pride comes before a fall. Even though I was subjected to random drug test, by my fifth day of being drug-free, I decided it was time for me to take a hit. I thought I would reward myself for being so good. And the fact that it was payday Friday made matters worse. The reason that I thought I would be okay was because in class, a lot of the students talked about the different types of things you could use to clean your urine, which will enable you to pass any urine test. Since I hadn't been using, I was able to save up some money, so I bought what they told me in order to have clean urine. Now I was ready to get me some crack. It was

Friday and class was over. I went to the spot to get me some rocks. When I had them in my hand, I felt terrified. A sudden fear came over me because of the realization of what I was about to do flooded my mind. Deep inside, I knew I was making a terrible mistake.

At this point, there was no turning back. Whenever you had rocks in your hand, you rationalized smoking them because of the amount of money you just spent. There's no way I'm going to just throw this away, even though you are making a tragic mistake. I used to look forward to Friday and being able to smoke. Now I had the crack in my hand, I was not sure what to do. I did finally smoke it. I got really high. I just couldn't enjoy it. Something had changed. Now all I could think about was, would my urine come up dirty? I had crossed the line and I had to rely on the stuff I had bought to clean my urine out. My logic was, since I only smoked a little bit this time, I'd be okay after I take my cure. Plus I had the rest of the weekend to clean myself out. This was the first time that I was so worried that I couldn't purchase any more.

I was done. I kept my money in my pocket for the remainder of the weekend. All I could think about was Monday morning class and if they were going to take a urine sample from me on Monday morning. My crackhead thinking got me to this point. To take a hit while clean and sober. Monday morning arrives and it was time to go to class. Soon as I got there, it was common practice for them to take a urine sample after being home all weekend. If you were going to fall, it will definitely be on the weekend. Some of the inpatient students also got weekend privileges and they were allowed to go home. As a standard practice, everyone had to give a urine sample. I peed in the cup and I went to my class. They never revealed to me the results of my urine test, so I thought the stuff was working, and I was good. Guess what, I kept getting high after leaving class. It went from just on Fridays, to a couple of days during the week. I thought I was fooling them. I figured this was going to be a breeze. I'd be out of here in a week and I could go back to work. Or at least that was what I thought.

The final week came, and there was no graduation ceremony. You were just released like every day before that. All I was told was to report to my manager on Monday morning. So what did I do? It was time to celebrate. I bought me some rocks after class because the urine test were over, and I did my thing. But in the bottom of my stomach, I really didn't know because remember they never told me the results of my urine tests. I just assumed they were good because they didn't kick me out of the class. Here I was again, wondering what Monday morning would reveal. Then came anxiety, no sleep, constant worrying. I blew it again. Monday morning came and I reported directly to my boss's office. Do not pass go, do not collect $200. And again, it was my boss, her boss, and the HR representative. This was not looking good and I was a little nervous.

After everyone showed up, we moved to a conference room. I was starting to feel that this wasn't going to be good because no one was saying anything and no one was smiling; the smile I came in with, I quickly removed. We all had a seat around a big conference table and the meeting began. First, they started out with a basic greeting. "How are you doing, Mr. Barnes?"

To which I replied, "Just fine."

Then they asked me, "How was your treatment?"

To which I said, "It was okay." I couldn't say it was good because I think they were about to drop a bomb on me. And here it comes. "Well, according to your test results, you tested positive for cocaine on all your tests during the whole process."

To which I replied, "That was why I requested inpatient care. All the people that were in the treatment with me were inpatients. I was the only one who could go home every day and the treatment facility was around the corner from where I brought my drugs." Basically, what I just said was, "It was all your fault!" Typical crackhead behavior. It was everybody else's fault. To that, they merely replied, "That's the only treatment available under your benefits plan." I had no more fight left in me. I blew it and I had to face whatever was coming my way. So they made their offer. I was told I could go back to work, but it would be very difficult to reach my targets because they would all be increased. Which meant I would probably be terminated, or "You could accept an offer we had put together for you." *Here we go!*

Eighteen years with a major corporation was about to go down the tubes, all because of my crack addiction. I was shocked that they were even going to make an offer after I had blown my chances in recovery. The recovery that I received full pay to complete. I couldn't even finish that. They said, "If you voluntarily resign, we will pay you your full pay with your medical and dental benefits for one year."

With my crackhead mind, I thought I had died and gone to heaven. All I could think was *I could party all year and not have to go to work.* I fixed my face to look as sad as I could and I told them, "Okay, I'll sign."

There were several documents I had to sign. I had to turn in all of my parts, give back my company vehicle, and I was no longer a Xerox employee. I only said goodbye to the people that were in the office. I was sure they didn't want me to make a spectacle or share my personal business with other employees. So they kept it simple and I left. The other plus was there would be no record of it that they could share with another employer if I were to find another job and use them as a reference. That way, I would have something to show for my eighteen years of employment with the Xerox Corporation. Even though I took the offer and left the company, I looked at it as an opportunity for a new start. I knew I had to do things differently. I'd experienced what crack could do to your life. It was now time for change.

Now, I had to figure out how to explain to my friends and family that I didn't work for that great company I used to brag about working for. I couldn't just isolate. I had to make sure I paid all my bills and not show my face too much. This whole situation was somewhat depressing and I was dealing with it untreated. When I'm faced with dilemmas, being an addict, I usually medicated myself with drugs or alcohol. With all this extra time on my hands, I found myself smoking more and more. I also hung out with others who were unemployed, even though I received a paycheck. I now realized if I didn't have something positive to occupy my time, the devil loved an idle mind, and if I didn't find something positive to keep myself busy, I was going to be in a world of trouble.

19

❦

Unemployed Crackhead

At the start of my loss of work, I just took It easy and things just got worse. My local dealers I knew personally would always give me crack upfront without payment, by the time I got my check, I owed most of it to them. I always abided to my rule to pay my crack dealers back first. Then I could get some more with no problem or no questions asked. I had good crack credit. Credit purchases were always a little smaller than cash purchases, but I didn't care as long as I got some. When you came back after that, because you were geeking, the rocks got even smaller.

That was just the way the game was played. Dealers knew at that point you'd take anything. Right now, I couldn't concern myself with how to buy crack on credit. I really needed to start thinking about how to get my life back on track. I had a year to figure out my next steps, because if I didn't stay busy, I was doomed. I wish I could say I got right back to work, because now I would have plenty of money if I could find a job to complement the pay I was receiving from Xerox; but I didn't. I did exactly what I wanted to do and that was take some time off. Since I was in the grips of my addiction, if I applied for a job, when I took a urine test, it would just come up dirty; and since I was getting a check anyway, I didn't really care. So needless to say, I stayed unemployed. Since I had nowhere to report to each morning, I spent more time getting high. Little bit by little bit, I was spiraling out of control. It got to a point that after spending all my money through the week, if it even lasted that long, I would be at the ATM till 12:01 Friday morning waiting for my next check to be deposited. I would be standing right there at the ATM, debit card in hand, inserting it over and over until there was a cash balance that I could withdraw from.

If I couldn't wait until Friday 12:00 a.m., I would write a check to myself and deposit it in my account for cash and withdraw the money. It didn't take long before the bank figured out my little scheme and put an end to it. I figured out all types of ways to get money when I was dead broke. The ATM got so tired of me robbing it, that it finally just kept my card. The ATM wouldn't give it back. It just displayed a message for me to come to the bank Monday morning to speak with a representative. Of course, I never showed up. Once, I was in the city playing the ATM game. I was hanging out with a dealer, who I guess you could say we kind of became associates, because I wouldn't call us friends. He was smoking crack, so he didn't mind fronting me more with the promise that soon as my check was deposited, I could give him his money back plus some extra. He was a little hesitant to believe that all of a sudden, I would have money in the bank and he made it clear that I better have money in the bank or things might get ugly. Since I had confidence that my check would be there, I continued to buy crack from him with the promise of paying him later.

As 12:00 a.m. showed up and I inserted my debit card into the teller machine. It said, "You have a zero balance". No problem, I'd just wait thirty seconds and try it again. This went on for about five or six tries, which lasted for twenty minutes and still no cash. The dealer was starting to get a little upset with me. I assured him that the money would be there. I tried one more time and there it was. I withdrew all of his money, plus some money for me to buy some more from him.

As I paid him, he made the comment that he should take all of my money. At this point, I was getting a little worried. I pleaded with him, "Come on man here's your money, give me a break". He said, "Get out of my face before I take all of your money". It would have been easy for him to jack a crackhead at one o'clock in the morning, never get caught, and no one would care. I quickly jumped in my car and took off. Just another situation that could have taken a bad turn.

Thank God it didn't. Feeling uneasy about this whole situation and the way it could have taken a wrong turn, I got some more money out of the bank, went to a different location to buy some crack, and got out of the city. Whenever I would get an uneasy feeling about situations or circumstances that I was dealing with, I always took that as a sign to go home. When I finally made it home, I smoked what I had and tried to go to sleep. That was a tough night and this was one of those nights that made me realize that it might be time to take a break from buying and smoking coke, especially in the city. Plus, my money was already getting low and I had already exceeded my withdrawal amount in one night; $400 up in smoke.

I remember being at the bank teller so high, I couldn't remember my four-digit pin number. After the fourth attempt, the machine just kept my card, which was probably the best thing that could have happened to me at the time. I would love to go back to my Bank of America history and check my transactions during that time in my life. I still use the same account to this day, but thanks be to God, my account is feeling much better these days. That same bank has extended me a $12,000 line of credit. Speaking of credit, now that I was unemployed, I still received a check, but I seemed to run through them pretty fast. I remember the time I received a check in the mail for $3,500. It was a loan from a creditor. Since I was a homeowner, I would get these in the mail every once in a while. This time I cashed it. I neglected to read the fine print, which said if I cash the check, I had to pay it back at 25 percent interest. Funny how when you were on crack you didn't see any of the small print, you just saw the big cash number. It took me years to pay it back and when I finally paid it all back, I paid back with penalties and interest over $5,000. Boy did they get me.

As the year of free paychecks progressed on, I did nothing to get clean. I just spent a lot of money on drugs; I barely paid my bills, and I never even thought about getting a job. Then it came. The last paycheck. Oh my goodness! You think It was never going to come to an end, but it did. I've had plenty of time to relax and get my thoughts together, but reality still caught me off guard and I had to do something quick. Like get a job. So I put together a resume and applied online for jobs. I applied for every job that was available in hopes that someone would give me a call for an interview. Then the interviews started to happen. There was hope that someone might hire me. I did everything I could to get myself cleaned up because I knew there would be a urine test in my future and I had to be clean. I started getting calls from companies scheduling me to come in and interview.

For some reason, even though I interviewed well, I never got hired, just rejections. At one point, I had been to so many interviews. I mixed up the information of one company with another company. When the interviewer asked me why I wanted to work for their company, I had to be honest and tell the interviewer that I didn't know the name of the company. At that point, she just frowned and said, "Mr. Barnes, this interview is over. Thank you for your time."

All I could do was apologize and walk out of her office. That was embarrassing to say the least. She just didn't understand that this was Thursday, and I had already been on four interviews since Monday. This taught me to do more preparation for each interview, have all my information ready, and to be knowledgeable about the company that I was interviewing for. A couple of days later, I had an interview with a company that serviced lotto machines and scratch off ticket machines. They scheduled a series of interviews with me, and the interviewing process was going great. The gentleman I was interviewing with thought I was a great candidate for the job. He said I had all the qualifications necessary to do the job, and since I worked on Xerox copy machines, fixing lotto ticket machines would be no problem for me. I made it through two of the interviews and the interviewer said he didn't see any reason why they wouldn't hire me. He thought I would be a great fit for the company. He commented on my great attitude. He said I had good customer service skills and that was important in this industry because I would be dealing with lots of different customers in the field.

I was feeling pretty good about getting this job. He told me once hired, I would receive a company vehicle, and the pay was higher than what I made at Xerox. I was on a cloud nine. Thinking, finally I was going to land the perfect job. And I did everything I could including abstaining from smoking crack. I wasn't going to let anything get in the way of me getting this job. So the interviewer said the last thing he needed was my driver's license info so they could check my driving record for insurance purposes. I didn't think I had a bad driving record, but I wasn't absolutely sure. I gave it to him and then all I could do was wait for the results.

As far as I was concerned, I was about to start my new job. Two weeks went by and I got the call. By this time, we were on a first-name basis because the interviews went so well, but the call wasn't what I expected. He said. "Sorry, Mark, we're not going to be able to hire you. You have excessive tickets on your driving record along with two suspensions of your driving privileges. Therefore, our insurance company feels you would be a liability." Translation, "Sorry, crack-head, no job for you!" Oh yeah, that was another byproduct of being a crackhead. You didn't pay tickets on time and they usually go all the way to suspension until you paid them. Crackhead behavior struck again. But when I look back, a job servicing lotto ticket machines, this probably wouldn't have been the best job for an addict.

Just think, they would have given me keys to lotto machines with access to lots of cash. I guess God was looking out for me way back before I gave my life to him. Whew! I continued to Interview and my past would get in the way of any success at finding a job. Then I saw an ad for a car salesman. The ad said they offered paid training. I do have the gift of gab; plus I've sold stuff before. This should be a piece of cake. So I applied and got the job, along with twenty other people. After the training was complete, they kept twelve of us. I was a bona fide car salesman. They gave us all our own separate desks and cubicles and the car selling began. I was very eager to get started. I was a go getter when it came to sales. We were on a showroom floor with other seasoned car salesmen as well. We were their competition and the older salesmen didn't appreciate us because we were taking their sales opportunities. It was like a feeding frenzy when a customer showed up to look at the cars. Since this was a larger dealership, there were plenty of customers to go around. I must go back a little bit before getting the salesman job. I was watching a TV evangelist during my desperate attempts to find a job, because I was reaching out to hear from God, as getting a job seemed to be tougher than I thought it would be. The preacher said to take a $1,000 seed and put it at your doorway right on the floor. Don't sow it to the ministry for one week.

All during the week, pray to God for your blessing. I did just that. If you were wondering where I got $1,000? I withdrew it from my 401(k) savings plan with Xerox. Now without saying my prayer was a new job and the minister said, "Believe that you will receive what you asked in Jesus's name, and you can have it". I wasn't sure, but I believed that was something written in the Bible.

At that time, I was desperate for a new job, so I was willing to do whatever the man of God told me to do. That was when a week later after sowing the seed, I got the salesman job. I truly believed it was an answer to prayer. One reason that let me know God truly had his hand on my success as a car salesman was, I immediately started making sales before any of my other coworkers did. The car sales business could be pretty cruel. If you didn't make sales, your manager kindly walked up to your desk and asked you to clean it out and "Come get your last paycheck, we no longer need you." And just like that, you were fired. I watched this happen to salesman after salesman.

The only thing that protected me was I was selling cars and my manager was very impressed with my numbers. After fifteen days on the job, I had already sold eight cars. I actually was selling at the same rate as the seasoned salesmen. Some of these guys had been selling cars for decades and I just came along, brand-new and started selling cars just as fast as they were. There was nothing special about me. I had no special skills; I knew it was the favor of God on me because of that seed I sowed into a ministry I had watched on TBN. It seemed like everyone I approached to help on the car lot wound up buying a car from me. The monthly number they wanted you to reach was at least fifteen cars. I did that my first month on the job. The one thing I did differently from the other car salesman was going on test drives. I never minded taking a customer out on a test drive in the car they were considering.

My manager frowned on it because he said I was taking too many customers on test drives and this used up too much time. But I continued to do it. My manager thought I should be able to gauge our customers' desire to purchase before taking them out on a test drive. I used the test drive to get to know the customer on a more personal basis. What better way to get to know someone than to go for a drive with them? That was my logic and it seemed to work.

Since I was getting results, my manager had to leave me alone and let me continue with my methods. They continued to let people go and I think we were down to two or three of the original twelve new hires. While working with the other sales reps, they would always talk about the hat trick. I asked them, "What is the hat trick?" They said it hadn't been done in quite some time, but the hat trick was selling three cars in one day. It was tough to do because the paperwork involved with selling a car took a lot of time itself. They didn't just let you spend $20,000 to $30,000 in thirty minutes. A complete car sale normally took about two hours to complete. I wasn't trying to do it; it wasn't in my plans that day, but it happened. I did the hat trick. I sold three cars in one day. This hadn't been done in ten years and I pulled it off.

It was no question that God was giving me favor on my new job. I started to get extra commission checks for the number of cars I sold in addition to my regular pay. My boss was very impressed with my work. When I sold three cars in one day, he was elated! I failed to mention that this car dealership was located on the west side of Baltimore City. It was a struggle every day to ride past all of my old crack spots. I was trying to give God the glory and stay on the right path, and I was doing good. One of the things I didn't know about car sales was when you did well and sold specific cars, you got cash bonuses. They actually gave you cash in your hand.

Since I was doing so well, I was getting these cash bonuses in my hand. After a day of work, I had to ride through the city to get home. Traveling through the city had never been a good thing for me. Especially with cash in my hand. So a couple of times I would treat myself to some crack after a hard day at work. Even still, I was able to maintain and not go overboard. One day, I got a letter from Kia;

it was an envelope with a check in it for selling the most Kia vehicles that month. I sold more Kia vehicles than any other salesman at the dealership, so they gave me a $300 bonus check. I was totally not expecting it. It came out of the clear blue sky, extra money. I received this check before my lunch break. I took my Kia check to the bank and cashed it on my lunch break; $300 in the hand of a crackhead in Baltimore City was never a good thing. I went and bought some rocks and started smoking on my lunch break. I never made it back to work. No phone call, no nothing, I just didn't return to work.

Once again, I got stuck. When I returned to work the next day, I gave some crazy excuse why I wasn't able to get back to work and they went for it. Remember, I was one of the top salesmen, so they overlooked it and gave me a break. We were open on Saturdays because Saturday was the big day for selling cars. We always started the day with a meeting to discuss the specials of the day. I smoked that Friday night because of all the money I had from selling cars. I arrived to work late and missed the start of the meeting.

When I did finally get to work, there was a gentleman on the showroom floor looking at cars. This was a great opportunity for me. I wouldn't have to go into the meeting late in front of everyone. Since the guy was looking for help, I walked up to him and asked him if I could help him. When he said, "Yes, I'm looking to buy a car," I knew this was my opportunity. I could just tell my boss the reason I didn't make it to the meeting was because I was helping a customer. But just to be safe, I walked into the meeting and told my boss that I was helping out a customer. My boss said; "Great job Mark, continue with what you are doing."

Once again, I dodged another bullet. To top it all off, I sold the car. Once again, when I didn't realize it, God was showing me tremendous favor on my new job. I attributed it back to when I sowed the seed into the TV evangelist's ministry. I was receiving a harvest because I sold more cars than anyone I was hired with. I was continuing to have success as a car salesman, but I still couldn't kick my drug issues. I would put it on the shelf for a little while, but I would always pick it back up. It eventually cost me my job as a salesman. The Saturday meetings, just working on Saturdays at all, led to my demise. Friday nights were big party nights for me, even though I knew I had to get up and go to work Saturday morning.

One Saturday, I didn't come in at all. I just couldn't get up and make it. Working on Saturday was crucial in the car sales business. Again, my manager gave me a break because I was doing so good. I worked for another month still selling more cars than my co-salesmen, but I missed another Saturday with no phone call; I just didn't come to work. I finally went in that Monday and the boss said, "That's it, you're done, clean out your desk."

He couldn't depend on me. I just wasn't reliable. He had enough. Crack got me again. The money I had made from being a car salesman quickly ran out. Once again, I was broke, with children to feed and a mortgage to pay. I applied for unemployment, but for some strange reason, I was denied. I was now between jobs again, and I needed money. I didn't want to bother my mother because two of my other brothers and I were always in her pockets, and I didn't want to reveal to my mother that I was still using crack. My youngest brother was able to avoid the road to drug abuse and alcohol abuse. I guess he watched his big brothers go down that road and he was wise enough to just say no! Now, I was faced with "How am I going to get some money, because my bills were starting to pile up and my mortgage was getting behind?"

20

The Big Check

I got a letter in the mail from the Xerox Corporation financial services. It just so happened that during this time, I had been away from Xerox for over a year, I didn't think much about the company that let me go. The letter said something about my 401(k) savings plan. That was when I realized I had money saved up in my 401(k) account that I could access in times of need. This definitely was a time of need. The phone number to the financial services company was on the letter, so naturally I called them up.

When I got the representative on the phone to ask about how much money I had in my 401(k) savings plan, she told me that I had $33,000 saved up over the eighteen years working with the Xerox Corporation. My next question was "How fast can I get that money sent to me?" She told me they would prepare the check and send it out in ten to fifteen business days. I was elated. I was able to call all my creditors and let them know that I would be paying them in the next couple of weeks. Deep down inside, I knew this wasn't going to be good. They were sending a crackhead a check for $33,000. I didn't give a second thought to this being my pension money and that I might want to roll it over into another savings account. All I knew was she was sending me a check. She asked me if I wanted all or just some of it?

Naturally being the crackhead that I was, I wanted it all. No more pension for me, I would worry about that later. Eighteen years of savings being shipped out in one check. The lady I spoke with let me know that the check would be arriving in ten business days and I said, "Great, send it!" Talk about anticipation. I was almost scared to receive that much money at one time. But in ten days, it arrived. I didn't even care that I had already lost $3,000 in finance charges, I just wanted my money. The early withdrawal had finance charges attached to it, but I could care less. I just wanted the money. Normal people deposit a check of that size in their bank account and patiently wait until the funds are available. Not me. I went to my bank with the check in hand, gave it to the teller, and she said a check of that size may take a week to clear.

That was way too long for a crackhead like me. I told her to give the check back to me and I'd figure out another way to cash it. I couldn't wait a week. I needed money now! Monique and I would communicate with each other every once in a while when crack was involved. Since I came into such a large amount of money, I knew I would be able to hook up with Monique again. Even though she dogged me and treated me like crap, I was still willing to give her a call, and I did. She was happy to hear from me; we did a little bit of catching up because it was a while since I had spoken with her. When I told her about the check and that I needed some way to cash it, she was more than willing to help and told me to come into the city because she knew where I could cash a check that size. You would think that would be a red flag for me, but actually it was an invitation because I knew we were going to get high and have sex.

When I look back on it, I realize how stupid I was, but when you were stuck on drugs, and you think you were in love, your mind played tricks on you, and you didn't always make decisions with common sense. So I headed into the city to go and pick up Monique, with my *check for $30,000. My problem was how was I going to cash it,* but Monique had the answer. I picked Monique up at her job, and right next to her job was a liquor store she was familiar with. That was when I had to reveal to Monique the amount of the check. When I did, her eyes almost jumped out of her head. I was sure she was thinking of how much crack we could smoke with that much money.

Her boss and the owner of the liquor store were friends. She told them about me needing my check cashed and since her boss was friends with the owner, he said, "No problem, I'll cash it for you for a certain percentage". I didn't care what the percentage was. All I knew was in a couple of minutes I was going to have $30,000 in my hand. I don't remember how much they took to this day, but I knew it was at least $1,000. Like I had $1,000 to just give away. But that was exactly what I did. That's right. I cashed a $30,000 check at a liquor store. Who in the world does that? Only someone on crack.

When they started to count the money out to pay me off, they had to use counting machines. I had never seen that much money in cash in my life. They counted out $30,000, or whatever it was because at this point, it was so much money, I was in awe. They gave it to me in $1,000 bundles with little paper wrappings holding them together. Then they stuffed it in brown paper bags. It looked like a drug deal exchange with a king pin drug dealer. I had never seen so much money in my life. And to think it was all mine. Once they gave me all the money, they escorted me out of the store to my car because that was too much money for anyone to be carrying around unarmed. I didn't have a gun, but they all did. All I knew was it was time to party! Monique and I in Baltimore City with $30,000 in cash on a Friday night. Truly, a recipe for disaster! We immediately bought a whole lot of crack and went to my place and went crazy. I paid up all my bills, I thought I put about $20,000 in the bank and I kept the rest with me. Way too much money to have in my pockets.

I smoked with Monique and I smoked without Monique. If I wasn't with her, I always made sure she had plenty of money in her pockets to smoke with. What a high roller I was. A fool and his money. Yes, I was supporting Monique's and my drug habit, and boy did we get high! I paid for us to smoke in hotel rooms, even though we didn't need to.

Once I rented us a room in a somewhat seedy motel because we were only using it to smoke in. We started smoking and the minute Monique took a hit, she got super paranoid and wanted to leave. We stayed in that room for a total of twenty minutes, then we left and never came back. What a waste of money. Like smoking crack wasn't a waste of money. Even though I paid my mortgage three months ahead, I went through that money like water. I had never in my life made so many bank teller withdrawals. I reached my withdrawal limit every day it seemed. It probably took all of three to four months to spend $30,000, and sure enough, I was broke again. Now I really had to get a job.

With the help of a cousin, I was able to land a job with his company building cellular tower antennas. It didn't pay a lot, but it was a good steady job. Like all my other jobs, I was well liked, a fast learner, and very productive. That was my truth, aside from smoking crack, I was a very productive member of society and a hard worker. Soon as I picked up that pipe all bets were off. I started off on the job doing well. It was manual labor, but I enjoyed it, and the people I worked with were good folks. I started to save some money, I even started dating a new girl, and she didn't use drugs. That was exactly what I needed, someone who didn't smoke crack. I figured if I didn't hang around people who smoked crack, then I wouldn't smoke crack. She was a young lady that I went to school with and she was a Christian girl. She went to church and she sang in the choir. This will be my opportunity to start going back to church and that was just what we did. She sang and once again, I got to start playing drums. Things were going great! She was also an athlete. She liked to jog and she played basketball.

Remember my one weakness when it comes to women? Big breast! She had huge breasts! I knew this was God sending me the woman for me. We jogged together, we hooped together, and she could shoot the lights out. I wasn't getting high. I was thinking, *finally I can have a regular life.* Not to mention she had her own place, so even though we would stumble with fornication, we would still try to be celibate, and just enjoy each other's company in hopes that our relationship would continue to grow. We were close in age, so we enjoyed a lot of the same things. We had been dating for several months and things were going great. Then I found out, in her childhood, she had suffered some childhood trauma. Since we had grown closer, she felt comfortable sharing what she had been through as a child. Due to her childhood trauma, she suffered from bipolar disorder.

As long as she stayed on her medication, she was fine. The day came when I would find out what would happen if she missed a couple days of taking her medication. I thought, *How bad can it be?* She was so sweet all the time. I had no idea of the seriousness of this disorder. I also felt obligated at this time to share with her about my little problem with crack cocaine addiction. She was very understanding because I made it clear that was in my past, and that I was done using crack cocaine. Boy, were we lying to each other. We still had major problems that we were dealing with. But we were trying. We were two people that wanted to get better and thought maybe we could do it together. We continued to attend church together, and things were looking pretty good. Then one day we had a minor disagreement. It was nothing big; I can't even remember what it was about. All I know was she went from zero to one hundred, just like that! She actually got physical and started to punch me. Nothing crazy, she wasn't going for blood, but she just started to fight me. I was not one to ever put my hands on a woman, so all I did was try to restrain her and hold onto her hands so she wouldn't continue hitting me.

At that point, I didn't understand where all this aggression was coming from. Then I remembered the bipolar disorder and thought maybe this was how it manifested itself. Then just as fast as she got hysterical, she began to calm down. That was when she realized that she had an episode. Then she began to cry because she knew that her disorder Showed up and I got to see it firsthand. She kept asking for my forgiveness and I did my best to comfort her and let her know not to worry, it's going to be okay. Then she was back to normal. That was my first introduction to a bipolar disorder moment. She was grateful that I handled it the way I did because she said her boyfriends in the past would get physical with her and put hands on her. I told her I would never hit a woman and she didn't have to worry about that. We could work through this together. She later explained that she was out of her meds and that was why she had an episode. I just told her to make sure she had plenty of her meds on hand in the future because I wouldn't want to go through that again. We laughed about it and put it behind us and continued with our relationship.

As far as I was concerned, I figured I was the perfect guy for her, and we'd be fine. Or would we? I just had to stay focused and not let my little issue surface. Being with her was working out just fine. As long as I stayed away from smoking crack, all was good. That lasted for approximately two months. We were playing basketball, jogging, and going to church together; our relationship was coming along just fine. It felt good to be away from the crack pipe. I was working at my new job every day, but I was an untreated addict. I wasn't aware that I really needed to be connected to some type of program or treatment constantly. If I had only known then what I know now, I may have not sunk to such a low point in my life. I thought, *if I just stayed with my girlfriend and kept going to work, everything would be fine.* I actually thought cocaine was behind me. I was finally done with smoking crack.

One of my problems was that I didn't distance myself from my old friends who were still using. I thought it was cool to hang around all of my old buddies. Just let them know that I didn't smoke cocaine anymore. This lasted for a little while until that one night when one of my friends showed up at my house at twelve o'clock midnight. Who visits at twelve o'clock midnight? No one but the crack man. I didn't tell him that it was too late for a visit, or to come back tomorrow. I couldn't get my mind or my mouth to tell him that I didn't fool around with that stuff anymore; I just said, "come on in".

And sure enough, he had that look on his face and crack in his pocket, and once again, it was on. I was so frustrated with myself because I knew I was about to fall again. I just couldn't say no. All of the thoughts about doing the right thing and being in a great relationship, I had totally forgotten. All I could think about at that point was getting high. He had some alcohol as well, so he had all the party elements. There was no way I could refuse a free party. The sad part about it was, it was only free in the beginning. This visit turned into a three-day binge because after he left, I was left with the obsession, I had to get some more. Since I had money in the bank from being clean and sober in my new relationship, I headed straight to Baltimore. I didn't show up to work for three days. When I didn't show up for work to pick up my paycheck, my coworkers showed up at my front door. It wasn't like me to not come to work or to call.

When they did arrive, they brought my paycheck with them. Of course, I had a quick lie about not feeling well for the last three days and now I was just starting to feel a little better, so I'd be back to work tomorrow. My cousin who helped get me the job was one of the people who showed up at my front door. I was sure he was the one who let them know where I lived. Even though I fed them all a big lie about why I didn't come to work, I was sure my cousin had a good idea of what the truth was. He, being a family member, knew about my issue, so he was a little upset about me not coming to work since he put his neck on the line to help me get the job in the first place. Even that was never enough because once again, I was about to blow off a great job, a brand-new relationship, and who knew what else. I managed to get myself together and made it to work the next day. Once again, I dodged another bullet.

After work that day, my girlfriend showed up at my door because she too was wondering why she hadn't seen or heard from me for three days. She asked me if I had slipped up and smoked crack again. I lied and said no. I had already confessed to her about my problem and since I wanted to hold on to the relationship, I told her that I was good. Since we didn't always see each other every day and spend time in each other's company that much, she believed me.

One thing about all crackheads, we are good liars. We can look you right in the face and lie to you without cracking a smile. A trait that I wasn't proud of, but it came in handy. I assured her that nothing like that had happened. Just think if I would have left it right there, I could have returned to a normal life and continued with my sobriety and my relationship. This would have just been a bump in the road. It only took a week before I had to test the waters again. I guess, since I had skated so successfully by the last episode, I could do it again, but I'd do it differently this time. I'd just get a dime, smoke it, and be done with it. These were my famous last words. This was truly the definition of insanity. Doing the same thing but expecting a different result. The one dime turned into $300. I was broke again.

Once again, I didn't show up for work, nor did I call. I just couldn't make it. Caused by another three-day binge in Baltimore City. When I finally returned home, I went to work the next day and they handed me my last check. My cousin was pissed! This time when my girlfriend showed at my door, I told her the truth. I messed up and went to Baltimore and got high. People who don't smoke, can't understand how you can do anything for three days in a row. She assumed I was cheating on her with my old girlfriend in Baltimore, and no matter what I said, she would not believe me. I didn't deserve for her to believe me. I actually didn't cheat on her with my ex, I cheated on her with crack. She couldn't find it in her heart to forgive me and I couldn't blame her, so she ended the relationship. Her logic was, who goes missing for three days at a time and isn't cheating.

So in one weekend I lost my job, lost my girlfriend, and pissed off a family relative. I really must have a problem because I did it over and over again. Whatever I seemed to gain, my addiction always took. When I look back, I see the devastation it brought in my life, but when you were in the middle of the storm it was harder to see what was happening around you. What seemed to be happening were brief victories followed by devastating storms. So I would look at the loss of a girlfriend and a job as a chance to start over with a clean slate. I tried to get back on that wagon and begin to string together some clean time on my own.

I actually found a meeting to go to at a local church. It was an Narcotics Anonymous meeting, but it was Bible-based, so I went. I had heard about other friends who went to meetings to get over their addictions. I wasn't having any luck doing it the way I was doing it, so why not give it a try. The meeting was held on Tuesdays at the church, and they actually fed you a great meal before the study began. This was perfect, so I began going. The people there were very nice. The majority of them were White, but that was okay with me because I was desperate and I needed help. They were all recovering addicts and they all believed in God.

After going for a while, I got to be friends with the guy who led the praise and worship. Before each meeting, we sang a couple of praise songs. This was awesome. When he found out that I played the drums, he offered to let me come to a rehearsal because he also had his own band and they needed a drummer. He knew I was in the beginning of my recovery, so he told me after I got some clean time under my belt, there might be an opportunity for me to join the band. This was a great incentive for me to remain clean. And that was what I did. After a month of showing up to the meetings and participating in the recovery program, he gave me the opportunity to join the band. I had to pack up my drum set, bring it to the rehearsal place, and start practicing with these guys. They were pretty much rock and rollers, but that was okay with me because I could pretty much play anything.

21

Band #3

I was just happy to be playing the drums again. I just knew this was what I needed to remain off of the pipe. I thought I could get clean, hear the Word, and play music. Once again, God was moving in my life, giving me the desires of my heart. We clicked as a band immediately. We mixed classic rock in with some spiritual songs and some originals. Things were going great. We had a pretty rigorous practice schedule, which allowed us to get a tight sound very fast. Our sound was unique but good.

For the sake of ease, I'd call the bandleader Joe. Joe had booked a small gig for us to play. We wanted to test our sound out on the public. One song that we played exceptionally well was a Jimi Hendrix's song "Fire." When we played it, the crowd went wild! Once the show was over, we got three more gigs from it, and we were on our way. Things were going well. The meetings were good, the band was good, and once again life was good. There was a young lady who also attended this meeting. She was very pretty with very large breasts, and a big booty for a White girl. All of my weaknesses. I tried to remain focused on the meetings and just remained friends with her. She, too, was trying to recover from drug addiction, and I really didn't want to be a hindrance to that or mess up my recovery. This White girl's body was unbelievable. I don't believe I had ever seen a White girl built like she was. I had to talk to her and since we went to the same meeting, we became friends. She had two sons and I had two daughters and they both happened to be the same age. We would talk at the meetings regularly about our children and our lives. Just general conversation. She took to me very fast. I should have seen this as a red flag, but all I saw was her fine body, and her large breasts.

So one day, we were chatting after the meeting and I invited her over to my place. To which she obliged. Her kids were with her parents and mine were with my mother since I had given up custody by now due to my problem, and she had the same issue. Her parents had custody of her children. We went to my place and everything was fine and cordial. We just sat and talked. We basically talked about our drug addictions and drugs of choice. You know, the things that drug addicts have in common. And like me, her drug of choice was crack. That was actually a reason to run for the hills. Two crackheads together, brand-new in recovery, not a good mix. But again, did I mention the T&A? Her body was unbelievable. So after we made small talk, I was walking her to the door to see her off. She was a registered nurse and had her own car, so this could wind up being a good thing, just not this early in recovery. I found out later that you should abstain from any relationships for at least one year when you were trying to get clean.

So while we were my front door saying goodbye, I helped her with her coat, and I turned her around to give her a little peck on the cheek. Our lips met and we got into a full on, deep passionate kiss. I stuck my tongue so far down her throat I could feel her tonsils and she returned the favor. Right in the doorway we started shedding clothes. Next thing you know we were upstairs in my bed getting busy. I should have known better. Here we go again! I was so weak when it came to large breasts and a big butt. I was trying my best to abstain from having sex since my last relationship. I knew in my heart fornication wasn't something that I should partake in. I was trying to be obedient to what God would want me to do. Also, I knew not to jump right back into another relationship. I knew I needed to give myself a chance to get ahold of this thing called sobriety.

It was funny when everything seemed to be going fine, Satan knew just what to bring your way to mess it all up again. I had the meetings, the new band, and good friends in the meetings to help me stay strong. How ironic that her name was also Monique. My history showed that I didn't have good luck with Moniques. We dated at first, then we grew closer as time went on. She was definitely the one who seemed to be falling fast. Maybe because I had the three-bedroom house, I'm just saying. Soon after we started talking, the kids started coming over with her. Like I stated earlier, even though she had boys and I had girls, they were the same age and they got along just fine. The next thing I knew, she moved in. Her parents were well off and they liked me a lot, mainly because I was a family man and took an immediate interest in their grandsons. I actually did like her boys. They were well-behaved and well-mannered. I also met the boys' dad. He also was a real nice guy and we got along good. He had no problems with me dating his ex-wife. He saw that I was good to his sons and they liked me. Both of the boys played recreational football, so I would show up to practice and throw the football with them.

At one point, I even helped out with the coaching. I was getting more entwined with this young lady's family as time went on. I must say, her children's father did warn me, he said; "she had a relapse problem, and to watch out". He didn't say a lot about her, but he did say to be careful because she could be crazy at times. An ominous warning. I felt since we were both in recovery together with a solid accountability group of Christian men and women, we'd be just fine. I finally got to meet her parents who lived in a big mansion in the city of Bel-Air. I thought, cool. She came from money. All her mom and dad wanted was for her to have a man who would take care of her and be good to their grandsons. They would love nothing more than to relinquish custody back to the mother, their daughter.

The grandmother was very skeptical because she had issues with her daughter and her continuous relapses. The boys' grandfather gave them anything they wanted. He owned a large tile and flooring business and money wasn't an issue. Even though the grandfather spoiled his grandsons, they were still good boys. Little did I realize what I was stepping into, but I was willing to give it a try because as long as I could keep that pipe out of my hands, I'd be alright. Things were looking good, my girls were doing good with their activities, her boys played football, and we would all go to the practices together. Her children's father would be there and we got along great, and that took a lot of the pressure off of me. I didn't have to be everybody's daddy.

I went to work, she went to work, so money wasn't a problem. I don't know; it seemed like things were starting to look like we could be a normal family. It was kind of nice to come home to a beautiful White woman every night with a great set of breasts and a loving household. I think this great life was going on for about two months when it happened. I came home like any normal night. This particular night, we had a break because we were such good parents, my baby mama had my girls and the grandparents kept the boys. I came home like any other Friday after a hard week of work. My set of large breasts were downstairs in the basement waiting for me. Just her and me alone together. She said, "Hey, honey, come downstairs." I was thinking, *Okay, time to get busy*. I got downstairs and she was sitting in the recliner.

As I approached, she put a balled-up fist toward me and turned it over, opened it up, and revealed two big rocks of crack cocaine. I just put my head down and sighed, "Oh no! We were doing so good."

To which she answered, "We have, and we'll just do these, and call it a night."

I said, "Are you kidding? We both know better than that."

You might ask, "Why didn't you just tell her 'No Way'! then flush it down the toilet." Well, I didn't have enough clean time, or enough knowledge, nor enough God in me to be that strong. The bad part was, we both had money, so it turned into a long night with multiple trips to Baltimore City. I was no match. Just the sight of some crack made me start to pass gas. When you started gas, there was no turning back. We were doing so good. Now, I really see why a relationship with anyone, especially another addict was a bad idea. If one of you fell, more than likely you were both going to fall, and we did. Her ex-husband tried to warn me, her mother and father gave me early clues that dating their daughter maybe a bad idea. I fell victim to a set of knockers; my weakness prevailed again.

Oh well, you live and you learn. What was evident was, she had to go, I could do bad all by myself. So in the days to follow as our finances started to unravel from continued smoking, so did our relationship. Once you got that train rolling, it was hard to bring it to a stop. The only good thing was that she had parents with money, and they were always right there to catch their daughter when she fell. This made it a little easier on me. I told her she had to leave. She hadn't moved too much of her stuff into my house, so the eviction was quick and easy. I was going to miss those big titties.

Our relapse caused us to go MIA from the meetings we were attending. I also stopped showing up for band practice with the brand-new band I just joined. Being that we were all addicts, when you stop showing up, they know exactly why. I soon got a call from the band leader to come pick up my drums. They knew if I wasn't serious about my recovery, I would just be a cancer to the other recovering addicts in the band. They made no bones about me being out of the band and that my drum set was ready for me to come and pick up. Wow, another band was gone, just like that.

God keeps opening up doors of opportunity. I enter, but I soon turn around and walk right back out of them. It was not that He closes them; I just kept turning around and would walk out of the door he opened for me to walk into. Now, the right thing to do would be for me to go back and say I messed up, start over again because you always get the chance to start over. The band opportunity was over, but they would've welcomed me back in the meetings with the free meals, but pride wouldn't allow that. I couldn't face those people after what I had done. Pride is a mother!

I was now once again on my own. My fall put me in one of those "what's the use" modes. Basically, I was having a pity party; woe is me. It seemed everything got worse this time. Each fall was worse than the previous. I had no job and the only income I received was unemployment. I got way behind in my bills and my house was going into foreclosure. I was being faced with some pretty tough decisions to make. I tried to stop the foreclosure on my house. I went online and found out what I could do to stop it. I had to go to Baltimore to the courthouse and file some specific documents for a chapter 11. I was filing for bankruptcy. It had reached that point. I got that done, and now, I had to wait for my reply documentation. I would have to then fill that paperwork out and take it back downtown and my house would be saved. When I finally received the documents by mail, I filled them out.

All of these documents were time sensitive; meaning I had to return them as soon as I received them filled out. Turn around was of the uttermost of importance. This was serious stuff, they were about to take my house, you know, the one I wouldn't pay the mortgage on. I received an unemployment check the day I had to turn the documents in. Why did I have to turn the documents in, you ask? I had to physically take the documents back to the courthouse because I took too long to do it by mail. There was no way I could file my documents at the courthouse in time unless I physically take them back to the courthouse.

Once again, my procrastination has gotten the best of me and my back was against the wall. It was good that I received an unemployment check because I needed money to take care of my business. I made it to downtown Baltimore and in a sober state of mind, with a whole lot of stuff to take care of, I decided to go get a rock, then I'd take care of my business to save my house. Needless to say, one rock turned into two, then three, then four, etc. I never made it to the courthouse. I blew it again, and this time, it might cost me my home where my daughters and I lived. *Oh no! What have I done! I can't lose my home! If I lose the house, everybody is going to know. Maybe if I just wait, it will all go away.* I filed part of the documents to complete my chapter 11 filing, maybe I was good. I didn't bother to follow up. I was so depressed about my situation I was getting into a bad space. I started to just not care anymore. This was a bad place to be. So I carried on day by day. Smoking crack, not smoking crack. I'd never forget the day when I had smoked all night and then those dreaded birds started chirping. It never fails, right around 6:00 a.m. the birds wake up and start singing that same old morning song. All this told me was that I had another all-nighter, up smoking crack again. The problem this time was my girls were home and they would soon be getting up and getting ready for school, and I still had some crack left. 6:00 a.m. and the alarm clocks started to go off. The girls were waking up.

Oh no! I had to put this pipe down and go get my kids ready for school. Okay, Shelby was a teenager; she was cool. She'd get herself ready, but Shaela was my baby, she was curios, needed help, and very inquisitive. I couldn't look like I'd been up all-night smoking crack. I got Shaela in the shower and then I ran downstairs to take another hit. Boy, was I sprung! Shaela was out of the shower calling for me. "Daddy, I'm done!" I ran back upstairs to get her dressed. Now Shelby was going to do Shaela's hair, so I ran back downstairs to take another hit. Shelby is done with Shaela's hair, she grabbed her breakfast, and she was out the door to catch the school bus. It was just Shaela and me. I ran back upstairs after a great big hit and I looked crazy! I couldn't even speak clearly right now, and my eyes are big as quarters. My eight-year-old is concerned and she looked at me with her pretty eyes all dressed up and ready for school and she said, "Daddy, are you okay?" I could have just melted. Even my baby knew something wasn't right.

I got it together and said, "Daddy is okay." Even though I was as high as a kite. I somehow managed to get myself somewhat together and get my daughter off to school. I will never forget that day. My youngest daughter realized that something was different about her daddy. Needless to say, that was one of those moments when you realize that Something had to change. If my youngest child was getting ideas, I knew my oldest had to know Daddy has a problem.

After that experience, I'd decided to give it a break for a while because apparently the cat was more and more getting out of the bag. I could no longer hide my problem. So I got a week or two under my belt; I was feeling better, I was doing better, and I guess I needed that wake-up call. A week or so passed, it was a normal Saturday morning. The girls and I got up for cartoons and breakfast. While I was preparing breakfast, the girls were enjoying their Saturday morning cartoons when I heard a knock at the door. We didn't usually get guests on Saturday mornings. I went and answered the door, and it was a White man there, and he asked, "Is Mark Barnes here?"

I answered, "Yes, I'm he."

He gave me his name and he said, "I just bought this house."

I immediately got defensive and said, "No, you didn't. There's no way you could have bought my house." I instantly remembered the chapter 11 filing that I didn't quite complete. But I told him that I took care of my chapter 11 issue and there was no way my house could have been up for sale.

He said, "Well, I'm pretty sure the house is mine, I bought it at an auction."

I said, "Well, I'm going to check into that because I'm pretty sure it's still my house."

He said, "Okay, sir, I'll be back later to finalize things with you." In anger, I shut the door but deep down inside, I knew it was over. I had lost my house and I didn't know what to do. A few days had passed, and the gentleman returned. He was nice, even when he didn't have to be because the house was his, and there was nothing I could do about it.

At this point, he just wanted to know when I was going to vacate. He asked me how much time I needed before I moved out. I really didn't know, so I just told him to give me two weeks. He was okay with that, so I had to figure out what I was going to do with my stuff. I had a three-story house completely filled with furniture from top to bottom and I didn't know what I was going to do with it. My life was coming apart at the seams. At first, I was a little stubborn and I didn't want to just give it away, meaning all of my stuff. Then I think God spoke to my heart and said to do just that; give it all away. So I started calling anyone I could think of and told them to come by and take whatever they wanted.

Since my life was coming apart due to my own bad decisions, I started to attend more church, and I was listening more intently to the voice of God. At least I was trying. Not listening got me to this point, so what did I have to lose? My daughters and I would give stuffed animals away to kids on the street. My daughters actually enjoyed giving them away. I guess I got into the spirit of giving. I had a universal gym that I gave to the pastor of the church. Now this was a little harder to part with, my drum set. I had just paid $400 for a brand-new double bass drum pedal and it was hard for me to part with it. I knew God had put on my heart who I was to give my drum set to. There was a little guy who used to sit beside me and watch me play drums when I played for the church. God told me to give my set to him.

When I told my friends about what I was going to do, everyone told me that I probably shouldn't give away my set, and they asked me if I was sure I was hearing from God. Deep down inside, I already knew that it was the voice of God telling me what to do, and I had to be obedient. One friend even told me that I could store my set at their house until I was ready to come and get it because I had a very nice set of Yamaha drums, and I couldn't possibly want to part with it that easily. This actually confirmed that I was making the right decision because I had so much opposition against me giving them away. So I packed them up and I headed to the little guy's house. I didn't even call to see if they were home; I just went there. I followed my heart. A single-parent mother raising her son.

I knocked at the door and she answered. I told her, "God told me to give this set of drums to your son." She just broke out in tears and said, "He wanted a set so bad, but I had no way of getting him one."

I said, "Well, here it is!"

The youngster was not home at the time, so I went in and set it up for him, so when he came home, he'd have a full set of drums waiting for him. The funny thing was, I felt better about giving the set away then I missed having them. I then realized it is better to give then it is to receive. My heart felt good. I gave away as much as I could but still had a lot of stuff. I slowly transitioned into my mother's house, but I would still go visit the house that I lost. I couldn't even call it my house anymore. It still hurt. But that day came when I went to visit it and my key didn't work. It just so happened this day I showed up, a truck with all of my stuff was pulling off. The new owner had hired a mover to come in and take all my stuff away. I had stereo equipment, bedroom furniture, living room furniture, dishes, everything was piled on the back of the truck. I watched as it pulled away. Even though I had lost all my possessions, God had given me a peace about losing it all. It was only material things and all material things can be replaced.

At this point, I basically had nothing but the clothes on my back. I had pretty much, through my addiction, lost everything I owned. It put things in a different perspective when you have nothing. But for some strange reason, I wasn't upset; my children didn't seem to be upset either. Thank God for my mother who was always there no matter how bad I had screwed up. The only thing I had at this point was the Dirty Ant. That was the name my daughter Shelby gave to my car. It was my old rust bucket Nova. It wasn't in the greatest of shape, but it worked. My old Chevy Nova I had abused, but it kept on running. Through the hacking, the riding around endlessly in it smoking crack, it really held up. Being back home with my mother was okay because I really didn't have any responsibilities and my mom enjoyed my company. My brothers weren't crazy about it, but as long as Mom was cool, all was good. My daughters split time between their mother and me, so things were kind of good, and I tried to be a good dad by always bringing them over to see and spend time with their grandmother because she loved spending time with her granddaughters.

Now you would think this would be a great time for me to get it together after all of the damage I had caused. I still managed to find time at night to sit in my room, at my mother's house, and smoke crack. And yes, even in my mother's house after a great big hit, I would get paranoid and started to hear things and just sit in my room and trip out. My mother ran her business out of her house and she kept large amounts of cash in her office drawer and I knew this. One thing I couldn't do was steal from her. I remember going into her office one night and looking at the money in the drawer, but I couldn't bring myself to take it. I knew that would crush my mother. I also knew that my brothers would demand that I leave her house, and at this point, I had nowhere else to go. Once I took a $20 bill, but I immediately put it back the first chance I got. Now my mother did have a tendency to leave money in her pockets. Like her coat pockets, or her sweater pockets, or maybe even in her pants pockets. If she left money in her pockets, I would sometimes help myself to that. After I did something like that, I'd feel pretty bad, but not that bad because I knew she would never miss it. The $20 I took, later for some reason or another, I told her about it. I also told her that I returned it, but after that, she never left money in the drawer in her office again.

Maybe that was best, so I wouldn't be tempted. Like I mentioned earlier in my story, I still had this never-ending quench to watch religious TV shows and I knew my relationship with God was getting stronger. I visited my brother's church more regularly and I took my girls with me. I had visited the altar a couple more times to repent of my drug use, but God didn't take it from me. I thought I left it at the altar, but I guess not because I would eventually fall. I knew God was up to something, I just didn't know what. I remember being at the altar praying and asking the Holy Ghost to help me. The ladies of the church surrounded me and started laying hands on me.

At this point, I was crying like a baby and one of the ladies said, "When you have that crack pipe in your mouth taking a hit, start praying in the Holy Ghost!" The first lady came by me, while I was standing at the altar, and slapped me on my right hand, then my left hand, and it was like someone had pulled the carpet from under my feet. The next thing I knew, I was on my butt in front of the whole church. I asked myself; "What in the heck is going on"? My mind was telling me, *This is it, that's what needed to happen. I was slain in the spirit! I'd never smoke crack again; it finally happened! God healed me!* As I sat there in front of the church crying my eyes out, I felt such freedom. I could feel the presence of God all over me. This was all new to me being slain in the spirit and all. Long ago, when I first started coming to the church, I had watched others being slain in the spirit. I told the pastor that I wasn't really sure about falling out in the spirit and I asked him about it. He told me to not worry about that. "Just let God work on you and read your Bible."

I said to him, "If I ever fall out like that, you'll know it's real because I don't necessarily believe like that." He didn't question my beliefs; he just told me to keep coming back.

For the most part, I did. Since I was at a bottom in my life, I was willing to try anything. I left church that day feeling pretty good about what just happened. I really thought I was done with crack. I tried to do everything they told me to do. I read my Bible, I continued to watch TV evangelist, and I did a lot of praying. One thing I hadn't done was to separate myself from my old friends. I tried to just stay to myself. One day I was home watching TV and I felt this feeling of just being lonely. I felt like I was all by myself. Not just the fact that I was in the house all by myself, but I just felt terribly lonely. It was weird because it was an extreme loneliness that I had never felt before. So I prayed.

I said, "God, I've decided to follow You now, Why do I feel so alone? I need You to comfort me right now. Your word says You are a comforter, and I need You. Amen."

Okay, I was done praying; now what do I do? I'd always been the neighborhood dad wherever I lived. Kids always gravitated to me because I liked to play. I played football, I took the neighborhood kids to the pool, and I barbecued and fed all the kids that didn't have food to eat. That was just the kind of guy I was; I loved kids. I was still home sitting in my loneliness when I heard a knock at the door. When I answered it, it was one of the young guys in my neighborhood. He was one of the kids I always threw the football with. Now any other day, I would have loved to go outside and play a game of catch with him, especially now with this spirit of loneliness hanging over me, but this time, when he asked if I would like to come out and play catch with the football, I answered, "No, I'm just going to relax." I didn't know where or when it happened, but I didn't feel lonely anymore. To me, it was a miracle because just five minutes before, I felt like I needed company; now, I didn't want any. It truly was a miracle that I wasn't lonely anymore. God answered my prayer. As I continued to walk with God and read his word, he would show up in different ways like this, letting me know he was real.

22

The Story of Joseph

I also learned how the enemy comes to kill, steal, and destroy. One of my buddies called me up and said he had some rocks and asked me if I wanted to smoke. Why couldn't I just say no? Even when God worked miracles in my life, I still made a conscious decision to do the wrong thing. I answered my buddy's call and I went to see him. Even though I was feeling convicted and I knew the spirit was speaking to me to not go, but the voices that told me to go were a little louder. All my friend did was get me started because when we finished and the money was gone, I knew I could just ride to Baltimore, start my hacking job, and get more money. So that was what I did.

It was a little different now because I was feeling more convicted about what I was doing. Something inside me was raging a war against decisions I was making out in the streets. I raised enough money to buy some rocks and the sun was down; it was early evening. Usually, I would just pull over on the side of any street to smoke. I had all of my tools and it was easy to quickly take a hit. This time, I packed my pipe, I lit my lighter, and I pulled on the pipe. When I let the smoke out, I started speaking in tongues. Just like the lady in church told me to do. It was weird; the more I prayed in tongues, the harder it was to smoke the crack pipe. I realized that I had to pray in tongues less, to finish smoking. There was something about this praying in tongues stuff.

When all the crack I had was gone, rather than continuing with hacking, I took my butt home. I guess it did make a difference because I would have hacked a little longer to continue smoking, but

I ended my evening a little earlier than usual. When I got home, I turned the TV on to TBN. I watched it until late at night. Thank God for twenty-four-hour religious TV. I also wouldn't run right back to the pipe after these godly experiences. I would read the Bible a little more and attend Wednesday night Bible study more regularly. I was trying my best to stay away from the pipe.

One day, while at my mother's house on a Saturday, I put my car in the shop. I got a ride from the shop to my mother's house, which was about four miles away. Not very far. When I got home, it just so happened my favorite Bible story was on: the story about Joseph. I loved the TV adaptation of that Bible story. I was intently watching it. It worked out perfectly because I could watch the show and kill some time while my car was being worked on. In the middle of watching it, I got a phone call from my old girlfriend. We had been talking a little more since our breakup over me smoking and staying out all night. She cared about my well-being and wanted me to do better. In the middle of our conversation, I started crying uncontrollably. I tried to continue with the conversation, but I couldn't stop crying enough to talk.

My friend asked me if I was okay. I said, "I think so", and I finally got myself together and continued to talk. Then all of a sudden, I started to cry again. I mean blubbering tears, the ugly-face crying. No matter how hard I tried, I couldn't gather myself. Again, she asked, "Are you okay, Mark?" I still couldn't gather myself enough to answer. That was when she said, "God is dealing with you, Mark. God is dealing with you!" I just hung up the phone, after getting myself together enough to tell her, "I'll talk to you later."

I didn't know what that meant: "God is dealing with you." After I hung up the phone, I continued watching Joseph, and then I was fine. I didn't cry another tear. Maybe God wanted me to continue watching Joseph. I don't know. After Joseph ended, I mean as soon as the credits were rolling, the phone rang again, and it was the mechanic, saying my car was ready to be picked up. Maybe I was supposed to watch Joseph because as soon as it was over, I had a total sense of peace come over me. I didn't have a worry in the world. I felt great. No tears, no worries, just great. It seemed so strange. My brother had picked me up when I dropped my car off at the shop to begin with, so he called me again to ask if I needed a ride to go and pick my car up.

For some crazy reason that I cannot explain, I wanted to walk. Yes, I know, my car was four miles away, and my brother wanted to take me to get it, but I just wanted to walk. My brother also thought it was strange that I wanted to walk that far to pick up my car. He told me to wait for him, he would come to pick me up and take me to get my car. I again told him that it was okay. I felt like walking. Then he got a little angry at me because I wouldn't accept his offer for a ride, when I just felt like walking, and for the life of me, I couldn't explain why. So that was what I did. I walked four miles to the shop to get my car and I enjoyed every minute of my walk.

It was a beautiful sunshiny day and I just had a certain peace. I guess it was the peace of God that I was experiencing at that moment. I wasn't sure why, but I didn't need company. When I look back, I realize, that was what it was; it was God's spirit comforting me. After watching Joseph, I guess that put me in a place where God's presence was all over me, and when you are in the presence of God, you don't need anyone else. I didn't know that then, but I know it now. Praise God!

It was a good walk and when I returned to my mother's house with my car, my brother was there wondering why I didn't accept his offer for a ride. I still had no explanation for why I wanted to walk, but he realized that I was okay with my walk and left it at that. I called my ex-girlfriend back to let her know I was okay after my crying fit with her on the phone earlier. I told her I think she was right. God was dealing with me. The story of Joseph, I could really relate to because I was feeling a little like him, like everything was turning against me. The only difference was, I was the cause of all of my troubles.

So now I was attending church a little more regularly and I enjoyed it. It seemed that was the only thing that was keeping me sober. I was starting to get some male friends at the church who had also struggled with drug addiction. The pastor was once a heroin addict. Apparently, God had me in the right place. I was able to openly share my experiences with my men's group, which helped me stay accountable.

JB was one person in my men's group in particular that I would talk to about my struggles with crack cocaine. He knew all about it because he once smoked it too. Heroin was his drug of choice that landed him in drug treatment. Now he had ten years of recovery under his belt, so he took me under his wing. I would still have times when I would fall and go get high, but he would have a hunch about it because I wouldn't show up to church or answer his calls. He never gave me a hard time when I fell and I admired that about him. He knew I needed more help than I was getting. So one day, JB asked me if I wanted to get some help. I thought, *Well, I'm going to church more. What other help can I get?* That was when he explained that he had a friend in California that was a part of a recovery program and she may be able to help me.

I was thinking, *California, I didn't know anyone in California.* How was I supposed to just pick up and leave my home and go west? I asked him if he was serious and he said he was. His friend told him if I got there, she'd have a bed for me and I'd be able to get into a six-month drug program. That was a lot to think about; leave everything I know to go to a place where I didn't know anyone. I told him I would think about it and get back to him. All I could think about was leaving my kids. Even though they were safe living with my mother, the thought of leaving them haunted me. I knew me leaving my children would crush them.

Then I thought, *Well, it's only six months*, and I'd come right back home. I told my mother and she was all in. She thought it was a great idea. She told me not to worry about the kids. "They'll be just fine. You just go and get some help."

It wasn't very hard to convince her. I was the only one that was skeptical. All I thought about was the gang violence going on in California because I was not a Blood or a Crip. What am I going to do? What was I going to wear? Did I have to make sure that I didn't wear the wrong color in the wrong place? I could get shot! All the gang stereotypes were running through my head because we didn't have gang violence where I was from. It seemed like that was all they talked about in California—the people being killed in drive-by shootings and the like. One thing I had learned in church was the Man of God I was sitting under, speaks to the congregation from God on decisions we may need help with. I definitely needed some spiritual direction for this decision. So I prayed. I said, "God, if I'm supposed to go to California. I need to hear it from the man of God's lips. He has to tell me, then I'll know it's from You, God. Amen!" Short, sweet, and to the point.

At this time, I didn't have anything. I lost my house and everything in it except what I gave away, so I had nothing to lose. It would have to be God's will before I up and left everything. It was a Wednesday night Bible study. It wasn't a large group, just a small gathering because not everybody showed up for Wednesday night Bible study, but I was desperate, and I needed to get my word from God so I showed up every chance I could to hear from God. I was sitting maybe four rows from the front, but in the middle of the row. Now, I was not necessarily here to get a direct message from God; in fact, I wasn't even thinking about my prayer for directions on my big decision, I was just trying to stay away from crack, and there ain't no crack in the church. The pastor stood behind the pulpit and instructed the congregation to turn to Genesis 12:1. He said, "Tonight's lesson is titled 'Go!'"

When I heard this, I just put my head in my hands, and I knew this was my word. Like Abraham, I was instructed to "go from your country, your people, and your father's household to the land I will show you." I didn't cry, but I felt like it. It was no question that I had to go. I wanted the man of God to give me my answer, and sure enough, he did. California, here I come. I knew I had to go. Not from my father's household, but from my mother's household. God had made for me one of the biggest decisions in my life. I had no relatives, no friends, or anyone I knew that lived in California. This truly was a leap of faith. I didn't know who to tell first. So I slept on it that night. Maybe I'd wake up tomorrow, I'd be back to normal, and the thought of leaving would be gone. No such luck!

When I got up the next day, I was more convinced that I was supposed to go. Once again, I had a peace about it. I called my brother, who had gotten me started going to church in the first place, and I told him about my new revelation. He was excited about it because he was the one who told me about the power of God. All of this just confirmed that God was leading me and answering my prayers concerning my next steps toward recovery and being in his will. Then I called JB to tell him to let his California connection know I was coming to get help.

As the wheels were put in motion, it was happening, I was leaving. Mom had mixed emotions about it because her son was leaving home. Even though she knew I needed help, she was still a little leery about me going that far and leaving my babies. Of course, my daughters didn't want Daddy to leave because for the most part, I shielded them from my addiction. I think my eldest had a good idea that Daddy was getting high. I let my girls know that I was going away for a little while, and that I would be back. So it was scheduled for me to catch a plane in two weeks.

The first week, everything was good. I pretty much stayed at home and spent most of the time with my daughters. We spent good quality time together and we went to church together. I saw the pastor and shared with him that I was going away to get help. He then explained that he could help me and why didn't I reach out to him for some counseling. He said he would have had no problem helping me with my addiction. That was when I told him, "You already helped me. God spoke through you on a Wednesday night Bible study. Through you, He explained to me what I was supposed to do." That was when I told him how I asked God to give me my instructions through the man of God.

He then said, "I can't argue with that, so go and do what God wants you to do." So he prayed for me and sent me on my way. I had a week left to go, and I had to get my airline ticket. My mother gave me the money, $300, to get my ticket. I don't know what got into me, but again, I came up with a bright idea. I was leaving in a week, and the ticket wasn't to cost the whole $300, so I could use a little to get a rock, and then I'd buy my ticket. I was about to start my recovery so I wouldn't be able to get high anymore; this was my last chance. Famous last words. One more time, I came up with a bright idea that eventually turned into a horrible idea. I started out with a $20 rock, then I went and bought a $50 rock, then another $50 rock.

By the end of the day and through the wee hours of the morning, I spent the whole $300. Immediately, the depression set in. Once again, I was reminded that I did it again. Now I was faced with having to explain to my mother what I did. That was how it was; when your guard was down and you were feeling confident, that was when your addiction sneaks up on you. I had one week to go, and I blew it! So now I had to crawl back to my mother with my tail between my legs, like I had done so many times before and fessed up that I had spent all my airfare money. Her disappointment in me was devastating. I really hated to disappoint my mother. You wouldn't think that since I had done it so many times before, and each time hurt more than the previous. Probably not as much as it hurt her. So when I confessed what I had done, she just looked at me with those sad eyes and said, "Mark, what is wrong with you?" She truly didn't understand addiction. She couldn't understand why I couldn't just stop. I needed an answer to that question myself. She refused to give me more money. But you know, there's nothing like a mother's love.

She said, "I'm calling your brothers." That is not what I wanted to hear. I thought to myself, *Oh no! Now I got to have them jump on my case as well.* My brothers were not as compassionate as Mom, and they were sick and tired of my mess. Especially the grief it caused my mom to have. My brothers wanted me gone in the worst way because I was causing my mother in her old age a lot of pain, emotionally and financially. My two brothers showed up to have a discussion with me and to lay me out for what I had done. We all met at my mom's office. They were pissed! They asked me the obvious question: "Why did you spend the money?"

To which I had no answer other than "I messed up." The fact remained I needed a ticket, and I knew they weren't putting any more money in my hands, and Mom was done forking out cash for me. So before I could even ask that question, my younger brother who was in the best financial position said, "Don't worry. I already bought your ticket. You leave Saturday morning." I didn't know whether to be happy or sad. But his last comment was, "You're getting out of here!"

I felt totally rejected at that point, but what could I say? All of this was not my doing and my brother was just going to fix it. I actually should have been thankful, but that feeling eluded me. To add insult to injury, both brothers told Mom not to let me sleep in the house, but to keep me locked in her office. I guess they thought I was going to steal from my mother, but like I said earlier, that was something I would never do. I truly understood where my brothers were coming from. They were just trying to protect Mom.

For the next week, I wasn't allowed to sleep in my mother's house. I had to sleep in her office with the door to the house locked. If I needed anything, or if I had to go to the bathroom, I had to knock on the door. I guess if I had to pee, I could just go outside like a dog. Boy, what have I gotten myself into? I really needed help. At this point, I had set in my mind that I could do this for a week. It was not like I had a choice, but I just prepared myself to sleep in her office until it was time for me to leave. Since there was nowhere for me to sleep in her office, I just decided to sleep outside in my car. The worst part of all was my daughters had to look at me through the glass window, which destroyed my youngest daughter. All she could do through this whole ordeal was cry. This tore a hole in my heart that I had never experienced before. And to think I was the cause of it all; it was all my fault. I thought it would be best for me to sleep in my car because my youngest daughter would just look at me through the office door window. She just looked at me and kept asking if I was okay. I couldn't take that.

That was when I thought it would be best if I just slept outside in my car. My mother gave me a blanket and a couple of pillows so I could at least be comfortable while sleeping outside. Remember, this is Maryland in November; It was cold! I had to say good night to my daughters one more time as I made my way outside to my car with my blanket and pillows. Once I got in my car, I reclined my seat back, got real cozy under my blankets, and I thought, *This isn't going to be so bad.* I turned the radio on to my favorite preacher and realized I'd be ministered to all night. I just had to remember to start my car every so often for heat and to charge the battery. This was my plan so the night wouldn't be so bad after all. Well, it wasn't fifteen minutes alone in my car before my daughters came running out of the house screaming, "Daddy, Daddy! Come back inside. Grandma has to tell you something." I went back in, thinking, *What is going on?* But it couldn't be bad because my girls were so excited when they came and got me.

As I walked back inside my mother's house, she had a big smile on her face. Oh, my brothers, the ones that served me my eviction, they were gone. I asked my mother, "What's going on?" My girls were halfway explaining when they came to get me. Something about "You don't have to sleep outside," but that was all they could get out in their excitement. My mother explained that she had just got off the phone with one of her clients who happened to be a pastor of a church, and she also had a daughter who was struggling with a crack addiction. Now, knowing how my mom was, I knew she was venting on the phone about me to her client. My mother couldn't keep a secret. Especially the one about her addict son who was now sleeping in her driveway about to be shipped off to California.

So in the midst of her sharing my problem with the minister, the minister said God put it on her heart to get me a hotel room to stay in for the six days remaining before I flew out to California. All I had to do was take my ID to the hotel and check into my room; it was all ready for me. I lost it! I immediately broke out into an uncontrollable cry. Then my daughter started crying because I was crying. My youngest asked me, Daddy, why are you crying?" I couldn't explain to her that it was because of the goodness of God. But I knew once again God was providing. I was overwhelmed with the joy of the Lord! Even Mom had to shed a tear because even though I had caused this whole situation, God's hand was still on me. I returned my mother's blankets and pillows. My daughters wanted to come too, and I allowed them to because they loved their dad. My mom said it was okay because she knew I wouldn't get into trouble while they were with me. At this point, I had no intentions of doing anything crazy in the six days before my departure. I knew I had to make the best of the last days with my family.

For the most part, I just tried to visit as many friends as I could to say goodbye. When I visited with friends, I didn't share a lot about the reasons why I was leaving because people had a tendency to try and talk you out of God's plans for your life. So I basically stayed focused on the plan. At this time, California was riddled with gang violence, so I asked anybody and everybody I knew that was from or recently visited California on how I should dress. I didn't want to show up in the wrong colors or look out of place because I knew there was a possibility that I could get caught up if introduced to the wrong people upon my visit. No one I spoke with was helpful, so I just had to trust that God had my back. I went to see my old girlfriend just to say goodbye, and we had somewhat of a rekindling. Maybe if I took care of my problem, we could get our relationship back on track. So we decided to give our relationship another try. We were going to attempt a long-distance relationship. We were officially dating again. Now I had another reason to do the right thing and to come back home.

My last week home flew by. Two more days before I left, I had one more thing to do. I owed my mechanic some money for some repairs that he did on my car, the Dirty Ant! Yes, remember my daughter named my car. It was a Chevy Nova that had seen better days, but it was reliable and cheap to maintain. I didn't want to leave any debts behind, so I took my car to my mechanic's shop. It was late Friday afternoon and no one was there. I signed the title of the car over to him and left the keys under the seat with a note, "Thanks for everything. The car is yours." I now owned nothing but the clothes on my back. I had nothing, but I felt great! I jogged back home. It was 3.5 miles to my hotel room.

It was now the day before I left, and I was feeling a lot of mixed emotions. The strange thing was with all that was about to happen in my life, I was not even thinking about getting high at all. I spent my last day with my mom and my kids. We talked about things to come. Daddy was going to get some help, and I'd be right back. Mom was a little worried, of course, but by now, we were talking about how it's all in God's hands. We had to just trust, believe, and pray!

The next morning came and my brothers who evicted me from my mom's house were evicting me from Maryland, taking me to the airport to fly to California. This would be my second trip to Cali, and I didn't know what to expect. The first time was with my mom for a Disney vacation; this time, it was to stop using crack! What a difference twenty years made. I wasn't nervous; I just had a lot of expectations because I was going to be at the mercy of the people receiving me at the airport. My life was truly in God's hands. Remember, I didn't have any friends or relatives to receive me at the airport. It would be nice to go visit an uncle or an aunt I hadn't seen in years, but that was not going to happen, just my new program counselor.

23

Welcome to California

The flight was cool. I got to California In the morning around 10:00 AM. The lady who received me was Debbie, she was a young White woman. Very polite and she seemed like all she wanted to do was help. I couldn't believe how warm it was after leaving 30 degrees in Maryland to 70 degrees in California. Yes, it was warm and sunny. Already I was thinking, *This won't be so bad after all.* Debbie and I had light conversation about me mostly and all the problems and mess I caused back home while in my addiction.

Debbie said to me, "Now you're taking your first steps in recovery so you can put all that behind you."

Of course, I had a thousand questions about the program, my living conditions, the meetings, and my meals. Could I work and make money? She answered them all. I felt a sense of calm talking to Debbie. I was all prepared to check into my room and meet the other addicts like myself. There was one little thing we had to do first. In order for me to qualify for the program, I had to be registered as homeless. And the way to achieve homeless status was to sign into a shelter. My first night in California had to be spent in a homeless shelter, a mission. Here we go! In order for me to get a bed, I had to be there by 4:00 p.m. First come, first serve. The beds ran out quickly, so if you didn't get there early, you didn't get a bed. The homeless people knew the system, so they lined up early in order to get a bed. I didn't know anyone and I didn't have anywhere to go. So I sat in the park across from the shelter. I actually was just like a homeless person sitting in the park looking at the pigeons and kids playing.

At 3:30pm, I made my way to the mission to stand in line for my bed. The line had already started, so I had to find my place in line because they also fed you at the mission. Talk about a humbling experience, but it was just what the doctor ordered. My first reality check. I almost didn't get a bed, but I didn't think God would allow me to spend my first night in California sleeping on the streets, so there was a bed left and I was able to get it. I got all signed in. The mission was also a church and we had to talk with the pastor. It was like an interview and I was good at that.

I told the pastor I knew God and I just stumbled a bit, I was trying to get back on the right path. He was very encouraging and he said, "You'll be just fine if you keep God first." Boy, was he right. So this was how I got to spend my first night in the Sunshine State on my road to recovery. After my interview, I signed my paperwork, and I was officially homeless. Once the interview portion was complete, I was in the facility, and I couldn't leave unless I wanted to smoke a cigarette. I was a crackhead that didn't smoke cigarettes. I was basically locked in. Now it was time to eat dinner. I must admit the meal was pretty good. Your basic baked chicken meal with a vegetable, a starch, and a roll with a carton of apple juice. Eating wasn't a priority to me even though I was hungry and I could eat. While eating, the trading began.

"Hey, man, if you don't want that roll, I'll take it. Are you going to eat your potatoes? If not, I'll take them!"

Just a little reminder of where I was and this was real. I had no control. They herded us through like cattle for each phase of the mission experience. I didn't make conversation with anyone, but I was very observant of my surroundings. I could tell I was in with the pros. They were no strangers to this mission and how it operated. I could tell because they would anticipate each command that was about to be given.

After we ate, we had a little time to chill before bedtime. If I remember correctly, bedtime was at 9:00 p.m. Wow, I had to go to bed at 9:00p.m. and I didn't have a choice. I didn't even make my kids go to bed at 9:00 p.m. But again, it wasn't up to me and the last thing I was going to do was be disobedient. They distributed fresh blankets and pillows with pillowcases, and they assigned us to our beds. A small twin bed just big enough to lay on. It was very obvious that this bed had seen better days, but I wasn't sleeping on the sidewalk so I couldn't complain. Actually, I was kind of excited about the whole process. It was truly a new experience and it wasn't that bad so far. Also, I knew the next day I would be picked up by my counselor and taken to my real recovery program. This was just a necessary step to get me to that process. I was lying in my cot thinking about tomorrow. There was no way I could sleep comfortably in a mission full of homeless people (me included).

As I lay there, and it got closer to the evening hours, I started to hear more activity. People were getting up all hours of the night to use the bathroom. Others were snoring so loud it was hard to fall into a deep sleep. When I think back, I recall a lot of people got turned away and denied a bed for the night. I imagined them sleeping in the streets tonight. Then I heard two people start to argue about who knows what. It almost escalated into a fight. Now I knew I had better keep my eyes open; these people were crazy! And guess what, I was right here with them. Through it all, I eventually fell asleep because at 6:00 a.m., I was awakened by a loud shout: "Time to get up!" The night spent at the mission was over, and at 6:00 a.m., we had to wake up. The good thing was a small continental breakfast and a hot cup of coffee were served before they sent us on our way. Most of my roommates left there and continued their lives of living on the streets until check-in time at the mission later that day, and that was their existence day in and day out. That had to be tough.

For me, I had an address to go to. Oh yeah, they didn't pick me up from the mission; they gave me an address and told me that it was five blocks away and for me to be there tomorrow morning when I left the mission. And that was what I did. I asked everyone I could, "How do I get to this address?" Even though it was five blocks away, I didn't want to get lost in Long Beach because I had heard so many things about the LA gang violence. To be honest, I was a little worried. I even asked a Long Beach city police officer. He was kind and he took time to help me. After getting directions from him, which I was confident would get me to my destination, since he was the police, I started walking in the direction he gave me. I had been walking for fifteen minutes and I still wasn't arriving at my destination, which should have only taken me five to ten minutes to reach. So I asked someone else and they explained that I was walking in the opposite direction of where I was trying to go.

Wow! The police officer sent me the wrong way. Maybe he just didn't know. I gave him the benefit of the doubt. Being a stranger in Long Beach I didn't want to have any preconceived notions. So after fifteen more minutes of walking, I found it, Atlantic Recovery! Now, even though I had been walking for at least half an hour, it was okay. I had just left Maryland in November with temps in the thirties to forties, so walking in Southern Cal in seventy-five to eighty degree temperatures was no problem. I remember during my walk, I came across a real orange tree.

For the first time in my life, I picked an orange off of a tree. It was in someone's yard, but it had oranges that hung over the fence, so I could reach them from the sidewalk. I peeled it, ate it, and it was good. Before that, the only oranges I had ever eaten had come from a grocery store. That was another first. Now I was standing in front of what will be my new home. I gathered my thoughts and went inside. It was a nice office with a receptionist. I told her my name, my counselor's name, and thank God, they were expecting me. My mind was telling me that since I had such a hard time finding the place, I might have missed my arrival time because what should have taken me fifteen minutes took forty-five. Maybe they would have said I was late and they didn't have any more beds available or some type of bad news, but they told me to have a seat, and someone would be with me shortly. Out came Debbie, the lady that picked me up at the airport. Finally, a familiar face. Debbie asked me if I had any trouble finding the place and I just replied, "A little bit, but that was okay."

After all, I did not want to seem ungrateful because I knew people were supporting me to get me this far in this process. I noticed while in the building there were people all around doing all types of chores like emptying trash, mopping floors, sweeping, trimming hedges, etc. I kind of got the hint that they must be the people in recovery. I didn't see any bedrooms, just offices. I guess this is the administration building. Sure enough, Debbie explained to me that they were patients and everyone had chores to do. Once I was all processed in, Debbie took me to my actual sober living facility where I would be living for the next six months. That was how long my program was. Six months then back home to Maryland. That was my plan. At first glance, it looked like a fairly decent apartment building. It had two floors with six apartments on each floor. The backyard didn't have any grass, just a garage and a cement patio area. There were addicts hanging around, kind of chilling because it was a nice day. Seventy-five degrees and sunny. The building was fairly clean because like the administration building, all of the patients had chores to do at the house.

For the most part, all tenants helped in maintaining the cleanliness since you didn't have to pay rent. Now I got to my room. No doors were locked so Debbie would knock twice then open the door. No. 6 was my room. Inside were three White guys; two small guys and one big burly guy. Debbie introduces them to me, Ken, Jim, and the big one—his name was Bill. I immediately sensed after hearing them say hello that the two smaller gentlemen were homosexuals. That didn't matter to me because I know drug addiction knows no bounds, and we were all addicts, and if they were here to get sober, I didn't care who helped me. All I knew was I needed some sobriety in my life.

Bill seemed to purposely come over as a real tough guy. I didn't know, maybe to make sure I didn't assume anything about his sexual preference because it was clear about Ken and Jim, they didn't try to hide their sexuality. All I know was when Debbie opened the door, we saw two gay guys and one big burly guy. Ken and Jim greeted me with two feminine sounding hellos, and a light handshake while Bill almost crushed my hand with his manly grip. At first, I thought there might be an issue with Bill because he came off as maybe being a little racist. I sensed it in how he spoke, almost like he was a little angry. Bill had the marine high and tight haircut, with a small Hitler mustache. Bill made a reference to jungle music as someone in another room was blasting some Parliament-Funkadelic. This let me know Bill was going to be difficult. He didn't hide his feelings. When Debbie left, she left me in the care of Jim. He was a Homosexual and he made no bones about it. This was fine with me because he was very nice to me and very welcoming. I needed this for my first introduction to life in a recovery home.

For the first couple of days, Jim took me under his wing and explained the processes to me. I was told I had to go to ninety meetings in ninety days. He also told me about the chores we were responsible for. He introduced me to the house leader, Greg, who was a brother, and he was cool. Overall, everybody in the house was cool, but remember, we were all addicts, and we were here because of our destructive behaviors. That being said, you had to take everything with a grain of salt. Just like jail if you were weak, you could be taken advantage of. Right off the bat, I discovered that there was a roach problem, but hey, who hasn't had roaches in their life. I was no stranger to roaches, even though we were responsible for keeping the place clean. One thing I failed to mention was the house was co-ed, men on the second floor, women on the first. I moved into my room and I was given the top bunk. I was so excited about getting my bed, I tried to do a hurdler's flop onto the bed. It was made of very cheap wood, and when I landed on it, the frame shattered. My first day and I started out by destroying property. I was told not to worry about it; they would have no problem repairing it and they did.

After they fixed my bed, I emptied my little bit of gym clothes into my three dresser drawers, and I was in. Now I've had a little bit of time to meet my fellow residents, male and female. Everyone I met seemed to be very nice. At the beginning, it looked like it was going to be a pretty fun experience. Everyone had plenty of food in their refrigerators. I was told the local grocery markets donate food to the recovery homes when they were called. The food that was usually about to expire, so just before it did or slightly after it did, they donated this food to the recovery homes. Since the rooms had their own kitchens, and we had plenty of food donated by the grocery stores, eating was never a problem. There was always someone cooking something and everybody didn't mind sharing. I had a little bit of money that mom sent me off with so I wouldn't be broke, in case I wanted to eat out. I soon found out that wouldn't be necessary. I must admit my first weekend here was okay. It was a chance to get situated and meet my roommates. Monday was the beginning of my program. I was about to find out why when I took a hit of crack, I spent all of my money to the point of ruining my life. And I wanted answers. They told me I was in the right place to get some answers, so I was very excited.

After we ate dinner, everyone was talking about a meeting that was starting in an hour. My question was, how are we getting there? We were walking someone said. I noticed that everyone was excited and anxious about going. They told me it wasn't mandatory, but if I was going to do ninety meetings in ninety days, I might as well get started now. Everyone seemed to be looking forward to going to this meeting, so I got a little excited too. How bad could it be? Plus, it was a group of guys and gals walking through the streets of Long Beach on a beautiful night. It was actually kind of cool. I began to see how I could really start to like this. This seemed like a nice way to start on my road to recovery. It wound up being a ten- to fifteen-minute walk, which, considering the weather, was no problem at all. The meeting was held in a church, which was even more nonthreatening. We all arrived and went inside.

I noticed at the entrance, there were many people gathering in front of the building. There were kids playing and people sitting out front having a cigarette and coffee. It was a very friendly atmosphere for this to be a meeting of recovering addicts. What I later realized was, a lot of people in recovery, like myself, have children. In the rooms of recovery, your children were welcome. "Since we can't always provide childcare when you are trying to get back on your feet." This made perfect sense to me. This was nothing like the little bit of recovery I had experienced back home. It was also surprising to see a room with over one hundred people in it. This was all new to me, but I loved it. They also served all the coffee you could drink for a dollar donation, if you had it; if you didn't, it was okay. I was feeling really good about what I was seeing. What I liked the most was the open arms; everyone was very welcoming. Once the meeting began, we started with prayer.

After the prayer, the business of the meeting and the format of the meeting was covered. It was actually structured and all participants knew how it worked. I was the only new guy in my mind, but they didn't make me feel that way. In the beginning, they called for newcomers. I was being very observant so I could follow protocol. I learned fast so when they called for twenty-nine days or less of clean time, I immediately stood up, went to the front, and got my newcomers chip and a big hug. I must admit that hug felt so good. I was on my way and that was my first step in the rooms of recovery. The only thing I was concerned about was, this was a meeting of Alcoholics Anonymous, my problem was smoking crack cocaine. Was this where I should be?

As the people began to share, there were many cocaine abusers in the room. I later learned most people graduate from alcohol to crack. That wasn't my story. I wasn't an alcoholic in the true sense of the word; after one or two drinks, I could stop. If I took one hit of crack, everything must go, and I was not stopping until my pockets were empty. I really enjoyed listening to people share their experiences while drinking alcohol and I could relate to a lot of their stories. I was taught to listen for the similarities, not the differences, so that was what I did. There were many similarities.

When the meeting ended, I didn't want it to be over. I really had a good time. I heard so much information that I could apply to my life immediately. I was like a sponge because I really had to turn my life around. Now that I had found out that the meetings were pretty cool, I did my best to reach out to people. I mentioned that I was from Baltimore because no one had ever heard of Aberdeen, Maryland. There were a few folks in the room that were from the East Coast and they came up and introduced themselves to me after the meeting and extended any help that I might need when going to other meetings. This would definitely help me to fulfill my ninety meetings in ninety days commitment. Since I enjoyed this particular meeting so much, I looked forward to finding other meetings that I could attend. I later found out there were plenty of meetings in my general area that I could attend. In a radius of about ten miles, there was a meeting somewhere just about every day. Some with large amounts of people, some with small, but there were plenty of meetings being held. They gave me a meeting directory with all the meetings in the general area listed with times and addresses.

As I looked through the directory, not being from Long Beach, I didn't have a clue where any of these locations were. They also gave me my first Big Book of Alcoholics Anonymous. I finally got the book with all the answers I was so desperately seeking. I took it back to my sober living residence and began to read the whole thing from cover to cover. I later found out you were supposed to go through the book with a sponsor. As each day passed, I got more involved in meetings. I settled into my new living conditions and made some friends in the sober living facility. While living there, I met people from every walk of life. From people who once had money, influence, no education, to people who were ex-prostitutes, ex-gang bangers, all sorts of folks trying to get off drugs. Of course, you had those that were court-ordered by a judge to come to a treatment facility. Some came just to have a roof over their heads and food to eat.

The majority of us were there because our lives had just reached rock bottom and we had come to the end of our ropes and there was no other way. Death or jail were the next stops for a lot of us. A saying that a lot of us use was, we were sick and tired of being sick and tired. We ultimately needed change in our lives. All of our ideas, plans, and schemes didn't work. I continued to find more meetings that I could walk to and I would have no problem attending ninety meetings in ninety days.

As I continued visiting different meetings, I found that they were very enjoyable. I became what was labeled "a meeting hound." this meant I was probably going to attend a meeting each day of the week including weekends, and sometimes multiple meetings in a single day. I really didn't have much else to do with my day. Once I finished my classes, which usually ended by midday, I had plenty of time to go to meetings. When you didn't have friends to visit or relatives to go see, then meetings were just fine. All the friends or associates that I met while in California were all associates by way of meetings. That was the common denominator we all had. We were usually related by our drug stories because we all had plenty of them. The majority of the meetings I attended were AA meetings. This was okay because most of the people at these meetings were coke or meth users and the stories for the most part were relatable. We hosted a meeting at my sober living on Wednesdays. It was mandatory for the residents to be there even though it was an open meeting to the public. People who didn't live there also attended our house meetings.

One of those was a beautiful girl named Kendra. She was very pretty and when she shared, she shared in a very profound way. Kendra also was very knowledgeable of the Big Book of Alcoholics. She had quite a few years of sobriety. Aside from her being gorgeous, it was also very attractive on how she shared from the Big Book of Alcoholics Anonymous with depth and weight. You could tell she was very serious about her program and she had been through the steps.

One day after a meeting, I introduced myself to her. She was very cool and receptive to my advance. In my mind, I thought maybe it was me she was attracted to. So here I am with about two months clean. I was starting to get my looks back. My physique was starting to fill back in. My smile was looking good because I always kept my teeth clean even when I was using. So Kendra and I were having a nice conversation. I told her about my issues and that I was from the East Coast. Most Californians enjoyed hearing about the East Coast. So as I told her a little bit of my story; she stopped me in the middle and said, "What are you doing on Sunday?" *I live in a sober living facility; I'm not doing anything on Sunday.* Of course, I didn't say that. I said absolutely nothing. I'd be right here. She told me to be ready next Sunday at 7:00 p.m.; she was coming to pick me up. In my mind, I was thinking that she was asking me out on a date because my conversation was so cool. I knew I got it together and I'd only been in Cali for a couple of months. That was one of the problems we addicts suffered from.

As soon as we got a little sober time under our belts, we went back to thinking we were big stuff and the women wanted us. That was what us men thought. My mind was telling me she wanted me, and being that I had always been or at least thought I was a ladies' man and a gentleman, I'd be ready for whatever. So she said no more than be ready; she was coming to pick me up in her vehicle. Don't forget I'd been walking for the past two months, so a ride in a car was a treat.

By now, I'd accumulated a few nice outfits, so I had to make sure that I was looking good for my date. Yes, I said date. When a woman said she was coming to pick you up on a Sunday night at 7:00 p.m., that was a date in my eyes. So I was eagerly anticipating my upcoming date. I got my outfit all picked out, I borrowed some cologne from a roommate, and now it was on. Sunday arrived and I'd had all day to prepare. I didn't have anywhere else to go and nothing else to do, so I waited patiently. It got to be around six thirty, I was all dressed up, my roommates and other tenants in the building started to ask me where was I going all dressed up like that. I just answered out with a friend. The time came for Kendra to arrive and I was sitting in front of my building because I didn't have a cell phone that she could call me on and let me know she had arrived. I wasn't going to miss her for anything. Then I heard a horn blow. I turned and saw a minivan. Okay, that was cool, wasn't expecting a minivan, but as long as it was a vehicle and I didn't have to walk, I was happy

The last couple of months, I had been on my feet walking everywhere I had to go. Getting a ride in any type of vehicle was a welcome change. Sure enough, it was her. I walked up to the van looking and smelling good. When I opened the door, there she was looking sweet as ever. I looked in the back seat and saw three polite children to which she immediately said, "Say hi to Mr. Mark!"

I was thinking, *What in the world is going on?* It was supposed to be just the two of us. I also had a little bit of money in my pocket to pay for dinner and a movie. But apparently, that was not the plan. So I asked, "What's up?" I really wanted to say, "Where are we going with these kids?" Or maybe all was not lost; maybe she had to drop them off first. Whatever the case, I was going along however it turned out.

By now, she understands I had the wrong intentions for whatever she had planned. So she explained to me with a big smile, "You'll see."

How could I argue, she had such a beautiful smile with pretty white teeth? So we took off, and as we rode, we entertained some small talk. The kids were very well behaved in the back seat. You could tell wherever we were going, they had been there before. This was a normal routine for them. The drive only took ten minutes. I knew we had arrived because I saw lots of people getting out of their cars and walking in the same direction. These people were well dressed and some were in casual clothes. I saw a lot of gold chains and jewelry. We finally found a parking space, and Kendra said, "We're here."

Whatever This place was, it was popular because the crowd of people arriving at this place was growing. We could barely find a parking space nearby, so we had to walk in the direction of the other folks who had also just arrived. It was quite a crowd of people, all heading in the same direction. Even her kids, once they got out of the van, didn't wait for their mother to walk with them; they just ran toward the building. When we arrived at the front door, there was a person there who greeted us with a handshake and a friendly hello. Apparently, that was his job to greet folks as they arrived. That was when I realized I was at a meeting. The gentleman who greeted us at the front door said, "Welcome to Crackheads on a Mission!"

I didn't know whether to laugh, smile, or what, so I just said, "Thank you" and "How are you doing?" And he gave me a great big hug and said, "Come on in and find a seat."

When he saw Kendra, he gave her the same hug along with, "What's up, Kendra!" So apparently, she was a regular. The kids immediately ran in and found the other children who frequently came there. That was when Kendra revealed that this was a meeting of Cocaine Anonymous! With her big pretty smile. Now it was all becoming clearer. When Kendra and I had our discussion at my sober living about me only attending Alcoholics Anonymous meetings, she knew I needed to attend a Cocaine Anonymous meeting; that was why she invited me to Crackheads on a Mission. Not only did she invite me, but she also came and picked me up and brought me there. I was flooded with different emotions. I was grateful. I was ashamed of my original intentions, thinking we were going on a date. I was also embarrassed because I knew she knew I thought it was a date because of the way I was dressed. She probably saw the shock on my face when I saw all the kids in her car when I opened the door. I was mostly thankful that a girl as fine as Kendra took the time out of her schedule to take me to a meeting that I truly needed in my recovery. I couldn't thank Kendra enough.

As we entered the meeting hall, I was a little apprehensive, but as I got further inside and got my cup of coffee, I knew I was in the right place. Even though I was from the East Coast, everyone there made me feel at home. It seemed a little cliquish at first, but I soon realized that a lot of the people in the room did drugs together. The difference I noticed from my AA meetings was, it was a little unruly and louder than what I'd been seeing in the meetings I'd attended.

Sometimes, the folks that would share their stories would get a little lengthy, but what I heard blew my mind. I heard my story! I heard people sharing about things they did that were the same things that I did while I was on crack. Some people did things a whole lot worse than the things I had done. But I had to hear it because now I knew I was not the only one who had experienced some of those things. I loved the sayings that I heard like, *keep coming back, and sit down and shut up, chase your life like you chased your death.* These profound sayings really hit home for me. If I had any doubts, they were now all gone. I'd found a new home. Even though they used the same book, these people gave the words in the Big Book of Alcohol Anonymous meaning, something I could latch on to. Something I could relate to. I now realized that the words in the Big Book of Alcoholics Anonymous could be related to my issues and problems. It didn't matter what your drug of choice was, it all applied. As I said before, the meeting was a little loud at times, but I was grasping at every word the people behind the podium would share.

At times, I couldn't hear all that was being said, which was a little irritating, then a guy got up and said, "If you're developing a resentment toward people in the room who are loud and you can't quite hear the speaker, then get your butt up and grab a seat in the front of the room." He must have read my mind because that was exactly what I was thinking. From that day on, I followed those instructions. I got to the meetings early enough to get a seat in the front of the room. I quickly realized God was using these people in the rooms to speak directly to me. I heard so much good sharing I didn't want the evening to end.

After all the powerful sharing, cross talking, cursing, etc., we sealed the meeting in prayer, giving God the glory. Wow! What a night! Kendra had to find me because I was meeting people and getting numbers and thanking the people who shared. I was like a kid in a candy store. God truly used Kendra to help me in my recovery because I needed Crackheads on a Mission more than they will ever know. But I later found out that was what it was all about, each one reaches one. Kendra saw the excitement on my face and I couldn't thank her enough. She was glad that I enjoyed myself. I didn't share how I was hoping the evening would turn out, but I was sure she knew, but that didn't matter because I got exactly what I needed, and that was what was important. We talked about it all the way back to my sober living. She offered to come and get me next week and I took her up on her offer. The funny thing was, when I got back home and shared my experience with a couple of guys in the house, most of them knew about Crackheads on a Mission.

I couldn't understand why the guys didn't go there, but what I found out was there were so many meetings in Southern California; people just found the meeting they liked and became regulars there. You had to discover your home group. This was a good ending to a Sunday night. I pulled out my Big Book and tried to go back and reread some of the quotes the people were sharing from the Big Book. I was truly inspired by the evening's events. It gave me a new perspective on the program I was enrolled in and a new desire on attending meetings. I realized that I had to get a sponsor to help me go through the Big Book of Alcoholics Anonymous. I had a meeting directory, so I started looking for meetings in my immediate area, and I found them. Some were close and some were far, but not too far. I had to figure out how to use public transportation. I was willing to do whatever I needed to do with this new vigor to get to meetings.

When I first got the mandate to do ninety meetings in ninety days, I thought that would be tough, but now I was excited about achieving this goal. God put Kendra in my path to kick-start the desire for meetings, and it worked. As I ventured out in my quest for meetings, I found out that in California, there were all kinds of meetings to attend. Some meetings were a little on the wild side, others were more reserved. Some were majority White, some were Black, some were Hispanic, and I mean they only spoke Spanish. But wherever you went, the message was still the same. And they all started with the serenity prayer. "God, grant me the serenity to accept the things that I cannot change, the courage to change the things that I can, and the wisdom to know the difference." You couldn't go wrong when you started off with prayer.

24

Working My Program

I started to get a small circle of meetings I could attend regularly. I was going to three meetings a day, walking. It was going to be no problem getting my ninety meetings in. I enjoyed meetings.

After a while, I was comfortable enough to share at some meetings. Not at Crackheads on a Mission. Those people had a lot of book knowledge and had been through the twelve steps of recovery outlined in the Big Book of Alcoholics Anonymous. They preferred that if you share you shared about recovery and not your drug use. In the beginning of my recovery, all I could talk about was what it was like while out there doing drugs. That was known as a drug-a-log, and that was all I had. I was still fresh off the streets in my addiction; I had no story of recovery to tell. Some meetings were filled with a lot of newcomers, so it was okay to share at those meetings. I didn't share often, I usually just listened. I made it a habit to sit in the front row because I wanted to hear everything. The meeting that my sober living offered was okay, but not like the outside meetings I attended. I got a lot of certificates of completion from my program, which would help me once I got back out in the world, and to possibly find a job. If your past ever came up in a job interview, you would have plenty of certificates to show your interviewer. This would help explain that you are working on your drug addiction by completing a program.

In the meetings, you heard people share their experience, strength, and hope. This made all the difference in the world, especially when you heard a story similar to your own. Now I was hearing over and over that I needed a sponsor. I'd been to enough meetings, and I'd met some brothers with some book knowledge; all I had to do was ask. The thing was, if you were ready for this step in your recovery, you had to be committed to it. You were asking someone to take the time out of their schedule to spend it with you. You must be serious because most people with that type of knowledge, and had been through the Big Book of Alcoholics Anonymous, took it seriously. Plus, it takes a while.

From what I'd heard, you definitely wanted to pick someone you think you could get along with because you'd be spending a lot of time together. I think I found my guy. He acknowledged at a meeting that he did advocate sponsoring, and he was available. When the opportunity presented itself, I asked that person I met from Crackheads on a Mission to sponsor me. He had ten years clean and sober at the time, and when we met, we hit it off and kind of had similar stories. One thing he said that resonated with me was the sound the rock made in the test tube after cooking it up. When he poured the rock out of the test tube, it rolled across the table.

I know it's a strange similarity, but I remembered that same experience as if it was yesterday. So I asked Terrence to be my sponsor, and he said yes. I had another reason to be excited on my road to recovery. We set up a date to start going through the Big Book. He told me my first assignment before we got together was to study and say the lay-aside prayer every day. "God, please lay aside everything I think I know about myself, the twelve steps, this book, the meetings, my disease, and you, God. That I may have an open mind and a new experience with all these things. Please let me see the truth. I did what I was told because everything I thought I knew got me here in the first place."

I was willing to do whatever I was told. That was what I heard again and again at the meetings. I had to be willing to follow instructions. I summed it up with "God, You take the wheel, I don't want to drive anymore." He allowed our meetings to be held at his apartment. Plus, who wanted to come to a sober living unless you lived there? I really enjoyed finally going through the steps with a brother who had some clean time under his belt. He had already taken several people through the book, so he knew what he was doing. The thing about recovery was, once you've had some time off of drugs, you started to come back to reality. You started to become responsible again. I found a church to attend and I enrolled at a trade school. God was starting to open up opportunities for me and I took advantage of them. My sponsor and I were starting to move through the steps at a good rate. I was very pleased with my progress and so was my sponsor. He explained to me that some people want this and some just go through the motions. I was of the first group, I wanted it. He explained to me that going through the steps was designed to help addicts have a spiritual awakening, a way to help them have a better relationship with God. In my case, I knew God, but my relationship with him wasn't good because of my drug addiction.

As we went through the process, I began to realize that I had to totally depend on God; He had to be all or nothing. As time went on, I did just that and God showed up in a major way. Sometimes God's timing can be a little scary; for instance, I was now nine months clean and sober and everything was going great. I was pretty much done with my programs and I had a ton of certificates of completion. Now I was enrolled in school and going through the steps with my sponsor when I got some news from the program supervisor. I was told that the government program that was sponsoring my program was ending and I would be responsible for paying my own rent at the sober living from now on. My rent would now cost me $400 a month if I wanted to continue staying in the sober living.

My mind was thinking, *What am I going to do now?* I remembered my mother telling me in one of our conversations that there was a letter there for me. I didn't pay it any attention thinking it probably was a bill that I owed. When I called to tell her about the bad news I had just received, she brought up the letter. The way she explained it this time was some money may be owed to me. I told her to send it to me. When it arrived, I saw that it was from an attorney. This really scared me, but it said something about equity I had from the sale of my house. The one I lost in foreclosure. Usually, when you lose a house due to foreclosure, you don't get any money back. You just lose your home, and that's it. However that letter seemed like a good thing, so I called the number, and sure enough, it was an attorney's office. I didn't get to speak to an attorney during that particular call, but I did leave my name and number so they could call me back.

I couldn't imagine any money being owed to me for a house that I lost in a foreclosure, but I had to find out. This particular number I left on the recording was the number of the phone that I had to share in my sober living. Yes, I had to share a payphone with ten other men. This was before cellphones were affordable. Now I was camping out near the pay phone because I didn't want to miss the phone call from the attorney's office. His receptionist did finally call back and I was able to get the phone call. I didn't know whether to be happy or scared. But the receptionist said the attorney would call me back later with details about the letter. So again, I had to wait for another phone call to the payphone. This particular phone call would be very important because I would find out if I actually had money coming my way. This was a tough time for me because I was going to be responsible for paying my rent by the end of the month.

I had different odd jobs, but none of them paid enough money to cover a $400 rent payment at my sober living facility. I was in my room on a Thursday morning and the hallway phone rang. I happened to hear it, so I ran to it, and answered it. Sure enough, it was for me. It was the attorney and he asked if he could speak to Mark Barnes. I said, "This is he!" Then he gave me the best news I could ever imagine. He told me I had a balance owed to me from the sale of my house. Remember, the one I lost in foreclosure. The attorney said, "I have a check here for $17,000."

I almost lost it on the phone. He asked me for my address so he could send it to me. I immediately gave him my address, thanked him, and hung up the phone. I didn't ask why; I just got off the phone and thanked God. I hadn't asked God to send me money to pay my bills, but He knew my needs, and He supplied my needs and above my needs. Talk about perfect timing. God made a way when I didn't see a way. Now I didn't have to worry about trying to find work to pay rent; I could concentrate on my program. I couldn't believe it, but it was true; God had my back. A week later, I had the check. I opened up a bank account with plenty of money. All I could think about was, if I had gotten this money while back at home, I would have smoked it all up. God knew what he was doing. I was attending a small church and I was a faithful tither. It was easy to tithe when all you had is $20 that you made helping someone paint a room: $2, no problem; $17,000, that was a big difference. I thought to myself, *What did you have before this check, and who did you say provided it?* That was a no-brainer. God was meeting all of my needs and above my needs. This was His money; He was just letting me steward it.

I wrote a check for $2,000 to sow into my church. I always made sure I gave above the tithe. I really felt good to be able to do that. I knew to be obedient with my awesome blessing, and I did. A week later, the pastor came to me and asked me about the check. He asked me if it was a mistake. It was a small church and that was probably the biggest one-time offering they had ever received. I explained the whole story to him and he said he admired my obedience. I told him I was realizing that you can't outgive God. I practice that to this day, and it's still true. He is my provider. Now that I was able to pay my rent, I could relax because I had stable living conditions back at my sober living. There was a bike rack at the sober living that had a few bikes locked to it. I had my eye on one particular bike for quite some time and it had never been moved. I asked the house leaders if it belonged to anyone, and they said no, and they told me that I could have it if I wanted it. It was a little rusted and needed some work, but it was just what I needed. I'd always been good with fixing bikes. They called in the maintenance people to cut the lock. I figured out what it needed, and since I had money, I totally restored it! I now had wheels! I could ride to all of my meetings now.

I'd had plenty of bikes in my life, but I was so proud of my new bike. With that much money, most people would have bought a used car, not me. All I needed was a bicycle, and now I had one. All you need in Southern California is a bicycle anyway because it's a bicycle town. It has its own bicycle lanes, it has a bike path on the beach, and the weather is so nice you can ride a bike all year long. I went from walking everywhere and not minding it, to riding everywhere and loving it. You would think I just got a new car because I was so appreciative of having transportation instead of walking. The public transportation (buses) had bicycle racks on the front of them so you could take your bike with you on the bus. This also increased my traveling range considerably. I had no problem getting to as many meetings as I could. Ninety meetings in ninety days was not a problem. I also had money in the bank. Things were looking up. Not to mention that I was also enrolled in trade school. My life was back on track.

Part of the reason I enrolled in school was because I wanted to improve my administrative skills, so when I finished my program, it would be easier to find work. I was coming to the end of all my programs and I was going to school full-time. I had money in the bank and a bike. Life was good, just think in a little while I could get ready to go back home. I'd learned about my addiction, and I now understood why I couldn't do anymore crack, smoke weed, or drink alcohol because it would set off a phenomenon of craving that I was powerless to stop once I start it. I just can't get it started because if I start, all bets are off. I got it now!

Then one day, I was walking down the street from my sober living to the corner store. I saw what I thought was a drug deal going on. I hadn't walked any more than a block from where I lived when I saw the deal going down. It was a sign that I was all too familiar with, a drug handoff. The dealer hands off the drugs and the user gives him the money, all in a handshake. A cold chill ran down my spine. All kinds of thoughts started to run through my mind. Any normal person would either not recognize what just happened or just ignore it and keep going about their day. My crackhead mind said, "Oh wow! I've got some money. I see who it is doing the selling, and he's near where I live. I'll go get some money out of the bank, come back and find him. I'll wait for the weekend and get a weekend pass. Get a hotel room, and get high all weekend, and come home Sunday night and no one will know anything."

Then I came to my senses and realized, "Are you crazy! You will get caught, and you will be homeless in California."

My program taught me to play the tape all the way through because I won't stop there. When I set off the phenomenon of craving, I wouldn't just buy one, I would keep spending my money until all of my money was gone. Then I wouldn't check back in until late, which would cause them to test me. My test results would be dirty and come up positive for cocaine use, which would cause them to throw me out of the program. Which would then cause me to be homeless in California. That was playing the tape all the way through. When I did that, I realized that I still had a problem. I still needed meetings, I still needed to continue with my sponsor, and above all, Jesus and I still had work to do. The difference now was that I stopped to think it all the way through. This meant there was some progress. Having that thought actually scared me a little. One thing was for sure: it was not time to go home just yet. I realized in that moment the devil was busy, and he would put temptations in my path, but God did provide a way of escape.

Once I got back home, I took out my Big Book of Alcoholics Anonymous and started reading it. I needed some reassurance right then and there because I got to see how my mind could be jilted and changed if I didn't fill it with the right information. Wow! I dodged that bullet. Also, I really needed to get more serious when reading God's word. I couldn't get complacent during this phase of my development. I had to stay focused on my recovery. School was going well, and it was almost time to graduate. My grades were good, and I really enjoyed being a student again. I met a lot of cool people and some not-so-cool people in school. I found myself being a big help in the school to my fellow students. Maybe because I was a little older and a lot of the students looked up to me. I'd been able to help with resume writing and interviewing skills. Before I came to California, I went on a lot of interviews, so I was pretty good at it. The staff at the school noticed how the students would come to me and ask for my help. I only did it because I enjoyed it. One day, the director of the school came to my classroom. While I was in class, he asked me to come to his office after class was over. Was I in trouble? Was there a problem with me graduating? I didn't know.

After class, I went to his office. I knocked on his door, and he said, "Come in and have a seat." So I did. He said, "I've notice that you are doing well in your classes."

I said, "Thank you, I've been working hard."

He said, "I also noticed that a lot of the students come to you for help."

I said, "Yes, but that's no problem I enjoy it. He said, "A position just became available for a placement director, would you be interested?" I was shocked because I hadn't even graduated yet. He told me, "That's okay. We would allow you to work around your class schedule." I thought, *This is crazy, they offered me a real job doing what I had been doing for free?* Since they would work around my class schedule, I told them I would be honored. We negotiated a salary, which was more than I had made in quite a while, and the job was mine. I knew this was nothing but the goodness of God. I had my own office and everything! I soon graduated from school, and I began to work full-time at my new position as a placement director. I started working with the graduates preparing them for the job market. I was successful at getting my grads jobs. I was responsible for hosting the school's job fair. I had to invite several companies to come and visit the school and explain to students what they were looking for in new hire candidates. I had to arrange for catering so that all the representatives could have lunch. This was quite an undertaking, but I pulled it off with the help of some of the other faculty. It was a huge success. One of the company representatives kept asking me if I wanted a job. This was very flattering, but I was already working at the school as a placement director. I actually had a good job, so I had to decline. He told me if I ever changed my mind to give him a call. I always said when you take drugs out of the equation, I was a shaker and a mover.

Drugs just got me off of my path to success; now I was back on it. Things were really going well for me. I was loving my new job; life was good. I had worked in my new position for about three months when we all got a call to a meeting with the school director. We all met only to find out that the school was closing down in a month and to prepare accordingly. We had to find new jobs. Well, it was nice while it lasted. That was a lesson in never getting too comfortable because God will start to ruffle the nest. I always remember when God closes one door, it's only to open another. Of course, I kept the number of the gentleman that wanted to hire me at my open house. So I gave him a call; his name was Scott. I called him and let him know about the situation at the school, and if the job offer was still available. Scott told me they actually filled the position, but he wanted to talk to his partner because he didn't want to let me get away. He put me on hold, and when he came back to the phone, he told me he would like me to come in for an interview. It was only a day or two later. I returned for the interview and they hired me on the spot. I was receiving one blessing after another. I guess God had to put me in positions where I could receive the blessings that He had for me.

One door closed and God immediately opened another. Now I was starting my new job, which was ten miles away, so I had to take the train from Long Beach to Gardena. Thank God for my bike because I was able to ride the bike to the train station in Long Beach, and then once I got off of the train with my bike in Gardena, I had to ride my bike two miles to my new office where I worked wearing a shirt and tie.

After working there a few months, I found out my boss was a recovering addict as well, going to meetings just like me. God ordered my steps to my new situation. He's working even when we don't realize it. We actually attended a few meetings together. He gave me my first one-year chip. Time went on and I finished all of my programs. I'm comfortable in the sober living because I had to pay rent and I could do it. But wouldn't you know it, my nest was being ruffled again.

I got notified that I had to move out of my sober living because I was late with one of my rent payments. I actually had the check to pay my rent in my hand, but it wouldn't clear the bank on Friday, the day rent was due, and the director at the sober living wouldn't wait. To me, it just didn't seem right. I had the check to pay my rent, but she wouldn't wait two days to receive the payment. It seemed a little fishy to me, but what could I say? I had to go. I was an ideal tenant at the sober living and I was well liked by all. I remembered that one of the previous tenants had moved out a couple of months earlier and got his own apartment. He had asked me if I wanted to be his roommate. I told him I was comfortable and I wanted to stay at the sober living. Now that the situation had changed, I reached out to him to see if he still needed a roommate, and sure enough, he did.

Once again, God was opening another door. I packed up my stuff, which consisted of a couple of black plastic trash bags, and I got a ride there, which took all of five minutes, and I now had my own place. The rent was $100 cheaper than I was paying at the sober living. My Father in heaven is so awesome! I was paying less rent, I had more room, and I had privacy, something I hadn't had for quite a while. I was actually getting used to being in a room with four other adults. But now, I had my own apartment with just one other roommate. I bought a futon to sleep on and I was no longer connected to any program. I was on my own. No more restrictions, no chores or curfews. I could come and go as I pleased. I saw how God was bringing me back in baby steps. He didn't allow me to have anything that I couldn't handle.

I still attended meetings and still worked with my sponsor. My living situation was cool because even though we had a one-bedroom apartment, it was plenty because we both were used to four grown men in one room sleeping on bunk beds. We basically moved into a mansion; plus, he was rarely there so things were working out just fine. Getting kicked out wound up being a blessing in disguise. God used it for my good. Now, as time went by, I was enjoying my job, riding my bike every day to the train, then two miles to the office and back. In a tie every day. I did this for a year straight and never complained. I actually enjoyed it. Then God did it again!

One of my coworkers on my job was getting rid of her car. She asked me if I was interested in purchasing it. By now, I was used to riding my bike every day. I rode my bike for a year with no problems. Owning a car wouldn't be a bad thing, but as I said before, Long Beach is a bike town, and I enjoyed riding the trains each morning and afternoon. Then she told me all she wanted was $1,500 for the car. That actually was a very good price. I didn't have it at the time so I really couldn't accept her offer. She was selling a four-door Camry. I believe the year was 2000. The car was in excellent shape. My boss got wind of what was going on and offered to put up the money for me to buy the car. He would allow me to make monthly payments back to him. Oh my goodness, I couldn't believe that he would make that offer for a new employee. I had to chalk it up to the favor of God. Each day that went by made me realize that coming to California was God's plan for my life. He opened door after door. I finally got the car and it was perfect! I couldn't believe my life was progressing. I had gotten my own place, a new job, and now my own car. Also, I was clean and sober for only a little over a year. I was living life drug- and alcohol-free. I had used substances for over twenty years of my life, crack for eighteen of those twenty years. I see how God was restoring my life day by day.

Now, if things weren't already good enough, my roommate came to me and said he was moving out. He was the manager of the building we lived in. He asked the building owners if I could step into his position as the building manager and continue paying the reduced amount of rent. The blessings of God were chasing me down. The owners of the building offered me the position of the building manager; of course, I said yes. Shortly after that, he moved out and left me with the majority of his furniture. All I brought to the apartment was two bags of clothes and a futon. It wasn't a lot of furniture, but I now had my own place. This was just too much. It brought me to tears how good God was being to an old crackhead like myself. I didn't deserve any of this. The job was great, I had a car, my own place, and a church home I belonged to. My mother was so proud of me, and my daughters were happy for their dad. God is good! Now there was only one thing left to do.

25

Shaela Comes to California

I called my mother and told her, "I think it's time for me to be a responsible parent again. It's not your job to raise my children." Since I turned over the custody of my girls to my mother, I said to her, "I am ready to be their dad again. Send them to me in California."

My eldest daughter, Shelby, was pregnant with my first grandson, so she wanted to stay in Aberdeen, but my youngest was just about to start high school, so I asked my mom to send her to me. A week later, I was a daddy again; well, I was raising my child on my own again. When I picked Shaela up at the airport, she was so happy to be back with her father, and I was happy to have her. God was putting my life back together piece by piece. It felt good living life on this side of the crack pipe. I was a productive member of society again. My daughter immediately fell in love with California, which was not hard to do. The church we belonged to had a great teen ministry so she found lots of good friends. We enjoyed the beach, bike riding, amusement parks, festivals, and everything Southern Cal had to offer. My eldest even came out to visit with my grandson after he was born. I tried my best to convince Shelby, my eldest, to stay, but she wanted to go back to be with her baby's father, and all I could say was okay.

But while I had them here, we had a ball! I had my family back together again plus one, which was wonderful. I did everything in my power to convince Shelby to stay with us in California, but she was dead set on going back home to Aberdeen. But we still had a great summer hanging out in California. The summer came to an end, and now it was time to enroll Shaela in school. It was time for Shaela to start high school in California. I was a little worried because we had lived all of our lives in Maryland. I wasn't sure if my daughter could adapt to school on the West Coast. To be honest, I was worried about the gang culture because I had heard so many stories about gangs in the meetings I attended. We didn't have gangs back in Aberdeen, so I just didn't know.

It was time to get my daughter registered into high school. Because of geographics, she was supposed to go to Long Beach Poly. I changed her high school to Wilson High School because I thought it would be a safer environment for her. I later found out that Long Beach Poly would have been just fine, but I didn't know, and I was only looking out for the welfare of my daughter. She did well and found many friends, but looking back, Poly probably would have been the better school for her. I have to admit that life was good. I was raising my daughter, working, and managing the building I lived in. I was now going to plan a trip back home. I could actually plan and pay for a trip back home. I had also taken up the game of golf; why not? It's Southern California with warm weather all year round. I booked me and Shaela's trip, and we went back home to visit, and everyone was so proud to see us doing so well.

By now, Shaela fell in love with California. So we would visit Maryland once a year in the summertime. I got Shaela through high school, and she graduated with good grades. The next step is college. I was excited about preparing her for her next steps, but she said she missed her mother and wanted to go back home to Maryland. Even though I wanted her to stay, I couldn't argue with her wanting to be with her mother because her mom wasn't in the best of health. So after her graduation, we flew back home for our normal summer vacation, but this time, it was for her to stay. I knew that wasn't a good decision, but she was eighteen, so I let her make up her own mind. I returned to California alone, and of course, life went on. I'll never forget my best friend Paul came to California to spend a week with me.

Remember, he was the only one I would call when I was stuck in Baltimore City on a crack binge. He wanted to see just how good his buddy was doing. I took off a week from work so I could spend it with him and his eight-year-old son. I told him just come on out and you both can stay with me. I planned a whole week's itinerary for us three to enjoy California. He and his son arrived on Saturday. When I picked them up at the airport, the first thing I did was get them an In-N-Out burger. Paul talks about that burger to this day. Then I took them to Venice Beach, and they loved it. On Sunday, we went to the Taste of Soul music festival. There, Paul got to meet his teen heartthrob from the TV sitcom *Good Times*, Thelma. We enjoyed all types of food and great live music, not to mention the thousands of people that were there. It was just an awesome good time. By Monday, we took a bike ride to the beach. He couldn't believe how close I lived to the Pacific Ocean. He and his son had such a wonderful time. On Tuesday, we went to Disneyland. That goes without saying how much fun we had there. On Wednesday, we went to Universal Studios. It was like the fun never seemed to end. I wanted to make sure my buddy had the vacation of a lifetime with his best friend who was no longer on the pipe. When we got up on Thursday morning, I asked him if he was ready for the day's events.

Paul just said, "Can we rest today?"

I said, "Are you sure? I've got more plans."

He said, "Let's just take it easy today."

To which I replied, "No problem."

On Friday, I took him and his son out for a round of golf. When we finished, he looked at me and said, "You are never coming back to Maryland." I had to laugh and said, "I think you're right." Maybe just to visit because that was where my family is, but I mainly wanted my friend to know that God was taking care of me and that things were back to normal. He and his son had a great week with his buddy, Mark! To top it all off, when it was time for Paul and his son to leave, his son asked if he could stay with Mr. Mark through the weekend and come back Monday.

To which Paul replied, "Are you crazy? Do you know what your mother would do to me if I came home without you, boy!"

I was actually touched by the request because he really meant it, and it only meant he, too, had a great time in California with me.

I thanked my best friend for visiting and sent him home with only good memories. It was important for me to show my best friend that God had turned my life around, and I had really recovered from my crack addiction. I'm sure that was what my buddy wanted to see. He got his friend back! He was the one I would call during some of my darkest times, so it was only fitting that he could see me back in control of my life. It felt really good to show him that God gave me my life back.

Whenever we talk about it, he tells me that it was one of his best vacations ever, and he couldn't wait to return. Vacation was now over, and it was time to get back to work. I really enjoyed my job, and now that I had a car, my boss allowed me to go out and bring in new business, instead of just making phone calls all day. This gave me a chance to go out and see more of California. In my travels, I did acquire new business, and for that, I thank God for his favor because I was selling import and export freight rates on container ships, and that was not necessarily my forte. I fixed copiers for eighteen years. The good thing was schooling actually prepared me more than I realized for this next phase in my life. I became pretty good at it. LA and Long Beach were the second largest ports in the country, and this area was saturated with freight forwarders. That was the proper name for what I did. Competition was tough, but for three years, I was able to maintain and acquire new sales for my company.

As time went on, things were getting a little tougher, especially to get new business. Since I was in sales, new business was always the objective. I guess, due to the economy, things were drying up. Getting new accounts seemed to be next to impossible. My boss also made it clear that my numbers were dropping. I was also getting a little burned on selling freight rates. My manager who was very cool came to me and asked if things were okay and if I was interested in continuing in this business. This was the same gentleman that did all he could to make sure I was hired. He took a special interest in my success, and he could see when things were tapering off.

Three years earlier, when he took a chance on me, I felt obligated to be honest with him, and I told him the truth about how I felt about the job. First, let me explain how God works behind the scenes when we don't even realize it. A month ago, I ran into a Canon representative at a restaurant while having lunch. I introduced myself and explained that I had worked for Xerox for eighteen years, and I was currently in the freight business.

After some small talk, I got a business card from the Canon representative and went on my way. Now, back to the present. My boss asked me if I was looking for another job because if my numbers didn't improve, the big boss was going to cut my salary. I told him I hadn't been looking for a new job. He then told me that I needed to pick up my productivity on the job because his boss was watching. With this new information, I decided to call the Canon representative that I met during lunch. She happened to be in sales, so she directed me to the service department. I spoke to a service manager who arranged for me to come in and interview, so I did.

When interviewing for big corporations, it was a three-phase interview process. The first interview was very positive. Since I've worked as a copier tech before, it was very easy to talk the talk and impress my interviewer with my copier skills experience. I already knew how to be a technician, and I had all the answers a service manager would want to hear. After that interview, my boss wanted to know if I had made any changes as far as looking for a new job was concerned. I explained to him that yes, I had been on an interview, and it was very positive. He asked if they offered me a job. Of course, I had to tell him no. I did let him know that the interview was very positive. He was concerned because his boss was starting to ask questions about my performance, and a salary reduction was going to happen in two weeks. All I could say was, I had to wait and see if they would call me back.

A week went by, and I had not gotten any new sales. That was when I got a call from the big boss. She wanted to speak with me in her office after lunch. All I could think was, *Here we go!* She was about to drop the bomb on me. Needless to say, I didn't eat any lunch. I turned on some radio ministry and sat in my car. I was worried, but I wasn't worried. I said, "God, it's in your hands." Lunch was over, and I walked into my boss's office along with my manager, and we all sat down. This boss was very meticulous about keeping records, and she kept all of the employees' productivity on spread sheets in a file. She began to pull out all the spreadsheets, showing me my numbers for the various quarters.

At this point, I was in a haze trying to prepare myself for the bad news she was about to drop on me. Then she got on the subject of commissions, and she talked about my productivity and what type of commission check I would receive based on my sales. This all took me by surprise. I wasn't prepared to hear about any commission check; I was prepared to hear that my check was about to be reduced. She continued to talk about my quarterly sales and that was when I vaguely heard her say, "For this quarter, your commission check is going to be $3,024.15." I know I didn't just hear what I thought I heard.

At this point, she had my total attention. That was when I asked her if she could please repeat what she had just said, and she did. It took everything in me to not start crying. Once again, I was overwhelmed by the news that I was not expecting to receive. God did it again! My boss did also mention that I needed to get my numbers back up, and that my salary would be cut next week if I didn't turn things around, as she handed me my check for over $3,000. I told her that I was working on it, and I would do much better. The funny thing was, my manager who was seated right beside me didn't know I was about to get a commission check. He was happy for me, though. This was truly shocking because I was sure this meeting was the precursor to more bad news. It was Christmas time, so it couldn't have come at a better time. It was like my Christmas bonus. I went back to my desk to digest what had just happened. I had to soak it all in. I knew it was God, and I couldn't wait to give back God's tithe on this increase I just received. I was clear on how to give back into God's Kingdom from an unexpected blessing, and boy was it unexpected.

After a great weekend, my seed was sown into my church's offering. I now had to return to work knowing my salary was about to be cut. It was like they gave me a bonus only to slowly take it back. I worked hard that week to try and get new business and save my salary. Monday nothing, Tuesday nothing, then Wednesday, I got a phone call. It was Canon calling me in for another interview. They wanted me to come in Friday. I could have jumped through the ceiling! I confirmed that I would be there, and it was not a problem. The good thing was my manager was my ally in this process. I ran into his office to let him know about my next interview. He, too, was excited for me because my excitement was infectious. He had no problem allowing me to be off Friday for my interview. I meant no disrespect to my boss because she was awesome as well; it was just business for her. And for that reason, I totally respected her; that's why I always worked hard for the company.

Truth be told, I was tired of the job; the people were great, the job was tough, and that market was saturated. In all actuality, that well had dried up and it was time to move on. I felt like the Israelites, you have to move with the cloud. I compared this to what eagles do with their babies in the nest. When it's time for the baby eagles to fly, the mother eagle makes the nest uncomfortable in the center. This, in turn, moves the baby eaglets closer and closer to the edge. When they finally get to the edge, the mother eagle pushes them out of the nest, and they start to fall, and before they hit the ground, she swoops under them and picks them up and brings them back up to the nest. She continues this process until they learn to fly. God made my nest more and more uncomfortable, which in turn made me reach out to a different company to eventually get my new job. He is so amazing!

Friday came, and I showed up to the interview suited and booted. I made sure that I looked as professional as I could—suit jacket and tie. Remember, I know how to interview; I used to teach it. This was interview #2, which was a good sign, so I was totally prepared for anything. I didn't know how extensive they went into my background, and I did have a few drug charges from my past back in Maryland. I wasn't sure if they would show up in a background check, but just in case, I brought all of my certificates of completion for all my programs and drug treatment training. If my past showed up, I had to show that I was a new person, and that I had treated all of my past behaviors. I was better now.

In my folder I brought to the interview, with my resume and recommendation letters; I also had my certificates. I'm sitting there in front of the interviewer's desk, handing him whatever he wanted to see from my folder, but not revealing too much too soon. He basically asked me questions about different scenarios I might find myself in, in an office environment. He wanted to know how I would deal with certain situations like an irritated customer or a problem machine. He wanted to know how I would defuse any situation that I might come across in an office environment. That was a piece of cake because I had done it all before, for eighteen years with Xerox. I actually shared real-life experiences that I had dealing with irate customers while working for Xerox. I explained to him that I worked the downtown territory for fifteen years. This was the most demanding territory. He was totally impressed.

During the interview, a few of my certificates for drug treatment had made it out of my folder and onto his desk as I ruffled through my resume and recommendation letters. I didn't pay attention to them because I was engaged in the interview. The interviewer called his manager into my interview and told him that he liked me, and asked if there were any questions that he might have for me. He was ready to make me an offer.

His manager said, "If Mr. Barnes is okay with you, go ahead and make him an offer." This was when I realized I had the job. I was about to be hired. I looked down at the desk and noticed all of my certificates, so I quickly gathered them all up and shoved them back into my folder. Since they were going to hire me, they didn't need to know about my drug past, and it was apparent they didn't do an extensive background check because they never asked me about any of my misdemeanor drug charges. They also didn't call Xerox and ask them why they let such a great tech get away.

My main concern was the criminal background. I knew if they did any type of check I would have never gotten the job. God had opened another door! Hallelujah! The big boss said he had no questions. "Go ahead and make him an offer." That day I got a $15,000 increase in pay! I couldn't wait to go back to my old job. Remember I was on pins and needles on my old job trying to hold onto it. I was stressing waiting to hear from Canon. During that wait, I received my commission check for $3,024.15. If I would have received the call from Canon the week before and got the job, my old boss would have never given me my commission check. She would have just congratulated me on my new job and sent me on my way. God orchestrated it so that I could get my commission check, then my new job.

When I look back, I see just how God had worked the whole thing out. God had everything happen according to his timing, and for that, I am truly grateful. I couldn't wait until Monday. Needless to say, I had a great weekend. I went out and played a round of golf with some of my friends, and of course, I shared how good God was to me. People weren't necessarily that concerned about my God, but I shared it anyway. My mother was extremely happy to see I was actually thriving in California all by myself. I could actually say that I was secure now. My brothers kicking me out of my mother's house was one of the best things that had ever happened to me. I won't tell them that; they'll have to read my book.

Now, it was Monday morning and time to go back to work. When I arrived, my manager hadn't gotten there yet, but the big boss was in. I couldn't spring it on her. I'd have to wait until my manager arrived. To be honest, I was doing absolutely no work. I know it was wrong, but deep inside, I was through with this job. It would be fine with me if they sent me home today, but we'd have to see what happens. My manager finally arrived. I went to his office and sprung the good news on him. I got the job, and I start on January 5th! He said, "Congratulations!" Then he said, "I'll be right back. I have to tell the boss." A couple of minutes go by and they both came to my desk. I could see the hint of a smile on my boss's face. They really both liked me because I got along with everybody, and I did work hard, and me leaving, though I was done with the job, was bittersweet. Here was the good part. Yep, more good news! It was December 15, ten days before Christmas. The boss decided for me to stay until Christmas, and after Christmas, I could use the rest of my vacation and then leave for the remainder of the year. She also said that she would not reduce my pay since I was leaving the company. "Don't worry about production, just show up each day and look like you're doing some work." Yes, that was exactly what they told me to do. "Look like you're doing some work." Trust me, I could do that. At this point, I was ecstatic; it really couldn't get any better than this. Believe it or not, yes, it could.

After showing up to work for two days and trying my best to look like I was doing some work, when actually all I was doing was playing on the internet, my manager came to me and said he and the boss have decided to let me go now. It didn't look good to the other employees who still had to produce while I just did nothing but play on the computer.

26

God Is so Good

My manager said, "We've decided to pay you until the fifth of January, full pay, and you can end your employment with us now."

I almost had tears in my eyes again as I gave them both a big hug and went around the office telling everyone my good news. I left that day and returned later that week on Friday for my last luncheon party with the whole office staff. I enjoyed those three years with CSL. One more chapter in my life on the other side of the crack pipe. Like I said before, God closes one door so that He can open another. It was getting a lot easier to see how God was blessing me. When I started walking in obedience, God really started moving on my behalf in a big way. Don't get me wrong; I'm not perfect in my walk, but I don't have to ask God to forgive me for nowhere near the amount of stuff I used to need forgiveness for. I do wake up every day and ask to be forgiven for things I know I did wrong, things I did wrong I may not be aware of, and wrong thoughts.

This allows me to start each day with a clean slate. Life has gotten better day by day, and it looks like there are more good things to come. I would soon be working for the Canon Corporation. I liked the way that sounded. Nothing like the stability of a large company. Well, Christmas was coming, I'm in beautiful Southern California, and the temps were in the seventies. Sometimes, I just have to stop and take in my surroundings. I just imagined if I could've grown up as a kid with this kind of weather, no rain-delayed Little League baseball games, no snow days, and the beach being fifteen minutes away; it's just incredible. It was the day before Christmas. I got money in my pocket, the weather was great, and I was off work. I booked a round of golf for this upcoming Saturday. I will never forget this as long as I live. I did drugs for a large part of my life, and this just pertains to my crack use, because this has never happened to me while smoking weed or drinking alcohol.

Us addicts all have recurring dreams about our drug use. Vivid dreams where you might have been using in the dream, and it's so vivid when you wake up, you look for the drugs that you were using in your dream. In this particular dream, I was smoking crack while sitting in my bed. The crack was on the nightstand beside the bed. I took a big hit off the pipe. Then all of a sudden, I woke up. I immediately started looking for the crack on my nightstand. It took about ten seconds before I realized it was a dream. I was also sweating profusely when I woke up. That was crazy, and it happens periodically years after you've stopped smoking.

Another instance was a vision that I had. This particular time, it was in the broad daylight at the golf course. This, too, I will never forget. I was paired up with three complete strangers, which is normal at the golf course unless you booked a round with friends. We were on the third or fourth hole, and we had just hit our tee shots. By then, we were all acquainted with one another so as we walked down the fairway to our next shot, we were just having a light conversation.

Now to paint this picture, it was a beautiful day; the sun was shining, it was me and three other gentlemen who I had only just met and we were walking down the middle of the fairway. In mid-conversation, I got a vision. In a moment's notice, I envisioned myself standing in Baltimore City in a dark, dank crack line about to purchase some crack like I had done so many times before. I mean, I was actually standing in line, and I remember that horrible feeling that I would feel while being in that miserable crack line, spending the last bit of my money. I remember I had my money folded in my hand; I had my trench coat and my tie on because it was right after a workday, and it was raining slightly.

It was just an all-around bad day. It was so real I could almost smell the Baltimore City air. While standing in the line, I heard the voice of God say, "When you were here, I already saw you HERE!"

And at that same moment, I was back in the middle of the fairway with the gentleman walking on the golf course. I burst into tears. I turned my back so no one would see me because it was an uncontrollable cry. I didn't want them to see me because I wouldn't be able to explain why I was crying so hard. I backed away from the group like I had something in my eye as they continued to walk on. I had to get myself together. What you must realize was, God took me back to a point where I had thrown in the towel. I had pretty much given up on life. I had concluded that I was going to die in the streets of Baltimore City as a crackhead. So when God showed me in an instant what he had brought me through, When I was no good; He saw me on the golf course playing golf on a beautiful Southern California day, when all I saw was me dying in the streets of Baltimore a crackhead; What a Vision!

Sometimes, I bring this story up in meetings when I have an opportunity to share, and it still brings me to tears every time I share it. A complete vision that took all of ten seconds if that long. He knew the plans He had for me. I couldn't see the forest before the trees. The grace of God is so big, we can't begin to realize His greatness. The youngsters will see visions and the old man will dream dreams, Acts 2:17. It's been a while since I've had a dream or a vision. I guess the further you get away from a hit, the less you dream about it. I don't miss it. God is renewing my mind as I read His word more and more.

Sixteen years later, I haven't had a hit of crack or a drink of alcohol or anything. I sometimes see all these new drinks they've come up with, and my mind does wonder what they would taste like. Or maybe on a hot day, a cold beer would be nice. But I'm quickly reminded of the mighty long way the Lord has brought me. I would not want to disappoint my Lord for all the great things He's given me. I've been given a brand-new fresh start in life. I could have been dead a long time ago. I think about taking a newcomer's chip at a Cocaine Anonymous meeting, and the thought of that is scary. Relapse is not an option for me.

The job at Canon is awesome; it has given me the ability to afford a decent life in Southern California. Not rich, but okay. So,

God, I never thought I would do it, but I guess it's done. It's like I don't even know how to bring this book to an end. Due to a pandemic, I've been laid off from my job after eleven years, and I've been procrastinating about beginning this book. The Lord spoke clearly to me after being laid off.

He said, "You now have time." And He's provided my finances and sustained me through the whole process of writing it. I had no more excuses, so I began to write, and now it's done. My hope is that my story helps someone who might be struggling with an addiction, can read this, and see how the God of the Bible can lead you to freedom like He did for me.

It's up to You now, God. I put pencil to paper and wrote a book to give You Glory! Amen!

Crack and back!

First spot I learned to buy   Methadone clinic
from in Edmonson Village

Penn Ave addict   Police posted up

Street corner sales spot in Edmonson village

Moniques' street in the Village_

Top of N. Ave. addict

Typical day in the city

CPSIA information can be obtained
at www.ICGtesting.com
Printed in the USA
JSHW020135200123
36474JS00002B/4